Middle School 2-2

기말고사 완벽대비

적중100

영어 기출 문제집

중2

동아 | 윤정미

Best Collection

구성과 특징

교과서의 주요 학습 내용을 중심으로 학습 영역별 특성에 맞춰 단계별로 다양한 학습 기회를 제공하여 단원별 학습능력 평가는 물론 중간 및 기말고사 시험 등에 완벽하게 대비할 수 있도록 내용을 구성

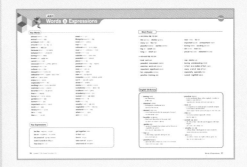

Words & Expressions

Step1 Key Words 단원별 핵심 단어 설명 및 풀이
Key Expression 단원별 핵심 숙어 및 관용어 설명
Word Power 반대 또는 비슷한 뜻 단어 배우기
English Dictionary 영어로 배우는 영어 단어

Step2 실력평가 단원별 수시평가 대비 주관식, 객관식 문제풀이

Step3 서술형 대비 학업성취도 및 수행능력평가 대비 서술형 문제풀이

Conversation

Step1 핵심 의사소통 의사소통에 필요한 주요 표현 방법 요약
핵심 Check 기본적인 표현 방법 및 활용능력 확인

Step2 대화문 익히기 상황에 따른 대화문 활용 및 연습

Step3 기본평가 시험대비 기초 학습 능력 평가

Step4 실력평가 단원별 수시평가 대비 주관식, 객관식 문제풀이

Step5 서술형 대비 학업성취도 및 수행능력평가 대비 서술형 문제풀이

Grammar

Step1 주요 문법 단원별 주요 문법 사항과 예문을 알기 쉽게 설명
핵심 Check 기본 문법사항에 대한 이해 여부 확인

Step2 기본평가 시험대비 기초 학습 능력 평가

Step3 실력평가 단원별 수시평가 대비 주관식, 객관식 문제풀이

Step4 서술형 대비 학업성취도 및 수행능력평가 대비 서술형 문제풀이

Reading

Step1 구문 분석 단원별로 제시된 문장에 대한 구문별 분석과 내용 설명
확인문제 문장에 대한 기본적인 이해와 인지능력 확인

Step2 확인학습A 빈칸 채우기를 통한 문장 완성 능력 확인

Step3 확인학습B 제시된 우리말을 영어로 완성하여 작문 능력 키우기

Step4 실력평가 단원별 수시평가 대비 주관식, 객관식 문제풀이

Step5 서술형 대비 학업성취도 및 수행능력평가 대비 서술형 문제풀이
교과서 구석구석 교과서에 나오는 기타 문장까지 완벽 학습

Composition

|영역별 핵심문제|
단어 및 어휘, 대화문, 문법, 독해 등 각 영역별 기출문제의 출제 유형을 분석하여 실전에 대비하고 연습할 수 있도록 문제를 배열

|서술형 실전 및 창의사고력 문제|
학교 시험에서 점차 늘어나는 서술형 시험에 집중 대비하고 고득점을 취득하는데 만전을 기하기 위한 학습 코너

|단원별 예상문제|
기출문제를 분석한 후 새로운 시험 출제 경향을 더하여 새롭게 출제될 수 있는 문제를 포함하여 시험에 완벽하게 대비할 수 있도록 준비

|단원별 모의고사|
영역별, 단계별 학습을 모두 마친 후 실전 연습을 위한 모의고사

on the textbook .... 교과서 파헤치기

- 단어Test1~2 영어 단어 우리말 쓰기와 우리말을 영어 단어로 쓰기
- 대화문Test1~2 대화문 빈칸 완성 및 전체 대화문 쓰기
- 본문Test1~5 빈칸 완성, 우리말 쓰기, 문장 배열연습, 영어 작문하기 복습 등 단계별 반복 학습을 통해 교과서 지문에 대한 완벽한 습득
- 구석구석지문Test1~2 지문 빈칸 완성 및 전문 영어로 쓰기

Contents

Lesson 7

Life in Space

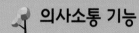 **의사소통 기능**

- 알고 있는지 묻기
  A: Did you hear about the new musical?
  B: Yes, I did. / No, I didn't.

- 궁금증 표현하기
  I'm really curious about it.

 언어 형식

- 현재완료
  I**'ve** never **seen** a blue sky.

- It ~ to부정사
  It's difficult **to walk on Earth.**

Words & Expressions

Key Words

- **adventure** [ædvéntʃər] 명 모험
- **air** [ɛər] 명 공기
- **amazing** [əméiziŋ] 형 놀라운
- **arrive** [əráiv] 동 도착하다
- **balloon** [bəlúːn] 명 풍선
- **container** [kəntéinər] 명 그릇, 용기
- **curious** [kjúəriəs] 형 궁금한, 호기심이 많은
- **dessert** [dizə́ːrt] 명 디저트
- **different** [dífərənt] 형 다른
- **difficult** [dífikʌlt] 형 어려운
- **ever** [évər] 부 줄곧, 내내
- **everywhere** [évriwὲər] 부 모든 곳에
- **excited** [iksáitid] 형 신난, 흥분한
- **exciting** [iksáitiŋ] 형 흥미진진한
- **exploration** [èkspləréiʃən] 명 탐험, 탐사
- **finally** [fáinəli] 부 마침내
- **fix** [fiks] 동 고치다
- **foreign** [fɔ́ːrən] 형 외국의
- **float** [flout] 동 뜨다, 떠가다
- **form** [fɔːrm] 동 형성하다, 만들어 내다
- **French** [frentʃ] 형 프랑스의
- **grass** [græs] 명 풀, 잔디
- **hear** [hiər] 동 듣다 (-heard-heard)
- **hill** [hil] 명 언덕
- **interesting** [íntərəstiŋ] 형 재미있는, 흥미로운
- **land** [lænd] 동 착륙하다
- **laugh** [læf] 동 웃다

- **lie** [lai] 동 눕다 (-lay-lain)
- **little** [lítl] 형 작은
- **marathon** [mǽrəθɑ̀n] 명 마라톤
- **musical** [mjúːzikəl] 명 뮤지컬
- **nearest** [níərist] (near의 최상급) 가장 가까운
- **other** [ʌ́ðər] 형 다른
- **poster** [póustər] 명 포스터
- **recently** [ríːsntli] 부 최근에
- **ride** [raid] 동 타다 (-rode-ridden)
- **save** [seiv] 동 구하다, 절약하다
- **secret** [síːkrit] 명 비밀, 기밀
- **shake** [ʃeik] 동 흔들다 (-shook-shaken)
- **shout** [ʃaut] 동 외치다
- **since** [sins] 접 ~한 이래로
- **soft** [sɔːft] 형 부드러운
- **spaceship** [spéisʃip] 명 우주선
- **space station** 우주 정거장
- **space suit** 우주복
- **swallow** [swɑ́lou] 동 삼키다
- **taste** [teist] 명 맛
- **thirsty** [θə́ːrsti] 형 목마른
- **thrilling** [θríliŋ] 형 아주 신나는
- **type** [taip] 명 종류, 유형
- **towards** [tɔ́ːrdz] 전 ~쪽으로, ~을 향하여
- **vegetable** [védʒətəbl] 명 야채, 채소
- **wet** [wet] 형 젖은
- **wind** [wind] 명 바람

Key Expressions

- **all night** 하룻밤 내내, 밤새도록
- **be born** 태어나다
- **be covered with** ~으로 뒤덮이다
- **be curious about ~** ~에 관해 궁금해 하다
- **don't have to+동사원형** ~할 필요 없다
- **each other** (둘 사이의) 서로
- **for example** 예를 들어
- **get on** ~에 타다
- **get wet** 젖다
- **here it is** (물건을 건네줄 때) 여기 있어
- **in surprise** 놀라서

- **in the air** 공중에
- **lie down** 눕다
- **not ~ anymore** 더 이상 ~ 않다
- **pull down** 아래로 끌어내리다
- **roll down** 굴러 내려가다
- **run up to ~** ~으로 달려가다
- **sound+형용사** ~처럼 들리다
- **take a walk** 산책하다
- **talk about ~** ~에 관해 말하다
- **try to+동사원형** ~하려고 시도하다

Word Power

※ 서로 반대되는 뜻을 가진 어휘

- □ **different** (다른) ↔ **same** (같은)
- □ **arrive** (도착하다) ↔ **depart** (출발하다)
- □ **difficult** (어려운) ↔ **easy** (쉬운)
- □ **excited** (신나는) ↔ **bored** (지루한)
- □ **land** (착륙하다) ↔ **take off** (이륙하다)
- □ **interesting** (흥미로운) ↔ **uninteresting** (재미없는)

- □ **little** (작은) ↔ **big** (큰)
- □ **near** (가까운) ↔ **far** (먼)
- □ **soft** (부드러운) ↔ **hard** (딱딱한)
- □ **wet** (젖은) ↔ **dry** (마른)
- □ **get on** (타다) ↔ **get off** (내리다)
- □ **intelligent** (똑똑한) ↔ **stupid** (어리석은)

※ 서로 비슷한 뜻을 가진 어휘

- □ **amazing** : **surprising** (놀라운)
- □ **fix** : **repair** (고치다, 수리하다)
- □ **form** : **build** (형성하다)
- □ **recently** : **lately** (최근에)

- □ **save** : **rescue** (구하다)
- □ **shout** : **yell** (외치다)
- □ **exciting** : **thrilling** (신나는)
- □ **land** : **touch down**(착륙하다)

English Dictionary

- □ **adventure** 모험
  → an unusual, exciting, and possibly dangerous activity, such as a trip
  여행과 같이 특이하고, 흥미진진하며, 위험할 수도 있는 활동

- □ **amazing** 놀라운
  → extremely surprising
  매우 놀라운

- □ **arrive** 도착하다
  → to reach a place, especially at the end of a journey
  특히 여행이 끝날 때, 어떤 장소에 도착하다

- □ **curious** 호기심 많은
  → interested in learning about people or things around you
  주변 사람 또는 사물을 알고자 하는 데 관심이 있는

- □ **exploration** 탐험, 탐사
  → the activity of searching and finding out about something
  무언가를 찾고 알아내는 활동

- □ **foreign** 외국의
  → belonging or connected to a country that is not your own
  자신의 나라가 아닌 나라와 관련되어 있거나 속해 있는

- □ **float** 뜨다
  → to stay on the surface of a liquid and not sink
  액체의 표면에 머무르고 가라앉지 않다

- □ **form** 형성하다, 만들다
  → to make something into a particular shape
  어떤 것을 특정한 모양으로 만들다

- □ **land** 착륙하다
  → to arrive on the ground or other surface after moving down through the air
  공중에서 아래로 이동한 후 땅이나 다른 표면에 도착하다

- □ **swallow** 삼키다
  → to cause food, drink, pills, etc. to move from your mouth into your stomach by using the muscles of your throat
  목의 근육을 사용함으로써 음식, 음료, 약 등을 입에서 배 속으로 움직이도록 하다

- □ **secret** 비밀
  → a piece of information that is only known by one person or a few people and should not be told to others
  한 사람이나 몇 사람만 알고 다른 사람에게는 말하지 말아야 하는 정보

- □ **spaceship** 우주선
  → a vehicle used for travel in space
  우주에서 여행하기 위해 사용되는 운송 수단

- □ **space station** 우주 정거장
  → a place or vehicle in space where people can stay
  사람들이 머물 수 있는 우주에 있는 장소나 탈것

- □ **towards** ~을 향해
  → in the direction of, or closer to someone or something
  누군가나 어떤 것의 방향으로 또는 더 가까이

01 다음 문장의 빈칸에 주어진 영어 설명에 해당하는 말을 쓰시오.

> Rada and Jonny thought about it all night and didn't tell Mom and Dad about it. It was their _____.

> a piece of information that is only known by one person or a few people and should not be told to others

02 다음 빈칸에 들어갈 말로 가장 적절한 것은?

> Jonny opened a milk container and shook it. The milk _____ed in the air and formed balls.

① float   ② reach
③ swallow   ④ fix
⑤ look

[03~04] 다음 영영풀이에 해당하는 단어를 고르시오.

03
> to move something down, using your hands

① roll down   ② be born
③ in surprise   ④ pull down
⑤ each other

04
> covered in or full of water or another liquid

① soft   ② dry
③ near   ④ simple
⑤ wet

05 다음 우리말에 맞게 빈칸에 알맞은 단어를 쓰시오.

> 언덕들이 있어. 그리고 언덕들은 부드러운 초록색의 잔디로 덮여 있지.
> ➡ There are hills, and they _____ _____ _____ soft green grass.

06 다음 빈칸에 공통으로 들어갈 말로 알맞은 것은?

> • He put a grape into his mouth and _____ed it.
> • One _____ doesn't make a summer.

① plan   ② land
③ swallow   ④ throw
⑤ laugh

07 다음 짝지어진 단어의 관계가 같도록 빈칸에 알맞은 말을 쓰시오.

> amazing : surprising = lately : _____

08 다음 빈칸에 들어갈 말로 알맞게 짝지어진 것은?

> • They looked at _____ other and laughed.
> • Rada and Jonny _____ down on the soft green grass and rolled down the hill.

① one – laid   ② each – rolled
③ every – lied   ④ each – lay
⑤ one – pulled

01 다음 빈칸에 들어갈 말을 〈보기〉에서 찾아 쓰시오. (필요하면 변형하여 쓰시오.)

> ┤ 보기 ├
>
> curious   excite   pull   cover

(1) It's also hard to jump there because Earth _____ you down.

(2) Hills are _____ with soft green grass.

(3) It was _____ to think about all the new things they were going to see and do.

(4) I'm really _____ about the space marathon.

02 다음 그림에 맞게 〈보기〉에서 단어를 골라 알맞은 표현을 쓰시오. (어형 변화 필수)

> ┤ 보기 ├
>
> cover pull roll down shake land

(1)   (2)   (3)

(1) A girl is _____ a bottle.

(2) A ball is _____ _____ the hill.

(3) An airplane is _____.

03 다음 빈칸에 공통으로 알맞은 단어를 주어진 철자로 시작하여 쓰시오.

(1) • You have to fill out a f_____ on their website.

　• The milk floated in the air and f_____ed balls. Jonny swallowed the balls.

(2) • The sailors saw l_____ in the distance.

　• The plane l_____ed safely at last.

04 다음 우리말과 같은 표현이 되도록 문장의 빈칸을 채우시오.

(1) 그들은 우주에서 태어났다.

　➡ They _____ _____ in space.

(2) Rada와 Jonny는 깜짝 놀라 아빠를 보았고, 그에게 둥둥 떠서 갔다.

　➡ Rada and Jonny looked at Dad in _____ and floated towards him.

(3) 모든 곳에 공기가 있기 때문에 너는 크고 무거운 우주복을 입을 필요가 없어.

　➡ You _____ _____ _____ wear your big heavy _____ _____ because there is air _____.

05 다음 영영풀이에 해당하는 단어를 〈보기〉에서 찾아 첫 번째 칸에 쓰고, 두 번째 칸에는 우리말 뜻을 쓰시오.

> ┤ 보기 ├
>
> space station exploration secret
> air space suit adventure

(1) _____ : the gases around you, which you breathe: _____

(2) _____ : a piece of information that is only known by one person or a few people and should not be told to others _____

(3) _____ : a special piece of clothing that astronauts wear in space: _____

Conversation

① 알고 있는지 묻기

A Did you hear about the new musical? 새로운 뮤지컬에 대해 들어 봤니?

B Yes, I did. / No, I didn't. 응. 들어 봤어. / 아니, 못 들어 봤어.

- 'Did you hear about ~?'은 '~에 대해서 들어 봤니?'라는 의미로 새로운 정보에 대해서 알고 있는지 묻는 표현이다. 비슷한 표현으로 'Do you know (about) ~?', 'Are you aware (of) ~?'와 현재완료를 사용해 'Have you heard about ~?'으로 들어 본 적이 있는지 물을 수도 있다.

  - A: Did you hear about the new store on Main Street? Main가에 있는 새 가게에 대해 들어 봤니?
    B: Yes, I did. / No, I didn't. 응. 들어 봤어. / 아니, 못 들어 봤어.

  - A: Are you aware that ice cream is from China? 너는 아이스크림이 중국에서 왔다는 것을 알고 있니?
    B: No. That's interesting. 아니. 그거 참 흥미롭구나.

  - A: Have you heard about the new waffle shop? 새 와플 가게에 대해 들어 본 적 있니?
    B: Yeah. I saw an ad about it on a poster. 응. 포스터에서 그것에 대한 광고를 봤어.

- 알고 있음을 표현할 때
  - I'm aware of the situation. / I've been told about it. / I've heard about it.

핵심 Check

1. 다음 대화의 밑줄 친 ⓐ의 의도로 알맞은 것은?

   G: Hojin, ⓐdid you hear about the speaking contest?

   B: No, I didn't. Where did you hear about it?

   G: From the school newspaper.

   ① 놀람 표현하기   ② 확신하는지 묻기
   ③ 알고 있는지 묻기   ④ 도움이 필요한지 묻기
   ⑤ 대안 묻기

2. 다음 주어진 문장과 같은 의미가 되도록 빈칸에 알맞은 말을 쓰시오.

   Did you hear about the accident?

   = _____ you _____ _____ the accident?

② 궁금증 표현하기

I'm really curious about it. 나는 그것에 대해 정말 궁금해.

■ 'I'm really curious about ~.'은 '나는 ~에 대해서 정말 궁금해.'라는 의미로 새로운 정보에 대하여 궁금증을 표현하거나 보다 많은 정보를 알고 싶을 때 사용하는 표현이다. 'I'd like to know more about ~.', 'I'm interested in ~, I want to know ~.' 등으로도 표현할 수 있다.

• The cat was naturally curious about its new surroundings. 그 고양이는 원래 새로운 환경에 호기심이 있었다.

• We are curious about why you never called us. 우리는 왜 네가 우리에게 전화를 하지 않았는지가 궁금하다.

■ '~하고 싶다, 궁금해지다'라는 의미는 'be[become] curious to+동사원형'으로 나타낼 수 있다.

• They were curious to find out who won the game. 그들은 누가 게임을 이겼는지 알고 싶다.

• I'm curious to know more about her. 나는 그녀에 관하여 더 알고 싶다.

핵심 Check

3. 다음 대화의 빈칸에 들어갈 알맞은 것은?

A: Why did you borrow the book about Mars?

B: It's because I'm curious _____ the universe.

① in   ② to   ③ for

④ with   ⑤ about

4. 다음 문장과 같은 의미로 사용될 수 있는 것을 <u>모두</u> 고르시오.

I am curious about this movie.

① I'd like to know more about this movie.

② I want to know about this movie.

③ I can tell you about this movie.

④ I don't know much about this movie.

⑤ I'm curious to know more about this movie.

Listen and Talk A-1

B: ❶Did you hear about the first spaceship ❷that went into space?

G: No, I didn't. ❸I'm curious about it.

B: This is a poster of the spaceship.

G: Really? I want to buy it.

B: 너는 우주에 간 첫 번째 우주선에 대해 들어 봤니?

G: 아니, 못 들어 봤어. 궁금하다.

B: 이것이 그 우주선 포스터야.

G: 정말? 그것을 사고 싶다.

❶ '~에 대해서 들어 봤니?'라는 의미로 새로운 정보에 대해서 알고 있는지 묻는 표현이다.

❷ that went into space는 주격 관계대명사절로 선행사인 the first spaceship을 꾸며주는 역할을 한다.

❸ 궁금증을 표현하거나 보다 많은 정보를 알고 싶을 때 사용하는 표현이다. 'I'd like to know more about ~.' 'I'm interested in ~, I want to know ~' 등으로 표현할 수도 있다.

Check(√) True or False

(1) G didn't know about the first spaceship that went into space.　T ☐ F ☐

(2) G has an interest in the spaceship.　T ☐ F ☐

Listen and Talk A-2

G: ❶Did you hear about the new book about Mars?

B: No, I didn't. ❷I'm really curious about Mars.

G: Look. It's ❸right here. ❹It's about Mars and its moons.

B: Great. I think I'll buy the book.

G: 너는 화성에 관한 새로운 책에 관해 들어 봤니?

B: 아니, 못 들어 봤어. 나는 화성에 관해 정말 궁금해.

G: 봐. 바로 여기 있어. 그것은 화성과 그것의 위성들에 관한 내용이야.

B: 멋지다. 이 책을 사야겠어.

❶ '~에 대해서 들어 봤니?'라는 의미로 새로운 정보에 대해서 알고 있는지 묻는 표현으로 'Do you know (about) ~?', 'Are you aware (of) ~?' 등으로 바꾸어 쓸 수 있다.

❷ 궁금증을 표현하거나 보다 많은 정보를 알고 싶을 때 사용하는 표현이다. 'I'd like to know more about ~.', 'I'm interested in ~, I want to know ~' 등으로 표현할 수도 있다.

❸ 여기서 right는 부사로 '바로'라는 뜻이다.

❹ be about은 '~에 관한 것이다'로 해석한다.

Check(√) True or False

(3) B knew about the book about Mars.　T ☐ F ☐

(4) B is going to buy the book about Mars.　T ☐ F ☐

Listen and Talk A-3

G: ❶Did you hear about the space marathon?

B: No, I didn't.

G: It's a marathon on a space station. Look at this video.

B: OK. ❷I'm really curious about it.

❶ '~에 대해서 들어 봤니?'라는 의미로 새로운 정보에 대해서 알고 있는지 묻는 표현으로 'Do you know (about) ~?', 'Are you aware (of) ~?' 등으로 바꾸어 쓸 수 있다.

❷ 궁금증을 표현하거나 보다 많은 정보를 알고 싶을 때 사용하는 표현이다.

Listen and Talk A-4

G: Did you hear about the new space food?

B: Yes, I did. It's ❶a type of ice cream.

G: Yes, and ❷here it is. It looks good.

B: I'm really curious about the taste.

❶ a type of: ~의 일종

❷ 상대방에게 물건을 건네줄 때 사용하는 표현으로 '여기 있다'는 의미이다.

Listen and Talk B

A: Look at this. ❶Did you hear about the new musical?

B: Yes, I did. I heard it has great songs.

A: Oh, I'm really curious about it.

❶ Have you heard about the new musical?로 바꾸어 표현할 수 있다.

Listen and Talk B

A: Look at this. Did you hear about the new musical?

B: No, I didn't.

A: I heard it has great songs.

B: Oh, ❶I'm really curious about it.

❶ 'I'd like to know more about it.'으로 바꾸어 표현할 수 있다.

Listen and Talk C

B: Subin, ❶did you hear about the new movie, *Life on the Moon?*

G: No, I didn't.

B: I heard it's really good.

G: ❷I'm really curious about the movie. What's it about?

B: It's about a man ❸who is trying to live on the moon.

G: ❹That sounds interesting.

B: Look. The movie is playing at the Space Theater here.

G: What time is the movie?

B: It begins at 2:30.

G: Let's eat lunch first and then see the movie.

B: OK. I'm hungry. Let's go!

❶ are you aware of the new movie로 바꾸어 쓸 수 있다.

❷ 궁금증을 표현하거나 보다 많은 정보를 알고 싶을 때 사용하는 표현이다. I'd like to know more about the movie.로 바꾸어 쓸 수 있다.

❸ who 이하의 문장은 선행사 a man을 수식하는 주격 관계대명사절이다.

❹ 'sound+형용사' 형태로 '그거 재미있겠다.'는 뜻이다.

Review 1

G: Tony, ❶did you hear about the movie, *My Hero?*

B: No, I didn't.

G: Well, I heard it's really good.

B: I'm really curious about the movie. What's it about?

G: ❷It's about a father who saves his son.

❶ '~에 대해서 들어 봤니?'라는 의미로 새로운 정보에 대해서 알고 있는지 묻는 표현으로 'Do you know (about) ~?', 'Are you aware (of) ~?' 등으로 바꾸어 쓸 수 있다.

❷ be about은 '~에 관한 것이다'로 해석하고, who saves his son은 선행사 a father를 수식하는 주격 관계대명사절이다.

Review 2

G: Did you hear about the new book, *Living in a Foreign Country?*

B: No, I didn't.

G: Look. It's right here. ❶It's about living in New York.

B: Great. I'm really curious about this book.

G: ❷Me, too.

❶ be about은 '~에 관한 것[내용]이다'는 뜻이고, 전치사 about 뒤에 동명사 living 형태를 사용한다.

❷ '나도 그래.'의 뜻으로 So am I.로 바꿔 쓸 수 있다.

● 다음 우리말과 일치하도록 빈칸에 알맞은 말을 쓰시오.

Listen and Talk A-1

B: Did you _____ _____ the first spaceship _____ went into space?

G: No, I didn't. I'm _____ _____ it.

B: This is a poster of the spaceship.

G: Really? I want _____ _____ it.

B: 너는 우주에 간 첫 번째 우주선에 대해 들어 봤니?
G: 아니, 못 들어 봤어. 궁금하다.
B: 이것이 그 우주선 포스터야.
G: 정말? 그것을 사고 싶다.

Listen and Talk A-2

G: _____ you _____ _____ the new book about Mars?

B: No, I didn't. _____ _____ _____ _____ _____ Mars.

G: Look. It's _____ _____. It's _____ Mars and its moons.

B: Great. I think I'll buy the book.

G: 너는 화성에 관한 새로운 책에 관해 들어 봤니?
B: 아니, 못 들어 봤어. 나는 화성에 관해 정말 궁금해.
G: 봐. 바로 여기 있어. 그것은 화성과 그것의 위성들에 관한 내용이야.
B: 멋지다. 이 책을 사야겠어.

Listen and Talk A-3

G: _____ _____ _____ _____ _____ the space marathon?

B: No, _____ _____.

G: It's a marathon on a space station. _____ _____ this video.

B: OK. _____ _____ _____ _____ it.

G: 너는 우주 마라톤에 대해 들어 봤니?
B: 아니, 못 들어 봤어.
G: 그것은 우주 정거장에서 하는 마라톤이야. 이 비디오를 봐.
B: 알겠어. 정말 궁금하다.

Listen and Talk A-4

G: Did you hear _____ the new space food?

B: Yes, I did. It's _____ _____ of ice cream.

G: Yes, and _____ _____ _____. It looks good.

B: I'm really _____ _____ the taste.

G: 너는 새로운 우주 음식에 대해 들어 봤니?
B: 응, 들어 봤어. 그건 일종의 아이스크림이야.
G: 응, 여기 있어. 맛있어 보인다.
B: 그 맛이 참 궁금하다.

Listen and Talk B

1. A: Look at this. Did you hear _____ the new musical?

   B: Yes, I did. I _____ it has great songs.

   A: Oh, I'm really _____ _____ it.

2. A: _____ _____ this. Did you _____ _____ the new musical?

   B: No, I didn't.

   A: I heard _____ _____ _____ _____.

   B: Oh, I'm really _____ about it.

1. A: 이것 봐. 새 뮤지컬에 대해 들어 봤니?
   B: 응, 들어 봤어. 좋은 노래들이 나온다고 들었어.
   A: 오, 정말 궁금하다.

2. A: 이것 봐. 새 뮤지컬에 대해 들어 봤니?
   B: 아니, 못 들어 봤어.
   A: 좋은 노래들이 나온다고 들었어.
   B: 오, 정말 궁금하다.

Listen and Talk C

B: Subin, did you hear _____ the new movie, *Life on the Moon*?

G: No, I didn't.

B: I heard it's really _____.

G: I'm really _____ _____ the movie. What's it _____?

B: It's _____ a man _____ is trying _____ _____ on the moon.

G: That sounds _____.

B: Look. The movie _____ _____ at the Space Theater here.

G: _____ _____ is the movie?

B: It _____ at 2:30.

G: _____ eat lunch first _____ _____ see the movie.

B: OK. I'm _____. Let's go!

Review 1

G: Tony, _____ _____ hear about the movie, *My Hero*?

B: No, I didn't.

G: Well, I _____ it's really good.

B: I'm really _____ about the movie. What's it _____?

G: It's _____ a father _____ saves his son.

Review 2

G: Did you hear _____ the new book, *Living in a Foreign Country*?

B: No, I didn't.

G: Look. It's _____ here. It's about _____ in New York.

B: Great. I'm really _____ _____ this book.

G: Me, too.

Conversation 시험대비 기본평가

01 다음 우리말에 맞도록 빈칸에 들어갈 알맞은 말을 쓰시오.

> 나는 화성에 관해 정말 궁금해.
>
> ➡ I'm really _____ _____ Mars.

02 다음 대화의 빈칸에 들어갈 말로 알맞은 것은?

> A: _____ the new movie, *My Father*?
> B: No, I didn't, but I'm curious about it.

① Are you curious about   ② Why don't we see
③ Tell me about   ④ Did you hear about
⑤ Are you interested in

03 다음 대화의 빈칸에 들어갈 말로 알맞은 것은? (2개)

> A: What are you looking at?
> B: I'm looking at this poster. _____
> A: It's Mars.

① I'd like to know where this place is.
② I know where this place is.
③ I want to know where this place is.
④ I have heard where this place is.
⑤ I'm amazed about this place.

04 다음 대화의 밑줄 친 우리말에 맞게 문장의 빈칸을 채우시오.

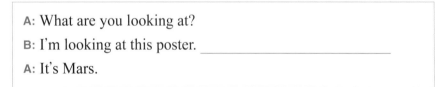

> A: 새 영화 New Moon에 대해 들어 봤니?
> B: No, I didn't, but I'm really curious about it.

➡ Did you _____ _____ the new movie, *New Moon*?

[01~02] 다음 대화를 읽고 물음에 답하시오.

> B: _____(A)_____ the spaceship that went into space?
>
> G: No, I didn't. I _____(B)_____ it.
>
> B: This is a poster of the spaceship.
>
> G: Really? I want to buy it.

01 위 대화의 빈칸 (A)에 들어갈 말로 알맞은 것은?

① Have you bought
② Have you seen the poster of
③ What do you think of
④ Did you hear about
⑤ Did you want to know about

02 위 대화의 빈칸 (B)에 들어갈 말로 알맞은 것을 <u>모두</u> 고르시오.

① am tired of   ② am surprised at
③ am full of   ④ am curious about
⑤ want to know about

03 다음 대화의 순서를 알맞게 배열한 것은?

> (A) OK. I'm really curious about it.
>
> (B) It's a marathon on a space station. Look at this video.
>
> (C) No, I didn't.
>
> (D) Did you hear about the space marathon?

① (A) – (B) – (C) – (D)
② (B) – (A) – (C) – (D)
③ (B) – (C) – (A) – (D)
④ (C) – (B) – (D) – (A)
⑤ (D) – (C) – (B) – (A)

[04~05] 다음 대화를 읽고 물음에 답하시오.

> G: Did you hear _____(A)_____ the new space food?
>
> B: Yes, I did. It's a type of ice cream.
>
> G: Yes, and (B)여기 있어. It looks good.
>
> B: I'm really curious _____(A)_____ the taste.

04 위 대화의 빈칸 (A)에 공통으로 들어갈 말로 알맞은 것은?

① with   ② about   ③ in
④ for   ⑤ at

05 위 대화의 밑줄 친 (B)의 우리말에 해당하는 표현을 주어진 단어를 포함하여 세 단어로 쓰시오.

➡ _____ (here)

06 다음 두 사람의 대화가 <u>어색한</u> 것은?

① A: What are you looking at?
  B: This picture. I want to know who the painter is.
② A: Did you hear about the new movie star, William Black?
  B: No, I didn't, but I'm curious about him.
③ A: Did you hear about the new TV show, *Hip Hop*?
  B: No, I didn't, but I'm curious about it.
④ A: Look at this. Did you hear about the new musical?
  B: No, I didn't. I heard it has great songs.
⑤ A: I'm really curious about the movie. What's it about?
  B: It's about a man who is trying to live on the moon.

서답형

07 다음 대화의 밑줄 친 우리말에 맞게 주어진 단어를 이용하여 영어로 쓰시오. (어형 변화 필수)

G: Tony, did you hear about the movie, *My Hero*?
B: No, I didn't.
G: Well, I heard it's really good.
B: I'm really curious about the movie. What's it about?
G: <u>그것은 아들을 구하는 아버지에 관한 거야.</u>

it / about / a father / who / save / son

➡ _____

08 다음 대화의 밑줄 친 부분의 의도로 알맞은 것은?

G: <u>Did you hear about the new book about Mars?</u>
B: No, I didn't. I'm really curious about Mars.

① 알고 있는지 묻기　② 의무 표현하기
③ 확신 표현하기　④ 궁금증 표현하기
⑤ 의견 묻기

[09~10] 다음 대화를 읽고 물음에 답하시오.

Bin: Subin, ⓐ<u>did you hear about</u> the new movie, *Life on the Moon*?
Subin: No, I didn't.
Bin: I heard it's really good.
Subin: I'm really ⓑ<u>curious about</u> the movie. What's it about?
Bin: It's about a man ⓒ<u>who are</u> trying to live on the moon.
Subin: That sounds ⓓ<u>interesting</u>.
Bin: Look. The movie is playing at the Space Theater here.
Subin: What time is the movie?
Bin: It ⓔ<u>begins</u> at 2:30.
Subin: Let's eat lunch first and then see the movie.

Bin: OK. I'm hungry. Let's go!

09 위 대화의 밑줄 친 ⓐ~ⓔ 중 어법상 어색한 것은?

① ⓐ　② ⓑ　③ ⓒ　④ ⓓ　⑤ ⓔ

10 위 대화를 읽고 답할 수 없는 질문은?

① What are they talking about?
② Is Subin interested in the new movie?
③ What is the movie, *Life on the Moon*, about?
④ What time does the movie begin?
⑤ What are they going to do after seeing the movie?

[11~12] 다음 대화를 읽고 물음에 답하시오.

D: Did you hear about the new space food?
B: _____(A)_____ It's a type of ice cream.
G: Yes, and here it is. It looks good.
B: I'm really _____(B)_____ about the taste.

11 위 대화의 빈칸 (A)에 들어갈 말로 알맞은 것은?

① Yes, I am.　② Yes, I did.
③ No, I don't.　④ No, I haven't.
⑤ Of course not.

서답형

12 위 대화의 빈칸 (B)에 들어갈 말에 대한 영어 풀이를 보고 주어진 철자로 시작하여 쓰시오.

wanting to know something, or to learn about the world

➡ c_____

[01~02] 다음 대화를 읽고 물음에 답하시오.

G: (A)새 책인 "Living in a Foreign Country"에 대해 들어 봤니?
B: No, I didn't.
G: Look. It's right here. It's about living in New York.
B: Great. (B)이 책이 정말 궁금해.
G: Me, too.

01 위 대화의 밑줄 친 (A)의 우리말에 맞게 주어진 단어를 이용하여 영작하시오.

> hear, the new book, *Living in a Foreign Country*

➡ _____

_____

02 위 대화의 밑줄 친 (B)의 우리말에 맞게 'curious'와 'really'를 이용하여 영작하시오.

➡ _____

03 다음 대화의 빈칸에 들어갈 말로 자연스러운 것을 〈보기〉에서 찾아 문장을 쓰시오.

A: _____ (A) _____
B: No, I didn't. _____ (B) _____
A: They are comfortable and not that expensive.
B: Oh, _____ (C) _____

┤ 보기 ├
- What about them?
- I'm curious about them.
- Did you hear about the new running shoes, *Speed*?

(A) _____
(B) _____
(C) _____

04 다음 대화의 밑줄 친 질문에 대한 답을 주어진 단어를 활용하여 조건에 맞게 영작하시오.

G: Tony, did you hear about the movie, *My Hero*?
B: No, I didn't.
G: Well, I heard it's really good.
B: I'm really curious about the movie. (A) What's it about?
G: _____

┤ 조건 ├
- 전치사를 사용할 것
- 관계대명사를 사용할 것
- 현재시제를 사용할 것

(a father, save, his son)

➡ It's _____.

05 다음 대화들을 순서대로 배열했을 때, 제일 마지막에 오는 문장을 쓰시오.

(A) I heard it's really good.
(B) Subin, did you hear about the new movie, *Life on the Moon*?
(C) I'm really curious about the movie. What's it about?
(D) It's about a man who is trying to live on the moon.
(E) That sounds interesting.
(F) No, I didn't.

➡ _____

Grammar

1 현재완료

- **I've** never **seen** a blue sky. 전 한 번도 파란 하늘을 본 적이 없어요.
- **Have** you ever **thought** about becoming a teacher?
  선생님이 되는 것에 대해 생각해 본 적이 있어요?

■ 현재완료는 'have[has]+과거분사'의 형태로 과거에 시작된 동작과 그 동작의 현재 상태를 동시에 표현한다.

■ 의문문은 'Have[Has]+주어+과거분사 ~?'이며, 부정문은 'have[has]+not[never]+과거분사'로 나타낸다.

- I **haven't smoked** for ten years. 나는 10년 동안 담배를 안 피우고 있어요.
- **Have** you **done** your homework already? 숙제를 벌써 했니?

■ 현재완료는 '계속(~해 왔다), 경험(~한 적이 있다), 완료(막[벌써] ~했다), 결과(~해 버렸다)'의 네 가지 용법으로 쓰인다. 계속적 용법은 보통 'for(~ 동안)+기간 명사'나 'since(~부터, ~ 이래로)+시간 명사'와 함께 쓰이며, 경험은 'once(한 번), twice(두 번), three times(세 번), ever(이제껏), never(한 번도 ~않다), before(전에)' 등과 같은 부사(구)와 함께 쓰인다. 완료 용법은 보통 'already(이미, 벌써), just(막, 방금), yet(아직, 벌써)' 등과 같은 부사와 쓰이고, 결과 용법은 과거에 발생한 사건이 현재 미치고 있는 결과를 포함한다.

- Mary **has studied** French for 5 years. 〈계속〉 Mary는 5년 동안 불어를 공부해 오고 있다.
- I **have** never **heard** such a sad story. 〈경험〉 나는 그런 슬픈 이야기를 들어 본 적이 없다.
- He **has** already **spent** all his money. 〈완료〉 그는 이미 자신의 돈을 다 써버렸다.
- The girl **has lost** her dog at the park. 〈결과〉
  그 소녀는 공원에서 그녀의 개를 잃어버렸다. (그 결과 (그녀의 개가) 지금 없다.)

■ 현재완료는 과거에 시작된 동작과 그 동작의 현재 상태를 동시에 표현하므로 명백한 과거를 나타내는 yesterday, ~ ago, last week 등의 부사(구)나 의문사 when과는 함께 쓰이지 않는다.

- He wasn't present at the meeting last week. (○)

  He hasn't been present at the meeting last week. (✕) 그는 지난 주 모임에 참석하지 않았다.

※ have[has] been to vs. have[has] gone to
  have[has] been to는 '~에 가 본 적이 있다'는 경험을 나타내고, have[has] gone to는 '~에 가고 없다'는 결과를 나타낸다. 그러므로 have[has] gone to는 3인칭만 주어로 쓸 수 있다.

핵심 Check

1. 다음 주어진 동사를 빈칸에 어법에 맞게 쓰시오.

(1) He _____ _____ English for ten years. (study)

(2) I have not _____ from her for six years. (hear)

(3) _____ you _____ a famous person before? (meet)

2 It ~ to부정사

- **It**'s difficult **to walk** on Earth. 지구에서는 걷는 것이 어려워요.
- **It** is good **to know** how to say hello. 인사하는 법을 아는 것이 좋다.

■ 비교적 긴 to부정사 부분이 문장의 주어로 쓰일 때 그 to부정사 부분을 일반적인 주어의 자리인 문장의 맨 앞에 두지 않고 문장 제일 뒤에 둔다. 대신 주어 자리에는 it을 넣어주는데 그것을 가주어 it이라고 부르고 문장 뒤로 간 to부정사 부분은 진주어라고 부른다. 이때 쓰인 it은 가주어이므로 구체적인 뜻이 없으며, '…하는 것은 ~하다'로 해석한다.

- **It** is easy **to play** the piano. 피아노를 치는 것은 쉽다.
  = **To play** the piano is easy.

- **It** is interesting **to watch** birds. 조류 관찰은 재미있다.
  = **To watch** birds is interesting.

■ It ~ to부정사의 의미상 주어
to부정사의 동작을 실제로 하는 사람을 to부정사의 의미상 주어라고 한다. to부정사의 의미상 주어는 to부정사 바로 앞에 'for+명사의 목적격'의 형태로 쓴다. It ~ to부정사 구문에서 to부정사의 의미상 주어가 없는 경우는 특별한 사람이 아니라 일반적인 사람이기 때문이다. 문장에 쓰인 형용사가 nice, kind, smart, wise 등과 같이 사람의 성향, 성격을 나타내는 말일 때는 'of+목적격'을 쓴다. 또한 to부정사의 부정은 to부정사 앞에 not[never]을 써서 'not[never]+to V'로 나타내며 '…하지 않는 것은 ~하다'로 해석한다.

- **It** is important for you **to choose** good friends. 네가 좋은 친구를 고르는 것은 중요하다.
- **It** is nice of you **to show** me the way. 길을 가르쳐 주셔서 감사합니다.
- **It** is easy **not to think** outside the box. 새로운 사고를 하지 않는 것은 쉽다.

핵심 Check

2. 다음 우리말과 일치하도록 빈칸에 알맞은 말을 쓰시오.

(1) 운동을 하는 것이 왜 중요할까요?
　➡ Why ＿＿＿＿ ＿＿＿＿ ＿＿＿＿ ＿＿＿＿ exercise?

(2) 구명 조끼를 입는 것이 안전하다.
　➡ ＿＿＿＿ is safe ＿＿＿＿ wear a life jacket.

(3) 내가 피아노를 치는 것은 쉽다.
　➡ It's easy ＿＿＿＿ ＿＿＿＿ ＿＿＿＿ ＿＿＿＿ the piano.

01 다음 빈칸에 알맞은 것을 고르시오.

> **A:** Isn't it good _____ with friends?
> **B:** Yes, of course.

① to travel in Korea
② travels in Korea
③ to traveling in Korea
④ of you to travel in Korea
⑤ your travel in Korea

02 다음 중 어법상 <u>어색한</u> 문장은?

① Have you ever seen a koala?
② The plane has just left for Seoul.
③ I have gone to Hong Kong.
④ Marianne has played the piano for 10 years.
⑤ I have already washed my hands.

03 다음 문장에서 어법상 <u>어색한</u> 부분을 바르게 고치시오.

(1) My parents have just return from the trip.

_____ ➡ _____

(2) Rada has eaten dinner with Jonny last weekend.

_____ ➡ _____

(3) How long do you have been in Canada?

_____ ➡ _____

(4) They've worked here for last year.

_____ ➡ _____

(5) That is nervous to sing in front of the class.

_____ ➡ _____

(6) It will be helpful reads the book.

_____ ➡ _____

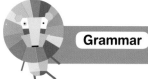

01 다음 중 어법상 바르지 <u>않은</u> 것은?

① Emily has caught a big fish and she is very excited.
② I've never heard her use bad language before.
③ They have lived in that house for more than 20 years.
④ When have you watched the new movie?
⑤ Hermionne has gone back to her country already.

 02 다음 중 어법상 바른 것은?

① It isn't easy studies English every day.
② It is so kind for you to lend me the book.
③ That's necessary to wear a helmet.
④ It's better run your own business if you can.
⑤ It has become common practice to chat online.

 03 다음 빈칸에 알맞은 말이 바르게 짝지어진 것은?

> • _____ the team won ten games this year?
> • It was hard _____ a science experiment.

① Is – to do   ② Is – done
③ Has – to do   ④ Has – done
⑤ Was – doing

 04 다음 문장의 빈칸에 들어갈 알맞은 것은?

> _____ is easy to play musical instruments.

① It   ② This   ③ That
④ What   ⑤ One

05 다음 대화의 빈칸에 들어갈 말로 알맞은 것은?

> M: Where's your homework, Peter?
> W: I'm sorry, but I have not finished it _____.

① just   ② already   ③ yet
④ for   ⑤ since

서답형

06 다음 괄호 안에서 알맞은 말을 고르시오.

(1) Alex (have / has) decided to visit an art museum in London.
(2) I (don't have / haven't) seen David today.
(3) Jane is not here now. She has (been / gone) to Stockholm to find work.
(4) Bella (has been / went) to the United States in 2011.
(5) It is always exciting (sleeps / to sleep) in a tent.
(6) It is impossible (of / for) them to get lost.

07 다음 중 어법상 옳은 것은?

① Angie has bought a new smartphone yesterday.
② Have she told you the good news yet?
③ I have gone to England once.
④ I have already seen the movie.
⑤ I've been learning English since ten years.

08 다음 중 밑줄 친 부분의 쓰임이 다른 하나는?

① It is impossible to live without air and water.
② It was not accepted in old days.
③ It's important for the students to do the project in three days.
④ It is dangerous to be in the street after dark.
⑤ It is better to be safe than sorry.

09 다음 질문에 대한 응답으로 알맞은 것은?

> Has he had any serious problems with ear in the past?

① Yes, he has.　② Yes, he is.
③ Yes, he does.　④ No, he isn't.
⑤ No, he doesn't.

서답형
10 주어진 어휘를 이용하여 다음 우리말을 영작하시오.

> 규칙적으로 휴식을 취할 필요가 있다.
> (it, a break, regularly, take, necessary, to)

➡ _____

11 다음 두 문장을 한 문장으로 바르게 연결한 것은?

> • Jack went back to his home.
> • And he is not here now.

① Jack went to his home.
② Jack went to his home already.
③ Jack hasn't been to his home.
④ Jack hasn't come back to his home yet.
⑤ Jack has gone to his home.

12 다음 우리말과 일치하도록 빈칸에 알맞은 단어로 묶은 것은?

> 비행기를 조종하는 것은 내 꿈 중 한 가지이다.
> ➡ _____ is a dream of mine _____ an airplane.

① It – fly　② It – to fly
③ That – fly　④ That – to fly
⑤ This – flying

13 다음 〈보기〉의 밑줄 친 부분과 용법이 같은 것은?

> ┤ 보기 ├
> He has worked for the company for more than 10 years.

① My mom has been sick since last week.
② She has gone to Japan.
③ Judy has been to America five times.
④ Kevin has already heard about the party at school.
⑤ Megan has lost her wallet on the train.

서답형

14 다음 문장에서 어법상 <u>어색한</u> 것을 바르게 고쳐 다시 쓰시오.

(1) It is difficult for me guess the ending of the story.

➡ _____

_____

(2) This is boring to read a science book.

➡ _____

(3) It is important read for an hour every day.

➡ _____

(4) I have worked in the hospital snack bar then.

➡ _____

(5) Jim has had a cat since three years.

➡ _____

(6) Garry has been to New York on business and he stays there now.

➡ _____

_____

서답형

15 다음 두 문장을 비슷한 뜻을 가진 한 문장으로 바꿔 쓰시오.

(1) Josh lost his smartphone. So, he doesn't have any smartphone now.

➡ _____

(2) Sophia started to live in Georgia five years ago. And she still lives there.

➡ _____

[16~17] 다음 우리말에 맞게 영작한 것을 고르시오.

16

> 너는 작년 이후로 아주 키가 컸다.

① You grew very tall since last year.
② You have grown very tall last year.
③ You have grown very tall for last year.
④ You have grown very tall as last year.
⑤ You have grown very tall since last year.

17

> 기말고사 후에 친구들과 어울리는 것은 정말 신이 나.

① It is very exciting hang out with my friends after finals.
② It is very exciting hangs out with my friends after finals.
③ It is very exciting to hang out with my friends after finals.
④ That is very exciting to hang out with my friends after finals.
⑤ That is very exciting hanging out with my friends after finals.

18 다음 중 어법상 <u>어색한</u> 것을 고르시오. (2개)

① It is necessary for Daniel to talk to his parents.
② It's nice for her to take care of her young sister.
③ It is fun to swim in the lake.
④ When have you watched the movie with her?
⑤ We have lived here since I was born.

Grammar **25**

01 다음 우리말에 맞게 주어진 어구를 바르게 배열하시오.

(1) Kelly는 10살 이후로 LA에서 살고 있다.
(Kelly, she, years, LA, has, was, lived, 10, old, since, in)

➡ _____

(2) 정부는 교육에 더 관심을 가지게 되었다.
(education, the government, interested, become, has, more, in)

➡ _____
_____

(3) 그는 그 소문에 대해 들은 적이 있어.
(the rumor, heard, he, has, about)

➡ _____

(4) 다른 나라들을 여행하는 것은 멋지다.
(countries, it, wonderful, travel, is, other, to, to)

➡ _____

(5) 그가 그 경기의 표를 구하는 것이 가능하니?
(the game, it, tickets, him, possible, get, is, for, for, to)

➡ _____

02 다음 우리말을 (1) to부정사 주어를 써서, (2) 가주어를 써서 영작하시오.

• 밤에 운전하는 것은 위험하다.
(1) _____
(2) _____

• 물건을 훔치는 것은 잘못이다.
(1) _____
(2) _____

03 그림을 보고, 주어진 어휘를 이용하여 자신의 경험에 대해 쓰시오. (현재완료 시제로 주어와 동사를 갖춘 완전한 문장으로 쓸 것.)

(1) (eat, nacho)

➡ _____
_____

(2) (have, to)

➡ _____
_____

04 다음 주어진 두 문장을 한 문장으로 바꿔 쓰시오.

(1) • Sonya visited New York again.
• It is her third visit.

➡ _____

(2) • I ate dinner a moment ago.
• So I am full now.

➡ _____

05 다음 문장을 It으로 시작하여 다시 쓰시오.

(1) To think about all the new things was exciting.

➡ _____

(2) To swim in the cool blue sea was great.

➡ _____

(3) To eat a lot of vegetables is good.

➡ _____

(4) That the pen is mightier than the sword is true.

➡ _____

06 다음 우리말을 괄호 안에 주어진 어휘를 이용하여 영작하시오.

(1) 나는 한 번도 일출을 본 적이 없다.
(a sunrise, see, never, 6 단어)

➡ _____

(2) 그는 영어를 20년 동안 가르쳐 왔다.
(teach, 7 단어)

➡ _____

(3) 이 물을 마셔도 안전한가요?
(this water, safe, drink, 7 단어)

➡ _____

(4) 내가 그 팀에서 축구를 하게 되어 운이 좋다.
(the team, lucky, me, 10 단어)

➡ _____

(5) 이를 매일 닦는 것은 중요하다.
(brush your teeth, important, 9 단어)

➡ _____

07 다음 문장에서 어법상 어색한 것을 고쳐 문장을 다시 쓰시오.

(1) When have you heard from Susan?

➡ _____

(2) Mr. Brown has lived in Jeju-do for 2010.

➡ _____

(3) Have you gone to Canada before?

➡ _____

(4) Use a ticket machine in the theater is easy.

➡ _____
_____

(5) It's important for her understands him.

➡ _____

08 다음 문장을 부정문과 의문문으로 각각 바꿔 쓰시오.

> They have already finished their project.

부정문 _____

의문문 _____

09 다음 두 문장의 의미가 같도록 빈칸에 알맞은 말을 쓰시오.

(1) It started raining last Saturday. It is still raining.

➡ It _____ last Saturday.

(2) Aiko went back to Tokyo. She is in Tokyo now.

➡ Aiko _____ to Tokyo.

Reading

The Best New Thing

Rada lived on a little world, far out in space. She lived there with her father, mother, and brother Jonny. Rada's father and other people worked on spaceships. Only Rada and Jonny were children, and they were born in space. One day, Dad told Rada and Jonny, "We're going back to Earth tomorrow." Rada and Jonny looked at Dad in surprise and floated towards him. Rada asked Dad, "What's it like on Earth?"

"Everything is different there. For example, the sky is blue," answered Dad. "I've never seen a blue sky," said Jonny. "The sky is always black here," said Rada. "You don't have to wear your big heavy space suits because there is air everywhere. It's also hard to jump there because Earth pulls you down," said Dad. "What else?" asked Rada. "There are hills, and they are covered with soft green grass. You can roll down the hills," answered Mom. "Dad, have you ever rolled down a hill?" asked Rada. "Yes, it's really amazing!" answered Dad. Jonny was thirsty, so he opened a milk container and shook it. The milk floated in the air and formed balls. Jonny swallowed the balls. "Jonny, if you drink milk that way on Earth, you'll get wet," said Mom.

be born 태어나다
in surprise 놀라서
towards ～을 향하여, ～ 쪽으로
space suit 우주복
pull down ～을 끌어내리다
be covered with ～으로 덮여 있다
ever 언젠가, 줄곧
container 그릇, 용기
swallow 삼키다

📎 **확인문제**

● 다음 문장이 본문의 내용과 일치하면 T, 일치하지 않으면 F를 쓰시오.

1 Rada and Jonny were born in space. ☐

2 The sky is always black in space. ☐

3 You don't have to wear your big heavy space suits because Earth pulls you down. ☐

4 You can roll down the hills which are covered with soft green grass. ☐

Later that night, Rada and Jonny talked a long time about Earth. It
늦게   =for a long time: 오랫동안   It: 가주어

was exciting to think about all the new things they were going to see
진주어   things와 they 사이에 목적격 관계대명사 which/that이 생략

and do. There was one new thing Rada and Jonny really wanted to do.
           thing과 Rada 사이에 목적격 관계대명사 which/that이 생략

They thought about it all night and didn't tell Mom and Dad about it. It
one new thing

was their secret. The next day, Rada's family got on a spaceship. "It's
(교통수단을) 타다

going to be a long trip," said Mom. "That's alright. I'm so excited!"
be going to+동사원형: 미래의 구체적인 계획을 통해 곧 일어날 것이라고 판단할 수 있는 일에 사용   = all right   excited는 과거분사지만 완전히 형용사화되어 so로 수식할 수 있음.

said Rada. The spaceship finally landed. "Dad, it's difficult to walk
가주어   진주어

on Earth," said Rada. "I know. Earth is pulling you down," said Dad.
pull down: 끌어당기다. 지구에 중력이 있음을 의미

Rada and Jonny couldn't float anymore. That was the first new thing.
우주에서는 공중에 떠다녔지만, 지구에서는 중력 때문에 더 이상 떠다닐 수 없음을 의미, 앞 문장 전체

"What's that sound?" asked Rada. "A bird is singing," said Mom. "I've
be동사 현재형+-ing: 현재진행형, 현재 하고 있는 동작을 나타낸다.

never heard a bird sing," said Rada. "And I've never felt the wind,"
현재완료(경험), '결코 들어 본 적이 없다' 지각동사 hear+목적어+동사원형/-ing   현재완료(경험), '바람을 한 번도 느껴 본 적이 없다'

said Jonny. These were all new things. Rada and Jonny ran up the
near의 최상급, '가장 가까운'

nearest hill. At the top, they looked at each other and laughed. Then
laughed 앞에 주어인 they가 중복되어 생략

they lay down on the soft green grass and rolled down the hill. That
lie(눕다)의 과거형. lie-lay-lain / lay-laid-laid: 놓다, 눕히다

was their secret! "This is the best new thing of all!" shouted Rada and
good의 최상급

Jonny. And they ran up to the top of the hill again.
~으로 뛰어 올라갔다

secret 비밀

all night 밤새도록

get on ~에 타다, ~에 오르다

each other 서로

lie 눕다

📎 **확인문제**

● 다음 문장이 본문의 내용과 일치하면 T, 일치하지 <u>않으면</u> F를 쓰시오.

1 It was exciting for Rada and Jonny to think about all the new things they were
going to see and do on Earth. ☐

2 Rada and Jonny thought about one new thing they really wanted to do on Earth and
told Mom and Dad about it. ☐

3 Rada has ever heard a bird sing. ☐

4 Rada and Jonny's secret was to lie down on the grass and roll down the hill. ☐

● 우리말을 참고하여 빈칸에 알맞은 말을 쓰시오.

1 The _____ New Thing

2 Rada lived on a little world, _____ _____ _____ _____.

3 She _____ _____ _____ her father, mother, and brother Jonny.

4 Rada's father and other people _____ _____ spaceships.

5 _____ Rada and Jonny were children, and they _____ _____ in space.

6 One day, Dad told Rada and Jonny, "We're _____ _____ _____ Earth tomorrow."

7 Rada and Jonny looked at Dad _____ _____ and floated towards him.

8 Rada asked Dad, "_____ _____ _____ on Earth?"

9 "Everything _____ _____ there.

10 _____ _____ , the sky is blue," answered Dad.

11 "_____ _____ _____ a blue sky," said Jonny.

12 "The sky _____ _____ here," said Rada.

13 "You _____ _____ wear your big heavy space suits because _____ _____ _____ everywhere.

14 It's also hard to jump there because Earth _____ _____ _____," said Dad.

15 "_____ _____?" asked Rada.

16 "There are hills, and they _____ _____ _____ soft green grass.

17 You can _____ _____ the hills," answered Mom.

18 "Dad, _____ _____ _____ _____ _____ a hill?" asked Rada.

19 "Yes, it's really _____!" answered Dad.

20 Jonny was thirsty, so he _____ a milk container and _____ it.

21 The milk _____ in the air and _____ balls.

22 Jonny _____ the balls.

23 "Jonny, if you drink milk that way on Earth, you'll _____ _____," said Mom.

1 최고의 새로운 것
2 Rada는 먼 우주의 작은 세계에 살고 있었다.
3 그녀는 아빠, 엄마 그리고 남동생 Jonny와 함께 그곳에서 살고 있었다.
4 Rada의 아빠와 다른 사람들은 우주선에서 일했다.
5 Rada와 Jonny만이 아이들이었고, 그들은 우주에서 태어났다.
6 어느 날, 아빠가 Rada와 Jonny에게, "우리는 내일 지구로 돌아갈 거야."라고 말했다.
7 Rada와 Jonny는 깜짝 놀라 아빠를 바라보았고, 그에게 둥둥 떠서 갔다.
8 Rada가 아빠에게, "지구는 어떤 곳인가요?"라고 물었다.
9 "그곳에선 모든 것이 다르단다.
10 예를 들어, 하늘은 파란색이지." 라고 아빠가 대답했다.
11 "전 한 번도 파란 하늘을 본 적이 없어요."라고 Jonny가 말했다.
12 "여기는 하늘이 항상 검은색이잖아요."라고 Rada가 말했다.
13 "그곳에는 모든 곳에 공기가 있기 때문에 크고 무거운 우주복을 입을 필요가 없단다.
14 또한 지구가 너희들을 끌어당기기 때문에 거기에서는 점프하는 것도 어렵단다." 아빠가 말했다.
15 "그 밖에 또 뭐가 있어요?" Rada가 물었다.
16 "언덕들이 있는데 그것들은 부드러운 초록색의 잔디로 뒤덮여 있단다.
17 언덕을 굴러 내려갈 수도 있어." 엄마가 대답했다.
18 "아빠, 언덕을 굴러 내려가 본 적 있어요?" Rada가 물었다.
19 "그럼. 정말 놀라워!" 아빠가 대답했다.
20 Jonny는 목이 말라서 우유 용기를 열어 그것을 흔들었다.
21 우유가 공기 중으로 떠서 방울을 형성했다.
22 Jonny는 그 우유 방울을 삼켰다.
23 "Jonny, 만약 네가 지구에서 그런 식으로 우유를 마신다면, 다 젖을 거야." 엄마가 말했다.

24 _____ _____ _____, Rada and Jonny talked a long time about Earth.

25 It was _____ to think about _____ _____ _____ _____ they were going to see and do.

26 There was _____ _____ _____ Rada and Jonny really wanted to do.

27 They thought about it _____ _____ and didn't tell Mom and Dad about it.

28 It was _____ _____.

29 The next day, Rada's family _____ _____ a spaceship.

30 "_____ _____ _____ _____ a long trip," said Mom.

31 "That's alright. I'm _____ _____!" said Rada.

32 The spaceship _____ landed.

33 "Dad, it's difficult _____ _____ on Earth," said Rada.

34 "I know. Earth is _____ _____ _____," said Dad.

35 Rada and Jonny _____ _____ _____ _____.

36 That was _____ _____ _____ _____.

37 "_____ that sound?" asked Rada.

38 "A bird _____ _____," said Mom.

39 "_____ _____ _____ a bird sing," said Rada.

40 "And _____ _____ _____ the wind," said Jonny.

41 _____ were all new things.

42 Rada and Jonny ran up _____ _____ hill.

43 At the top, they looked at _____ _____ and laughed.

44 Then they _____ _____ on the soft green grass and _____ _____ the hill.

45 That was _____ _____!

46 "This is the _____ _____ _____ of all!" shouted Rada and Jonny.

47 And they ran _____ _____ _____ _____ of the hill again.

24 그날 밤 늦게, Rada와 Jonny는 지구에 대해서 오랜 시간 이야기했다.

25 그들이 보고, 하게 될 모든 새로운 것들을 생각하는 것은 흥미로웠다.

26 Rada와 Jonny가 정말로 하고 싶었던 한 가지 새로운 것이 있었다.

27 그들은 밤새 그것에 대해서 생각했고 엄마와 아빠에게는 그것을 말하지 않았다.

28 그것은 그들의 비밀이었다.

29 다음날, Rada의 가족은 우주선에 올랐다.

30 "긴 여행이 될 거야." 엄마가 말했다.

31 "괜찮아요. 정말 신나요!" Rada가 말했다.

32 우주선이 마침내 착륙했다.

33 "아빠, 지구에서는 걷는 것이 어려워요." Rada가 말했다.

34 "그래. 지구가 너를 끌어당기고 있거든." 아빠가 말했다.

35 Rada와 Jonny는 더 이상 떠다닐 수 없었다.

36 그것이 첫 번째 새로운 것이었다.

37 "저건 무슨 소리죠?"라고 Rada가 물었다.

38 "새가 노래하는 거야." 엄마가 말했다.

39 "새가 노래하는 것을 들어 본 적이 없어요."라고 Rada가 말했다.

40 "그리고 저는 바람을 느껴 본 적도 없어요."라고 Jonny가 말했다.

41 이러한 것들이 모두 새로운 것들이었다.

42 Rada와 Jonny는 가장 가까운 언덕으로 뛰어 올라갔다.

43 꼭대기에서, 그들은 서로를 쳐다보고 웃었다.

44 그리고 나서 그들은 부드러운 초록 잔디에 누워서 언덕 아래로 굴러 내려갔다.

45 그것이 그들의 비밀이었다!

46 "이것이 모든 것들 중에서 최고의 새로운 것이에요!" Rada와 Jonny는 외쳤다.

47 그리고 그들은 언덕 꼭대기로 다시 뛰어 올라갔다.

● 우리말을 참고하여 본문을 영작하시오.

1 최고의 새로운 것
➡ _____

2 Rada는 먼 우주의 작은 세계에 살고 있었다.
➡ _____

3 그녀는 아빠, 엄마 그리고 남동생 Jonny와 함께 그곳에서 살고 있었다.
➡ _____

4 Rada의 아빠와 다른 사람들은 우주선에서 일했다.
➡ _____

5 Rada와 Jonny만이 아이들이었고, 그들은 우주에서 태어났다.
➡ _____

6 어느 날, 아빠가 Rada와 Jonny에게, "우리는 내일 지구로 돌아갈 거야."라고 말했다.
➡ _____

7 Rada와 Jonny는 깜짝 놀라 아빠를 바라보았고, 그에게 둥둥 떠서 갔다.
➡ _____

8 Rada가 아빠에게, "지구는 어떤 곳인가요?"라고 물었다.
➡ _____

9 "그곳에선 모든 것이 다르단다.
➡ _____

10 예를 들어, 하늘은 파란색이지."라고 아빠가 대답했다.
➡ _____

11 "전 한 번도 파란 하늘을 본 적이 없어요."라고 Jonny가 말했다.
➡ _____

12 "여기는 하늘이 항상 검은색이잖아요."라고 Rada가 말했다.
➡ _____

13 "그곳에는 모든 곳에 공기가 있기 때문에 크고 무거운 우주복을 입을 필요가 없단다.
➡ _____

14 또한 지구가 너희들을 끌어당기기 때문에 거기에서는 점프하는 것도 어렵단다." 아빠가 말했다.
➡ _____

15 "그 밖에 또 뭐가 있어요?" Rada가 물었다.
➡ _____

16 "언덕들이 있는데 그것들은 부드러운 초록색의 잔디로 뒤덮여 있단다.
➡ _____

17 언덕을 굴러 내려갈 수도 있어." 엄마가 대답했다.
➡ _____

18 "아빠, 언덕을 굴러 내려가 본 적 있어요?" Rada가 물었다.
➡ _____

19 "그럼, 정말 놀라워!" 아빠가 대답했다.
➡ _____

20 Jonny는 목이 말라서 우유 용기를 열어 그것을 흔들었다.
➡ _____

21 우유가 공기 중으로 떠서 방울을 형성했다.
➡ _____

22 Jonny는 그 우유 방울을 삼켰다.
➡ _____

23 "Jonny, 만약 네가 지구에서 그런 식으로 우유를 마신다면, 다 젖을 거야." 엄마가 말했다.
➡ _____

24 그날 밤 늦게, Rada와 Jonny는 지구에 대해서 오랜 시간 이야기했다.
➡ _____

25 그들이 보고, 하게 될 모든 새로운 것들을 생각하는 것은 흥미로웠다.
➡ _____

26 Rada와 Jonny가 정말로 하고 싶었던 한 가지 새로운 것이 있었다.
➡ _____

27 그들은 밤새 그것에 대해서 생각했고 엄마와 아빠에게는 그것을 말하지 않았다.
➡ _____

28 그것은 그들의 비밀이었다.
➡ _____

29 다음날, Rada의 가족은 우주선에 올랐다.
➡ _____

30 "긴 여행이 될 거야." 엄마가 말했다.
➡ _____

31 "괜찮아요. 정말 신나요!" Rada가 말했다.
➡ _____

32 우주선이 마침내 착륙했다.
➡ _____

33 "아빠, 지구에서는 걷는 것이 어려워요." Rada가 말했다.
➡ _____

34 "그래. 지구가 너를 끌어당기고 있거든." 아빠가 말했다.
➡ _____

35 Rada와 Jonny는 더 이상 떠다닐 수 없었다.
➡ _____

36 그것이 첫 번째 새로운 것이었다.
➡ _____

37 "저건 무슨 소리죠?"라고 Rada가 물었다.
➡ _____

38 "새가 노래하는 거야." 엄마가 말했다.
➡ _____

39 "새가 노래하는 것을 들어 본 적이 없어요."라고 Rada가 말했다.
➡ _____

40 "그리고 저는 바람을 느껴 본 적도 없어요."라고 Jonny가 말했다.
➡ _____

41 이러한 것들이 모두 새로운 것들이었다.
➡ _____

42 Rada와 Jonny는 가장 가까운 언덕으로 뛰어 올라갔다.
➡ _____

43 꼭대기에서, 그들은 서로를 쳐다보고 웃었다.
➡ _____

44 그리고 나서 그들은 부드러운 초록 잔디에 누워서 언덕 아래로 굴러 내려갔다.
➡ _____

45 그것이 그들의 비밀이었다!
➡ _____

46 "이것이 모든 것들 중에서 최고의 새로운 것이에요!" Rada와 Jonny는 외쳤다.
➡ _____

47 그리고 그들은 언덕 꼭대기로 다시 뛰어 올라갔다.
➡ _____

[01~04] 다음 글을 읽고 물음에 답하시오.

Rada lived on a little world, far out _____ⓐ space. She lived there with her father, mother, and brother Jonny. Rada's father and other people worked on spaceships. Only Rada and Jonny were children, and they were born in space.

One day, Dad told Rada and Jonny, "We're going back to Earth tomorrow."

Rada and Jonny looked at Dad in surprise and floated towards him.

Rada asked Dad, "What's (A)it like _____ⓑ Earth?"

"Everything is different there. For example, the sky is blue," answered Dad.

"I've never seen a blue sky," said Jonny.

"The sky is always black here," said Rada.

01 위 글의 빈칸 ⓐ와 ⓑ에 들어갈 전치사가 바르게 짝지어진 것은?

① for – to ② in – for
③ in – on ④ from – to
⑤ for – on

02 위 글의 밑줄 친 (A)it과 문법적 쓰임이 같은 것을 모두 고르시오.

① I think it strange that she wants them.
② How's it going with you?
③ It was wine, not water, that you drank.
④ It is impossible to get there in time.
⑤ As it happened, I left the book at home.

03 위 글의 종류로 알맞은 것을 고르시오.

① book report ② article
③ biography ④ essay
⑤ science fiction

04 위 글의 내용과 일치하지 않는 것은?

① Rada lived far out in space with her family.
② Rada and Jonny were born in space.
③ When Rada and Jonny heard they were returning to space, they were surprised.
④ Dad said everything was different on Earth.
⑤ The sky was always black in space.

[05~08] 다음 글을 읽고 물음에 답하시오.

"You don't have to wear your big heavy space suits because there is air everywhere. It's also hard to jump there because Earth pulls you down," said Dad.

"What else?" asked Rada.

"There are hills, and they are covered with soft green grass. You can roll down the hills," answered Mom.

"Dad, ⓐhave you ever rolled down a hill?" asked Rada.

"Yes, it's really amazing!" answered Dad.

Jonny was thirsty, so he opened a milk container and ____(A)____ it. The milk floated in the air and formed balls. Jonny swallowed the balls.

"Jonny, ⓑ만약 네가 지구에서 그런 식으로 우유를 마신다면, 다 젖을 거야," said Mom.

서답형

05 위 글의 빈칸 (A)에 shake를 알맞은 형태로 쓰시오.

➡ _____

06 아래 〈보기〉에서 위 글의 밑줄 친 ⓐ의 현재완료와 용법이 같은 것의 개수를 고르시오.

① He has lost his pen.
② We have visited Paris before.
③ I have learned English since 2015.
④ She hasn't cleaned her room yet.
⑤ How many times have you seen it?

① 1개　② 2개　③ 3개　④ 4개　⑤ 5개

서답형

07 위 글의 밑줄 친 ⓑ의 우리말에 맞게 주어진 어휘를 이용하여 11 단어로 영작하시오.

> drink, that way, get wet

➡ _____

중요

08 다음 중 Rada와 Jonny가 지구에서 처음 경험하게 될 일이 아닌 것을 고르시오.

① 우주복을 입을 필요가 없는 것
② 점프를 쉽게 할 수 있는 것
③ 부드러운 초록색의 잔디로 뒤덮여 있는 언덕을 보는 것
④ 언덕을 굴러 내려가는 것
⑤ 우유 방울을 삼키는 대신 마시는 것

[09~11] 다음 글을 읽고 물음에 답하시오.

Later that night, Rada and Jonny talked a long time about Earth. ⓐIt was (A)[exciting / excited] to think about all the new things they were going to see and do. There was one new thing Rada and Jonny really wanted to do. They thought about ⓑit all (B)[night / nights] and didn't tell Mom and Dad about ⓒit. It was their secret.

The next day, Rada's family got (C)[on / off] a spaceship.

"It's going to be a long trip," said Mom.

"That's alright. I'm so excited!" said Rada.

서답형

09 위 글의 밑줄 친 ⓐit, ⓑit, ⓒit이 가리키는 것을 본문에서 찾아 영어로 쓰시오.

(A) _____

_____

(B) _____

(C) _____

서답형

10 위 글의 괄호 (A)~(C)에서 문맥이나 어법상 알맞은 낱말을 골라 쓰시오.

(A) _____ (B) _____ (C) _____

11 위 글에서 알 수 있는 Rada와 Jonny의 심경으로 가장 알맞은 것을 고르시오.

① upset　　　② confused
③ worried　　④ disappointed
⑤ expectant

[12~15] 다음 글을 읽고 물음에 답하시오.

The spaceship finally (A)[landed / took off].

"Dad, it's difficult to walk on Earth," said Rada.

"I know. Earth is (B)[pulling / pushing] you down," said Dad.

Rada and Jonny couldn't float anymore. That was the first new thing.

"What's that sound?" asked Rada.

"A bird is singing," said Mom.

"I've never heard a bird sing," said Rada.

"And I've never felt the wind," said Jonny. These were all new things.

Rada and Jonny ran up the nearest hill. At the top, they looked at each other and laughed. ⓐThen they lie down on the soft green grass and rolled down the hill. That was their secret!

"This is the best (C)[familiar / new] thing of all!" shouted Rada and Jonny.

And they ran up to the top of the hill again.

서답형

12 위 글의 괄호 (A)~(C)에서 문맥상 알맞은 낱말을 골라 쓰시오.

(A) _____ (B) _____ (C) _____

서답형

13 위 글의 밑줄 친 ⓐ에서 어법상 **틀린** 부분을 찾아 고치시오.

_____ ➡ _____

14 위 글의 제목으로 알맞은 것을 고르시오.

① Oh, It's Difficult to Walk on Earth!
② Be Careful! Earth Is Pulling You Down!
③ Guess What? I Can't Float Anymore!
④ New Things They Experienced on Earth
⑤ How to Roll Down the Hill

중요

15 위 글의 내용과 일치하지 **않는** 것은?

① 지구에서는 걷는 것이 어렵다고 Rada가 아빠에게 말했다.
② 지구에서 Rada와 Jonny는 더 이상 떠다닐 수 없었다.
③ Rada는 새가 노래하는 것을 들어 본 적이 있다.
④ Jonny는 바람을 느껴 본 적이 없다.
⑤ Rada와 Jonny는 부드러운 초록 잔디에 누워서 언덕 아래로 굴러 내려갔다.

[16~18] 다음 글을 읽고 물음에 답하시오.

"You don't have to wear your big heavy space suits because there is air everywhere. (①) It's also hard to jump there because Earth pulls you down," said Dad.

(②) "There are hills, and they are covered with soft green grass. (③) You can roll down the hills," answered Mom.

(④) "Dad, have you ever rolled down a hill?" asked Rada.

(⑤) "Yes, it's really amazing!" answered Dad. Jonny was thirsty, so he opened a milk container and shook it. The milk floated in the air and formed balls. Jonny swallowed the balls.

"Jonny, if you drink milk that way on Earth, you'll get wet," said Mom.

16 위 글의 흐름으로 보아, 주어진 문장이 들어가기에 가장 적절한 곳은?

> "What else?" asked Rada.

① ② ③ ④ ⑤

17 다음 빈칸 (A)~(C)에 알맞은 단어를 넣어 우주에서 우유 먹는 법을 완성하시오.

> In space, you can't drink milk in the same way as people do on Earth. First, you open a milk container and ___(A)___ it. Then, the milk floats in the air and forms ___(B)___ . Finally, you can ___(C)___ the balls.

(A) _____ (B) _____ (C) _____

18 위 글을 읽고 대답할 수 <u>없는</u> 질문은?

① Why is there no need to wear your big heavy space suits on Earth?

② Why is it difficult to jump on Earth?

③ What can you do on the hills that are covered with soft green grass?

④ When did Dad roll down a hill?

⑤ When Jonny was thirsty, what did he do?

[19~21] 다음 글을 읽고 물음에 답하시오.

The spaceship finally landed.

"Dad, it's difficult to walk on Earth," said Rada.

"I know. Earth is pulling you down," said Dad.

Rada and Jonny couldn't float anymore. That was the first new thing.

"What's that sound?" asked Rada.

"A bird is singing," said Mom.

"I've never heard a bird sing," said Rada.

"And I've never felt the wind," said Jonny.

ⓐ<u>These were all familiar things.</u>

Rada and Jonny ran up the nearest hill. At the top, they looked at each other and laughed. Then ⓑ<u>그들은 부드러운 초록 잔디에 누워서 언덕 아래로 굴러 내려갔다</u>. That was their secret!

"This is the best new thing of all!" shouted Rada and Jonny.

And they ran up to the top of the hill again.

19 What was the first new thing to Rada and Jonny? Fill in the blanks with the suitable words. (6 words)

➡ It was that _____ .

20 위 글의 밑줄 친 ⓐ에서 흐름상 어색한 부분을 찾아 고치시오.

_____ ➡ _____

21 위 글의 밑줄 친 ⓑ의 우리말에 맞게 주어진 어휘를 이용하여 13 단어로 영작하시오.

on the soft green grass

➡ _____

_____

[22~24] 다음 글을 읽고 물음에 답하시오.

The next morning, Rada's family went to a park. Rada said to Dad, "Dad, I've never ___ⓐ___ a bike before." "Let's ___ⓑ___ bikes, then," said Dad. They then ___ⓒ___ bikes together. The weather was great, and it was so fun.

In the afternoon, Rada's family went to the beach. Jonny said to Mom, "I've never swum before." "Let's swim, then," said Mom. It was great to swim in the cool blue sea.

At night, Rada and Jonny talked about living on Earth. "It's wonderful to live on Earth," Rada said to Jonny. "Yes. It's great to be here," Jonny said.

22 위 글의 빈칸 ⓐ~ⓒ에 ride를 알맞은 형태로 쓰시오.

ⓐ _____ ⓑ _____ ⓒ _____

23 위 글을 읽고 Rada의 가족이 한 일을 우리말로 쓰시오.

오전: _____

오후: _____

밤: _____

24 What did Rada and Jonny think about living on Earth? Answer in English in a full sentence.

➡ _____

_____

[25~27] 다음 글을 읽고 물음에 답하시오.

Later that night, Rada and Jonny talked a long time about Earth. ⓐIt was exciting ⓑto think about all the new things they were going to see and do them. There was one new thing Rada and Jonny really wanted to do. They thought about it all night and didn't tell Mom and Dad about it. It was their secret.

The next day, Rada's family got on a spaceship. "It's going to be a long trip," said Mom.

"That's alright. I'm so excited!" said Rada.

25 아래 〈보기〉에서 위 글의 밑줄 친 ⓐIt과 문법적 쓰임이 같은 것의 개수를 고르시오.

① It is warmer than yesterday.
② It is important to choose good friends.
③ Look! It's going up that tree.
④ It is impossible to master English in a month or two.
⑤ I think it necessary that you should do it at once.

① 1개 ② 2개 ③ 3개 ④ 4개 ⑤ 5개

26 위 글의 밑줄 친 ⓑ에서 어법상 틀린 부분을 찾아 고치시오.

—————— ➡ ——————

27 What was Rada and Jonny's secret? Answer in English.
(8 words)

➡ ——————————————

[28~30] 다음 글을 읽고 물음에 답하시오.

The spaceship finally landed.

"Dad, it's difficult to walk on Earth," said Rada.

"I know. Earth is pulling you down," said Dad.

　Rada and Jonny couldn't float anymore.
That was the first new thing.

"What's that sound?" asked Rada.

"A bird is singing," said Mom.

"ⓐI've never heard a bird to sing," said Rada.

"And I've never felt the wind," said Jonny.

These were all new things.

Rada and Jonny ran up to the nearest hill.
At the top, they looked at each other and
laughed. Then they lay down on the soft
green grass and rolled down the hill. That
was their secret!

"This is the best new thing of all!" shouted
Rada and Jonny.

And they ran up to the top of the hill again.

28 위 글의 주제로 알맞은 것을 고르시오.

① final landing of the spaceship

② new things Rada and Jonny experienced
on Earth

③ the gravity of the Earth

④ the way Rada heard a bird sing and
Jonny felt the wind

⑤ Rada and Jonny who enjoyed rolling
down the hill

29 위 글의 밑줄 친 ⓐ에서 어법상 틀린 부분을 찾아 고치시오.

—————— ➡ ——————

30 위 글을 읽고 대답할 수 없는 질문은?

① Why is it difficult to walk on Earth?

② Was it possible for Rada and Jonny to
float on Earth?

③ Has Jonny ever felt the wind?

④ What did Rada and Jonny do at the top
of the hill?

⑤ How many times did Rada and Jonny
run up to the top of the hill?

[01~03] 다음 글을 읽고 물음에 답하시오.

Rada lived on a little world, far out in space. She lived there with her father, mother, and brother Jonny. Rada's father and other people worked on spaceships. Only Rada and Jonny were children, and they were born in space.

One day, Dad told Rada and Jonny, "We're going back to Earth tomorrow."

ⓐRada와 Jonny는 깜짝 놀라 아빠를 바라보았고, 그에게 둥둥 떠서 갔다.

Rada asked Dad, "What's it like on Earth?"

"Everything is different there. For example, the sky is blue," answered Dad.

"I've never seen a blue sky," said Jonny.

"The sky is always black here," said Rada.

01 위 글의 내용과 일치하도록 다음 빈칸 (A)와 (B)에 알맞은 단어를 쓰시오.

> In space, there were no (A)_____ except Rada and Jonny (B)_____ were born there.

02 위 글의 밑줄 친 ⓐ의 우리말에 맞게 한 단어를 보충하여, 주어진 어휘를 알맞게 배열하시오.

> surprise/ towards / looked / him / and / Rada and Jonny / floated / Dad / at

➡ _____

_____

03 다음 빈칸에 알맞은 단어를 넣어 우주와 지구의 차이점을 완성하시오.

> The _____ of the sky in space is different from that on Earth.

[04~06] 다음 글을 읽고 물음에 답하시오.

"You don't have to wear your big heavy space suits because there is air everywhere. It's also hard to jump there because Earth pulls you down," said Dad.

"What else?" asked Rada.

"There are hills, and they are covered with soft green grass. You can roll down the hills," answered Mom.

"Dad, have you ever rolled down a hill?" asked Rada.

"ⓐYes, it's really amazing!" answered Dad.

Jonny was thirsty, so he opened a milk container and shook it. The milk floated in the air and formed balls. Jonny swallowed the balls.

ⓑ"Jonny, if you will drink milk that way on Earth, you'll get wet," said Mom.

04 위 글의 내용과 일치하도록 다음 빈칸 (A)~(D)에 알맞은 말을 쓰시오.

	in space	on Earth
wear your big heavy space suits	(A) _____	(A) need not
to jump	easy	(B)_____
how to have milk	swallow the milk (C)_____	drink milk

05 위 글의 밑줄 친 ⓐYes, 뒤에 생략된 말을 쓰시오. (2 단어)

➡ _____

06 위 글의 밑줄 친 ⓑ에서 어법상 **틀린** 부분을 찾아 고치시오.

_____ ➡ _____

[07~09] 다음 글을 읽고 물음에 답하시오.

The spaceship finally landed.

"Dad, it's difficult to walk on Earth," said Rada.

"I know. Earth is pulling you down," said Dad.

ⓐRada and Jonny couldn't float anymore. That was the first new thing.

"What's that sound?" asked Rada.

"A bird is singing," said Mom.

"(A)I've (_____) heard a bird sing," said Rada.

"And (B)I've (_____) felt the wind," said Jonny.

These were all new things.

Rada and Jonny ran up the nearest hill. At the top, they looked at each other and laughed. Then they lay down on the soft green grass and rolled down the hill. That was their secret!

07 위 글의 밑줄 친 (A)와 (B)가 각각 다음 문장과 같은 뜻이 되도록 빈칸에 공통으로 들어갈 알맞은 한 단어를 쓰시오.

(A): This is the first time I've ever heard a bird sing,

(B): This is the first time I've ever felt the wind,

➡ _____

08 위 글의 밑줄 친 ⓐ를 다음과 같이 바꿔 쓸 때 빈칸에 들어갈 알맞은 말을 쓰시오.

Rada and Jonny could _____ _____ float.

09 What was Rada and Jonny's secret? Fill in the blanks with the suitable words.

It was that they _____ _____ on the soft green grass and _____ _____ the hill.

[10~12] 다음 글을 읽고 물음에 답하시오.

Rada lived on a little world, far out in space. She lived there with her father, mother, and brother Jonny. Rada's father and (A)[another / other] people worked on spaceships. Only Rada and Jonny were children, and they were born in space.

One day, Dad told Rada and Jonny, "We're going back to Earth tomorrow."

ⓐRada and Jonny looked at Dad in surprise and ran towards him.

Rada asked Dad, "(B)[How / What] is it like on Earth?"

"Everything is (C)[different / similar] ⓑthere. For example, the sky is blue," answered Dad.

"I've never seen a blue sky," said Jonny.

"The sky is always black ⓒhere," said Rada.

10 위 글의 괄호 (A)~(C)에서 문맥이나 어법상 알맞은 낱말을 골라 쓰시오.

(A) _____ (B) _____ (C) _____

11 위 글의 밑줄 친 ⓐ에서 흐름상 어색한 부분을 찾아 고치시오.

_____ ➡ _____

12 위 글의 밑줄 친 ⓑthere와 ⓒhere가 가리키는 것을 본문에서 찾아 쓰시오.

ⓑ _____ ⓒ _____

교과서

구석구석

One Minute Speech

Did you hear about the new book, *Dave's Adventures*?
상대방이 알고 있는지 물어보는 표현이다
This book is about Dave and his adventures in the woods.
~에 관한 것이다
The main characters are Dave and a big bear. The story is fun.

Are you curious about the book?
be curious about ~: ~에 관해 궁금해하다
Then you should read it!

구문해설 · adventure 모험 · be about ~에 관한 것이다 · main character 주인공
· curious 궁금한, 호기심 있는

새 책인 Dave의 모험에 관해 들어 봤니? 이 책은 Dave와 숲에서의 그의 모험에 관한 거야. 주인공은 Dave와 큰 곰이야. 이야기가 재미있어. 그 책에 관해 궁금하니? 그러면 그것을 꼭 읽어 봐야 해!

Read and Complete

1. Rada's family lived in space. One day, they decided to go back to Earth.
decide는 to부정사를 목적어로 취한다.
2. Rada's family talked about life on Earth. They talked about the blue sky and

hills which are covered with green grass.
주격 관계대명사+be동사: 생략 가능
3. The next day, Rada's family got on a spaceship. It was a long trip to Earth.
get on: 타다, 오르다, get off: 내리다
4. When they arrived on Earth, Rada and Jonny ran up the nearest hill and
arrive on: ~에 도착하다   형용사 near의 최상급
rolled down it. That was the best new thing to them.
the hill

구문해설 · in space: 우주에서 · decide: ~을 결정하다 · be covered with: ~으로 뒤덮여 있다
· roll down: 굴러 내려가다

1. Rada의 가족은 우주에서 살고 있었다. 어느 날, 그들은 지구로 돌아가기로 결정했다.
2. Rada의 가족은 지구의 생활에 대해 이야기했다. 그들은 파란 하늘과 초록색 잔디로 뒤덮인 언덕에 대해 이야기했다.
3. 다음날, Rada의 가족은 우주선에 올랐다. 그것은 지구로의 긴 여행이었다.
4. 그들이 지구에 도착했을 때, Rada와 Jonny는 가장 가까운 언덕으로 뛰어 올라가 아래로 굴러 내려갔다. 그것은 그들에게 최고의 새로운 것이었다.

Around the World

1. Russia sent the first dog into space. It was small, and its name was Laika.
the+서수: 최초의   the dog's
2. Yuri Gagarin went into space for the first time.
처음으로, 최초로
3. The USA sent the first human to the moon. His name was Neil Armstrong.
~을 …로 보냈다
4. Russia built the first space station. It flew around the Earth almost 3,000
날아다녔다. 선회했다   지구
times.

구문해설 · space station: 우주 정거장 · almost: 거의 · times: ~ 번, ~ 배

1. 러시아는 우주에 최초의 개를 보냈다. 그것은 작았고, 이름은 Laika였다.
2. Yuri Gagarin이 최초로 우주에 갔다.
3. 미국은 달에 최초의 인간을 보냈다. 그의 이름은 Neil Armstrong이었다.
4. 러시아가 최초의 우주 정거장을 건설하였다. 그것은 거의 3천 번 지구 주변을 돌았다.

Words & Expressions

01 다음 주어진 두 단어의 관계가 같도록 빈칸에 알맞은 단어를 쓰시오.

> excited : bored = take off : _____

02 다음 글의 빈칸 ⓐ와 ⓑ에 들어갈 단어로 바르게 짝지어진 것은?

> • You ⓐ_____ wear your big heavy space suits because there is air everywhere.
> • It's also hard to jump there because Earth ⓑ_____.

① have to – rolls you down
② must not – pulls down you
③ don't need to – pulls you up
④ don't have to – pulls you down
⑤ cannot – pulls down you

[03~04] 다음 영영풀이에 해당하는 것을 고르시오.

03

> to come out of a mother's body

① be curious about   ② roll down
③ be born   ④ swallow
⑤ get on

04

> to arrive on the ground or other surface after moving down through the air

① land   ② float
③ take off ④ get on
⑤ form

05 다음 빈칸에 공통으로 들어갈 말을 쓰시오.

> • That desk takes up too much _____.
>   *take up: 차지하다
> • There are 90 parking _____s in this parking lot.
> • On June 18, China sent its first spacewoman into _____.
>   *spacewoman: 여성 우주비행사

06 다음 밑줄 친 부분의 뜻이 잘못된 것은?

① This is a poster of the spaceship. (우주선)
② It's a type of ice cream. (종류)
③ Rada and Jonny looked at Dad in surprise. (놀라서)
④ They were born in space. (태어났다)
⑤ On sunny days, people go to parks and lie down on the grass. (구르다)

Conversation

07 다음 대화를 순서에 맞게 바르게 배열한 것은?

> (A) Yes, and here it is. It looks good.
> (B) Yes, I did. It's a type of ice cream.
> (C) Did you hear about the new space food?
> (D) I'm really curious about the taste.

① (A) – (B) – (D) – (C)
② (B) – (A) – (C) – (D)
③ (C) – (A) – (B) – (D)
④ (C) – (B) – (A) – (D)
⑤ (D) – (B) – (C) – (A)

[08~10] 다음 대화를 읽고 물음에 답하시오.

> B: Subin, did you hear about the new movie, *Life on the Moon*?
> G: No, I didn't.
> B: I heard it's really good. (①)
> G: I'm really curious about the movie. (②)
> B: It's about a man who is trying to live on the moon. (③)
> G: That sounds interesting.
> B: Look. The movie is playing at the Space Theater here. (④)
> G: What time is the movie?
> B: It begins at 2:30. (⑤)
> G: Let's eat lunch first and then see the movie.
> B: OK. I'm hungry. Let's go!

08 주어진 문장이 들어갈 위치로 알맞은 것은?

> What's it about?

①   ②   ③   ④   ⑤

09 다음 질문에 대한 답을 위 대화에서 찾아 쓰시오.

> Q: What is the movie, *Life on the Moon*, about?

➡ _____

10 위 대화의 내용과 일치하지 않는 것은?

① Subin heard the new movie is really good.
② Subin has an interest in the new movie.
③ The new movie is playing now.
④ They are going to see the movie after eating lunch.
⑤ The movie is about a man trying to live on the moon.

11 다음 그림을 보고 제시된 〈조건〉에 맞게 아래 대화의 빈칸을 완성하시오.

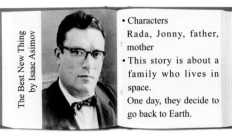

┤ 조건 ├
(1) 'hear'를 사용할 것.
(2) 'really'와 'curious'를 사용하여 새로운 정보에 관심을 나타내는 표현을 쓸 것.
(3) 축약형을 사용하여 세 단어로 쓸 것

> A: (1) _____ the new book, *The Best New Thing*?
> B: No, I didn't.
> A: I heard it's really interesting.
> B: (2) _____
>   (3) _____
> A: It's about a family who lives in space.
> B: That sounds interesting.

12 다음 대화의 밑줄 친 부분에 대한 설명으로 적절하지 않은 것은?

> G: ⓐDid you hear about the new book, *Living in a Foreign Country*?
> B: No, I didn't.
> G: Look. It's ⓑright here. ⓒIt's about living in New York.
> B: Great. ⓓI'm really curious about this book.
> G: ⓔMe, too.

① ⓐ: 상대방이 어떤 정보를 알고 있는지를 묻는 말이다.
② ⓑ: 형용사로 '올바른'의 의미다.
③ ⓒ: 새 책의 내용에 관해 설명하는 말이다.
④ ⓓ: 새로운 정보에 대해 궁금증을 표현하는 말이다.
⑤ ⓔ: 상대방의 말에 자신도 그렇다고 동의하는 표현이다.

13 다음 빈칸에 들어갈 말이 나머지와 <u>다른</u> 하나는?

① It was easy _____ me to find his new house.

② It was foolish _____ you to believe him.

③ It's difficult _____ me to play the piano well.

④ It was exciting _____ him to play soccer with his friends.

⑤ It can be dangerous _____ her to drive fast.

14 다음 빈칸에 들어갈 표현이 순서대로 바르게 짝지어진 것을 고르시오.

> I _____ him since I _____ a child.

① have known – was

② have known – has been

③ have known – had been

④ knew – was

⑤ knew – has been

15 다음 밑줄 친 부분의 쓰임이 나머지 넷과 <u>다른</u> 것은?

① I <u>have eaten</u> French food before.

② Jane <u>has been</u> to Jeju-do many times.

③ She <u>has</u> never <u>met</u> a movie star.

④ <u>Have</u> you <u>tried</u> to protect the environment?

⑤ My English <u>has improved</u> since I moved to Australia.

16 다음 문장을 주어진 말로 시작하여 다시 쓰시오.

(1) Tony must hand in his report by tomorrow.

➡ It is necessary _____

_____.

(2) You should be careful when you cross the street.

➡ It is necessary _____

_____.

17 다음 ⓐ~ⓗ 중 옳은 것을 <u>모두</u> 고르면?

> ⓐ Has Daniel found his wallet yesterday?
> ⓑ I have lost my backpack.
> ⓒ I've never gone to Egypt before.
> ⓓ How long has Mr. Williams worked for this company?
> ⓔ I have taught English since 10 years.
> ⓕ It's important follows the rules.
> ⓖ That is a pity that you cannot come to my party.
> ⓗ It's fun to ride a horse.

① ⓐ, ⓒ 　　　　② ⓑ, ⓒ, ⓓ

③ ⓑ, ⓓ, ⓗ 　　　④ ⓓ, ⓔ, ⓗ

⑤ ⓓ, ⓔ, ⓖ

18 다음 밑줄 친 부분의 쓰임이 <u>다른</u> 하나는?

① It's hard <u>to fix</u> a bike.

② It's nice <u>to take</u> a walk in the park.

③ It's necessary <u>to learn</u> English.

④ He has gone never <u>to return</u>.

⑤ It is exciting <u>to cook</u>.

19 다음 중 어법상 <u>어색한</u> 문장은?

① It is bad for your teeth to drink too much soda.

② It was exciting to watch the baseball game.

③ It is important for you to be careful all the time.

④ James has eaten too much and he is sick now.

⑤ Peter, have you finished your project yesterday?

Reading

[20~22] 다음 글을 읽고 물음에 답하시오.

One day, Dad told Rada and Jonny, "We ⓐ <u>are going</u> back to Earth tomorrow."

Rada and Jonny looked at Dad in surprise and floated towards him.

Rada asked Dad, "ⓑ<u>지구는 어떤 곳인가요?</u>"

"Everything is different there. ___(A)___, the sky is blue," answered Dad.

"I've never seen a blue sky," said Jonny.

"The sky is always black here," said Rada.

20 위 글의 빈칸 (A)에 들어갈 알맞은 말을 고르시오.

① However
② Therefore
③ In addition
④ For example
⑤ That is

21 위 글의 밑줄 친 ⓐare going과 문법적 쓰임이 같은 것을 <u>모두</u> 고르시오.

① He is studying English in his room.
② What is she doing now?
③ She is leaving Seoul tonight.
④ Who is singing a song there?
⑤ He is coming here next week.

22 위 글의 밑줄 친 ⓑ의 우리말에 맞게 5 단어로 영작하시오.

➡ _____

[23~24] 다음 글을 읽고 물음에 답하시오.

"You don't have to wear your big heavy space suits (A)[because / though] there is air everywhere. It's also hard to jump there because Earth pulls you down," said Dad.

"(B)[How / What] else?" asked Rada.

"There are hills, and they are covered with soft green grass. You can roll down the hills," answered Mom.

"Dad, have you ever rolled down a hill?" asked Rada.

"Yes, it's really amazing!" answered Dad.

Jonny was thirsty, so he opened a milk container and shook it. The milk floated in the air and formed balls. Jonny swallowed the balls.

"Jonny, (C)[if / unless] you drink milk that way on Earth, you'll get wet," said Mom.

23 위 글의 괄호 (A)~(C)에서 문맥상 알맞은 낱말을 골라 쓰시오.

(A) _____ (B) _____ (C) _____

24 위 글의 내용과 일치하지 <u>않는</u> 것은?

① 지구에서는 크고 무거운 우주복을 입을 필요가 없다.
② 지구에서는 점프하는 것이 어렵다.
③ 지구에서는 언덕을 굴러 내려갈 수도 있다.
④ 아빠는 언덕을 굴러 내려가 본 적이 있다.
⑤ Jonny는 목이 말라서 우유 용기를 열고 그것을 마셨다.

[25~27] 다음 글을 읽고 물음에 답하시오.

Later that night, Rada and Jonny talked a long time about Earth. It was exciting ⓐto think about all the new things they were going to see and do. ⓑThere was one new thing Rada and Jonny really wanted to do. They thought about it all night and didn't tell Mom and Dad about it. It was their secret.

The next day, Rada's family got on a spaceship.

"It's going to be a long trip," said Mom.

"ⓒThat's alright. I'm so excited!" said Rada.

25 위 글의 밑줄 친 ⓐto think와 to부정사의 용법이 <u>다른</u> 것을 <u>모두</u> 고르시오.

① He opened the door, only to find the room empty.

② It is difficult to know oneself.

③ He has many children to look after.

④ She was very happy to get the birthday present.

⑤ To see is to believe.

26 위 글의 밑줄 친 문장 ⓑ에 생략된 한 단어를 넣어 문장을 다시 쓰시오.

➡ _____

_____

27 위 글의 밑줄 친 ⓒThat이 가리키는 것을 본문에서 찾아 쓰시오.

➡ _____

[28~30] 다음 글을 읽고 물음에 답하시오.

The spaceship finally landed.

"Dad, it's difficult to walk on Earth," said Rada.

"I know. Earth is pulling you down," said Dad.

Rada and Jonny couldn't float anymore. That was the first new thing.

"What's that sound?" asked Rada.

"A bird is singing," said Mom.

"I've never heard a bird sing," said Rada.

"And I've never felt the wind," said Jonny. (①) Rada and Jonny ran up the nearest hill. (②) At the top, they looked at each other and laughed. (③) Then they lay down on the soft green grass and rolled down the hill. (④) That was their secret! (⑤)

"This is the best new thing of all!" shouted Rada and Jonny.

And they ran up to the top of the hill again.

28 위 글의 흐름으로 보아, 주어진 문장이 들어가기에 가장 적절한 곳은?

These were all new things.

①　　②　　③　　④　　⑤

29 다음 문장에서 위 글의 내용과 <u>다른</u> 부분을 찾아서 고치시오.

Rada has ever heard a bird sing and Jonny has ever felt the wind.

_____ ➡ _____

_____ ➡ _____

30 본문의 내용과 일치하도록 다음 빈칸에 알맞은 단어를 쓰시오.

To Rada and Jonny, the _____ _____ _____ of all was to lie down on the soft green grass and roll down the hill.

출제율 95%

01 다음 짝지어진 단어의 관계가 같도록 빈칸에 알맞은 말을 쓰시오.

intelligent : stupid = rough : _____

출제율 90%

02 다음 영영 풀이에 해당하는 단어는?

in the direction of, or closer to someone or something

① along   ② out   ③ towards
④ into   ⑤ across

출제율 85%

03 다음 대화의 밑줄 친 (A)와 같은 의미의 문장을 주어진 단어를 활용하여 쓰시오.

G: Did you hear about the space marathon?
B: No, I didn't.
G: It's a marathon on a space station. Look at this video.
B: OK. (A)I'm really curious about it.

➡ _____ (interest)

출제율 95%

04 다음 대화의 밑줄 친 부분 중 어법상 어색한 것은?

G: ⓐDid you hear about the new book, *Living in a Foreign Country*?
B: ⓑNo, I didn't.
G: Look. It's right here. It's about ⓒto live in New York.
B: Great. ⓓI'm really curious about this book.
G: ⓔMe, too.

① ⓐ   ② ⓑ   ③ ⓒ   ④ ⓓ   ⑤ ⓔ

출제율 100%

05 다음 글의 밑줄 친 (A)~(E)의 해석으로 틀린 것은?

Later that night, Rada and Jonny (A)talked a long time about Earth. It was (B)exciting to think about all the new things they were going to see and do. There was one new thing Rada and Jonny really wanted to do. They thought about it (C)all night and didn't tell Mom and Dad about it. It was their (D)secret. The next day, Rada's family (E)got on a spaceship.

① (A) 오랜 시간 이야기했다
② (B) 흥미진진한
③ (C) 밤새
④ (D) 비밀
⑤ (E) 우주선에서 내렸다

[06~07] 다음 대화를 읽고 물음에 답하시오.

B: (A)너는 우주로 간 첫 번째 우주선에 대해 들어봤니?
G: No, I didn't. I'm curious about it.
B: This is a poster of the spaceship.
G: Really? _____ (B)

출제율 85%

06 위 대화의 밑줄 친 (A)의 우리말에 맞게 주어진 문장의 빈칸을 채우시오.

Did you _____ _____ the first spaceship _____ went _____ space?

출제율 95%

07 위 대화의 (B)에 들어갈 말로 알맞은 것을 고르시오.

① What about you?
② I want to buy it.
③ I'm sorry to hear that.
④ I haven't heard about it.
⑤ I'm very interested in fashion.

[08~10] 다음 대화를 읽고 물음에 답하시오.

B: Subin, (A)did you hear about the new movie, *Life on the Moon*?

G: No, I didn't.

B: I heard it's really good.

G: (B)그 영화가 정말 궁금해. What's it about?

B: It's about a man _____ ⓐ

G: That sounds interesting.

B: Look. The movie is playing at the Space Theater here.

G: What time is the movie?

B: It begins at 2:30.

G: Let's eat lunch first and then see the movie.

B: OK. I'm hungry. Let's go!

출제율 95%

08 위 대화의 빈칸 ⓐ에 들어갈 말을 주어진 단어를 배열하여 의미가 통하도록 문장을 완성하시오.

> is / to / live / the / trying / who / on / moon

➡ _____

출제율 90%

09 위 대화의 밑줄 친 (A)와 같은 의미가 되도록 '현재완료'를 사용하여 문장을 쓰시오.

➡ _____

출제율 85%

10 위 대화의 밑줄 친 (B)의 우리말에 맞게 주어진 어휘를 배열하여 대화를 완성하시오.

> really / about / I'm / curious / the / movie

➡ _____

출제율 100%

11 다음 빈칸에 알맞은 말이 순서대로 짝지어진 것은?

> • I have known her _____ 10 years.
> • I have known her _____ 2010.

① for – during   ② during – for

③ for – since   ④ since – for

⑤ as – for

출제율 90%

12 다음 우리말을 주어진 어휘를 이용하여 영작하시오.

(1) 그는 삼십 분째 잠들어 있다. (sleep)

➡ _____

(2) 그 유명 인사는 방금 공항에 도착했어.
(the celebrity, the airport, arrive)

➡ _____

(3) Sue는 전에 프랑스에 가 본 적이 없다.
(be, never, to)

➡ _____

(4) 나는 새로 온 그 학생의 이름을 잊어버렸다.
(그래서 지금 생각나지 않는다.)
(forget, the new student)

➡ _____

(5) 다양한 의견을 나누는 것이 중요해.
(share, various, important, to)

➡ _____

(6) 네가 내 생일을 기억해 줘서 고마워.
(nice, remember, to)

➡ _____

출제율 95%

13 다음 중 어법상 적절한 문장은?

① It's great to is here.

② It's fun to playing with friends.

③ It is boring fish in the lake.

④ It's exciting for us having you here.

⑤ It is better to drink ice tea in summer.

14 다음 중 어법상 바르지 <u>않은</u> 것은? (출제율 90%)

① I have known him since I was young.
② Have you gone to London before?
③ It has been cold and cloudy for the last three days.
④ The banana has not turned brown yet.
⑤ How long have you known her?

15 다음 두 문장이 같도록 할 때 빈칸에 알맞은 것은? (출제율 95%)

> To predict the future is impossible.
> ➡ It is impossible _____ the future.

① predict
② predicts
③ to predicting
④ predicting
⑤ to predict

[16~17] 다음 글을 읽고 물음에 답하시오.

> One day, Dad told Rada and Jonny, "We're going back ⓐ Earth tomorrow."
> Rada and Jonny looked ⓑ Dad ____ⓒ____ surprise and floated ⓓ him.
> Rada asked Dad, "What's it (A)like ⓔ Earth?"
> "Everything is different there. For example, the sky is blue," answered Dad.
> "I've never seen a blue sky," said Jonny.
> "The sky is always black here," said Rada.

16 위 글의 빈칸 ⓐ~ⓔ에 알맞지 <u>않은</u> 전치사를 고르시오. (출제율 100%)

① to
② at
③ with
④ towards
⑤ on

17 위 글의 밑줄 친 (A)like와 같은 의미로 쓰인 것을 고르시오. (출제율 85%)

① Does he <u>like</u> to go there?
② She was <u>like</u> a daughter to me.
③ I <u>like</u> playing the piano.
④ There are many things of <u>like</u> shape.
⑤ How did you <u>like</u> it?

[18~20] 다음 글을 읽고 물음에 답하시오.

> "You don't have to wear your big heavy space suits ____ⓐ____ . ⓑIt's also hard to jump there because Earth pulls you down," said Dad.
> "What else?" asked Rada.
> "There are hills, and ⓒthey are covered with soft green grass. You can roll down the hills," answered Mom.
> "Dad, have you ever rolled down a hill?" asked Rada.
> "Yes, ⓓit's really amazing!" answered Dad.
> Jonny was thirsty, so he opened a milk container and shook ⓔit. The milk floated in the air and formed balls. Jonny swallowed the balls.
> "Jonny, if you drink milk that way on Earth, you'll get wet," said Mom.

18 위 글의 빈칸 ⓐ에 들어갈 알맞은 말을 고르시오. (출제율 90%)

① because they are so heavy
② so that you can jump easily
③ because there is air everywhere
④ because Earth pulls you down
⑤ so that you can roll down the hills

✏️ 출제율 95%

19 위 글의 밑줄 친 ⓑ와 바꿔 쓸 수 <u>없는</u> 말을 <u>모두</u> 고르시오.

① To jump there is also hard

② That's also hard jumping there

③ It's also hard for you to jump there

④ Jumping there is also hard

⑤ That's also hard to jump there

✏️ 출제율 90%

20 위 글의 밑줄 친 ⓒthey, ⓓit, ⓔit이 가리키는 것을 각각 영어로 쓰시오.

ⓒ _____

ⓓ _____

ⓔ _____

[21~23] 다음 글을 읽고 물음에 답하시오.

Later that night, Rada and Jonny talked a long time about Earth. ⓐ<u>It was exciting to think about all the new things they were going to see and do.</u> There was one new thing Rada and Jonny really wanted to do. They thought about it all night and didn't tell Mom and Dad about it. It was their secret.

The next day, Rada's family got on a spaceship.

"It's going to be a long trip," said Mom.

"That's alright. I'm so ___(A)___ !" said Rada.

✏️ 출제율 90%

21 위 글의 빈칸 (A)에 들어갈 알맞은 말을 고르시오.

① bored   ② interesting

③ pleasant   ④ excited

⑤ surprised

✏️ 출제율 95%

22 위 글의 밑줄 친 문장 ⓐ에서 all the new things와 they 사이에 들어갈 수 있는 말을 <u>모두</u> 고르시오.

① which   ② who   ③ that

④ what   ⑤ whom

✏️ 출제율 95%

23 위 글의 내용과 일치하지 <u>않는</u> 것은?

① 밤 늦게, Rada와 Jonny는 지구에 대해서 오랜 시간 이야기했다.

② Rada와 Jonny는 지구에서 그들이 보고, 그리고 하게 될 모든 새로운 것들을 생각했다.

③ Rada와 Jonny는 정말로 하고 싶었던 한 가지 새로운 것이 있었다.

④ 부모님은 Rada와 Jonny가 정말로 하고 싶어 하는 한 가지 새로운 것에 대해 듣고서 흥미로워 하셨다.

⑤ "긴 여행이 될 거야."라고 엄마가 말했다.

[24~25] 다음 글을 읽고 물음에 답하시오.

The spaceship ⓐ<u>finally</u> landed.

"Dad, it's difficult to walk on Earth," said Rada.

"I know. Earth is pulling you down," said Dad.

Rada and Jonny couldn't float anymore. That was the first new thing.

"What's that sound?" asked Rada.

"A bird is singing," said Mom.

"I've never heard a bird sing," said Rada.

"And I've never felt the wind," said Jonny.

ⓑ<u>These</u> were all new things.

✏️ 출제율 90%

24 위 글의 밑줄 친 ⓐfinally와 바꿔 쓸 수 <u>없는</u> 말을 고르시오.

① at last   ② consequently

③ after all   ④ in the end

⑤ in the long run

✏️ 출제율 100%

25 위 글의 밑줄 친 ⓑThese가 가리키는 것 세 가지를 본문에서 찾아 우리말로 쓰시오.

(1) _____

(2) _____

(3) _____

서술형 실전문제

01 다음 그림을 보고 아래 〈조건〉에 따라 대화를 완성하시오.

It tastes like Gimchi.

┤ 조건 ├

(A) new snack에 대한 정보를 알고 있는 지 묻는 말을 hear를 사용하여 쓸 것.

(B) 새로운 정보에 대하여 궁금증을 표현할 때 사용하는 표현을 전치사 about을 이용하여 쓸 것.

A: (A) _____

B: No, I didn't.

A: It tastes like Gimchi.

B: Oh, (B) _____

02 다음 대화의 밑줄 친 우리말을 주어진 어휘를 배열하여 완성하시오.

A: Did you hear about the new game, *MVP*?

B: No, I didn't, but I'm curious about it.

A: It's a baseball game. 네가 좋아하는 선수를 선택하고 경기할 수 있어.

you / a player / can / who / choose / you / and / like / play

➡ _____

03 다음 빈칸에 알맞은 단어를 〈보기〉에서 골라 쓰시오.

┤ 보기 ├

before   ago   since   for

(1) I caught a cold two weeks ago. I have caught a cold _____ two weeks.

(2) Yesterday I adopted a pet. I have never had a pet _____.

(3) Joe started to live in Seoul from 2010. Joe has lived in Seoul _____ 2010.

04 다음 대화를 읽고 아래 물음에 영어로 답하시오.

Andy: Subin, did you hear about the new movie, *Life on the Moon*?

Subin: No, I didn't.

Andy: I heard it's really good.

Subin: I'm really curious about the movie. What's it about?

Andy: It's about a man who is trying to live on the moon.

Subin: That sounds interesting.

Andy: Look. The movie is playing at the Space Theater here.

Subin: What time is the movie?

Andy: It begins at 2:30.

Subin: Let's eat lunch first and then see the movie.

Andy: OK. I'm hungry. Let's go!

(1) What are Subin and Andy talking about?

➡ _____

(2) What will Subin and Andy do before they see the movie? (4 단어로 쓸 것)

➡ _____

05 가주어 It을 사용하여 주어진 문장과 같은 의미가 되도록 쓰시오.

(1) To answer his questions was easy.

➡ _____

(2) Camping food is easy to cook.

➡ _____

(3) Seoul is safe and comfortable to live in.

➡ _____

(4) She was very wise to say so.

➡ _____

06 다음 두 문장의 의미가 같도록 문장의 빈칸을 완성하시오.

(1) He was born in Busan and he still lives in Busan.

➡ He _____ _____ in Busan _____ he was born.

(2) I read the book twice and I read it again today.

➡ I _____ _____ the book _____ _____.

(3) Somebody took my umbrella, so I don't have my umbrella now.

➡ Somebody _____ _____ my umbrella.

[07~09] 다음 글을 읽고 물음에 답하시오.

"You (A)[have to / don't have to] wear your big heavy space suits because there is air everywhere. It's also (B)[easy / hard] to jump there ⓐbecause Earth pulls down you," said Dad.

"What else?" asked Rada.

"There are hills, and they are covered with soft green grass. You can roll down the hills," answered Mom.

"Dad, have you ever rolled down a hill?" asked Rada.

"Yes, it's really (C)[amazing / amazed]!" answered Dad.

Jonny was thirsty, so he opened a milk container and shook it. The milk floated in the air and formed balls. Jonny swallowed the balls.

ⓑ"Jonny, if you drink milk that way on Earth, you'll get wet," said Mom.

07 위 글의 괄호 (A)~(C)에서 문맥이나 어법상 알맞은 낱말을 골라 쓰시오.

(A) _____ (B) _____ (C) _____

08 위 글의 밑줄 친 ⓐ에서 어법상 틀린 부분을 찾아 고치시오.

_____ ➡ _____

09 다음 빈칸 (A)와 (B)에 알맞은 단어를 넣어 엄마가 밑줄 친 ⓑ처럼 말한 이유를 완성하시오.

It's because milk will spill out of the container and make you (A)_____ _____ if you open a milk container and (B)_____ it on Earth.

*spill: (액체가) 흐르다, 쏟아지다; 쏟다

01 주어진 어휘와 가주어 It을 이용하여 3 문장 이상을 쓰시오.

보기

learn a new language	see a doctor	exercise regularly
learn Chinese	go to the beach	search information

(1) _____

(2) _____

(3) _____

(4) _____

(5) _____

02 다음 내용을 바탕으로 Rada와 Jonny가 지구에 도착한 다음 날 했을 새로운 경험에 대한 글을 쓰시오.

The next morning, Rada's family went to a park.

Dad, I've never ridden a bike before.

OK. Let's ride bikes.

In the afternoon, they went to the beach.

Mom, I've never swum before.

Let's swim, then.

At night, Rada and Jonny talked about living on Earth.

It's wonderful to live on Earth.

Yes. It's great to be here.

The next morning, Rada's family went to a park. Rada said to Dad, "Dad, I've never (A)_____ before." "Let's ride bikes, then," said Dad. They then (B)_____ together. The weather was great, and it was so fun.

In the afternoon, Rada's family went to the beach. Jonny said to Mom, "I've never (C)_____." "Let's swim, then," said Mom. It was great (D)_____ in the cool blue sea.

At night, Rada and Jonny talked about (E)_____. "It's wonderful to live on Earth," Rada said to Jonny. "Yes. It's great to be here," Jonny said.

단원별 모의고사

01 다음 단어에 대한 영어 설명이 어색한 것은?

① in surprise: feeling or showing surprise because of something unexpected
② container: something that you keep things in
③ lie: to be or to get into a position with your body flat on something
④ roll down: to move something down, using your hands
⑤ thrilling: exciting and interesting

02 다음 짝지어진 단어의 관계가 같도록 빈칸에 알맞은 말을 쓰시오.

> different : same = _____ : depart

03 다음 영영풀이에 해당하는 단어를 고르시오.

> to stay on the surface of a liquid and not sink

① float   ② swallow   ③ lie
④ roll   ⑤ arrive

04 다음 중 짝지어진 대화가 어색한 것은?

① A: Did you hear about the new running shoes, *Speed*?
  B: No, I didn't. What about them?
② A: Did you hear about the new restaurant, *Rose*?
  B: Yes, I did. It has good service.
③ A: The new snack tastes like Gimchi.
  B: Oh, I'm curious about it.
④ A: Did you hear about the new song, *Loving You*?
  B: No, I didn't. It's a Korean pop song.
⑤ A: Did you hear about the new TV show?
  B: No, I didn't.

[05~06] 다음 대화의 빈칸에 들어갈 말로 알맞은 것을 고르시오.

05

> G: _____
> B: No, I didn't. I'm really curious about Mars.
> G: Look. It's right here. It's about Mars and its moons.
> B: Great. I think I'll buy the book.

① Have you ever been to Mars?
② Did you know Mars has its moons?
③ Did you hear about the new book about Mars?
④ Do you want to know about Mars?
⑤ Did you buy the book about Mars?

06

> G: Tony, did you hear about the movie, *My Hero*?
> B: No, I didn't.
> G: Well, I heard it's really good.
> B: I'm really curious about the movie.
> _____
> G: It's about a father who saves his son.

① What about you?
② What is going on?
③ Is it good?
④ Look at this video.
⑤ What's the movie about?

[07~09] 다음 대화를 읽고 물음에 답하시오.

Andy: Subin, did you hear about the new movie, *Life on the Moon*?

Subin: No, I didn't.

Andy: I heard it's really good.

Subin: _____(A)_____ What's it about?

Andy: It's about a man who is trying to live on the moon.

Subin: That sounds interesting.

Andy: Look. The movie is playing at the Space Theater here.

Subin: What time is the movie?

Andy: It begins at 2:30.

Subin: Let's eat lunch first and then see the movie.

Andy: OK. I'm hungry. Let's go!

07 위 대화의 빈칸 (A)에 들어갈 말로 알맞은 것은?

① I want to know more about the man.

② I'm really curious about the movie.

③ I'm not interested in the movie.

④ What do you want to know about the movie?

⑤ I'm not really curious about it.

08 What are they going to do after this dialogue? (6 단어로 답할 것)

➡ _____

09 위 대화를 요약한 글이다. 빈칸에 들어갈 알맞은 말을 쓰시오.

Andy and Subin are talking about the movie, *Life on the Moon*. It is _____ a man _____ is trying to live on the moon.

10 다음 대화의 내용과 일치하면 T, 일치하지 않으면 F에 표시하시오.

Girl: Did you hear about the new book, *Living in a Foreign Country*?

Boy: No, I didn't.

Girl: Look. It's right here. It's about living in New York.

Boy: Great. I'm really curious about this book.

Girl: Me, too.

(1) They are talking about living in New York. (T / F)

(2) The boy is interested in the new book. (T / F)

11 다음 대화의 빈칸에 들어갈 말은?

G: Tony, did you hear about the movie, *My Hero*?

B: No, I didn't.

G: _____

B: I'm really curious about the movie. What's it about?

G: It's about a father who saves his son.

① I don't know about the movie, either.

② I want to know what the movie is about.

③ Why don't we see the movie?

④ What time does the movie begin?

⑤ Well, I heard it's really good.

12 다음 대화의 마지막 말 앞에 올 순서가 바르게 배열된 것은?

> (A) No, I didn't.
> (B) Great. I'm really curious about this book.
> (C) Look. It's right here. It's about living in New York.
> (D) Did you hear about the new book, *Living in a Foreign Country*?

> G: Me, too.

① (A) – (C) – (B) – (D)
② (B) – (C) – (D) – (A)
③ (C) – (D) – (A) – (B)
④ (D) – (A) – (C) – (B)
⑤ (D) – (B) – (A) – (C)

13 다음 중 어법상 어색한 것을 고르시오.

① I've never swum before.
② When have you visited Italy?
③ She has lost her notebook in the classroom.
④ I have just finished my project.
⑤ Have you ever been to Spain before?

14 다음 주어진 문장의 밑줄 친 부분과 쓰임이 같은 것은?

> It was interesting to watch sci-fi movies.

① How long does it take to go to the station?
② It was Mike that we visited yesterday.
③ It was difficult for me to answer the question.
④ Start a new file and put this letter in it.
⑤ It will take time to get to the new city hall.

15 다음 문장에서 어법상 어색한 것을 바르게 고치시오.

(1) Have you found your umbrella an hour ago?

_____ ➡ _____

(2) I started to play the piano long time ago. And I still enjoy playing it. So, I played the piano since a long time.

_____ ➡ _____

(3) I have never gone to London.

_____ ➡ _____

(4) Search information using the Internet is easy.

_____ ➡ _____

(5) It's necessary of you to wear a helmet.

_____ ➡ _____

16 다음 우리말을 주어진 어휘를 이용하여 영작하시오.

(1) 그는 10살 때부터 그녀를 알았다.
(know, since, ten years old)
➡ _____

(2) 그는 아직 숙제를 끝마치지 못했다. (finish)
➡ _____

(3) 그들은 그 영화를 네 번 보았다.
(see the movie)
➡ _____

(4) 그녀는 파리로 가 버렸다. (현재 여기에 없다.)
(have)
➡ _____

(5) 이 웹사이트를 방문한 것이 도움이 되었다.
(helpful, this web site)
➡ _____

(6) 아이가 큰 개를 목욕시키기는 힘들다.
(a child, wash, hard, to)
➡ _____

[17~18] 다음 글을 읽고 물음에 답하시오.

One day, Dad told Rada and Jonny, "We're going back to Earth tomorrow."

Rada and Jonny looked at Dad in surprise and floated towards him.

Rada asked Dad, "What's it like on Earth?"

"Everything is different there. For example, the sky is blue," answered Dad.

"ⓐI've never seen a blue sky," said Jonny.

"The sky is always black here," said Rada.

17 다음 빈칸 (A)와 (B)에 알맞은 단어를 넣어 지구와 우주의 하늘의 색깔에 대한 설명을 완성하시오.

On Earth, the color of the sky is (A)_____ from that in space. It's (B)_____, not black.

18 위 글의 밑줄 친 ⓐ의 현재완료와 용법이 <u>다른 것을 모두</u> 고르시오.

① How long <u>have</u> you <u>known</u> Mr. Green?
② I <u>have</u> just <u>finished</u> my work.
③ I <u>have visited</u> New York three times.
④ She <u>has been</u> ill for a week.
⑤ <u>Have</u> you ever <u>written</u> a letter in English?

[19~21] 다음 글을 읽고 물음에 답하시오.

"You don't have to wear your big heavy space suits because there is air everywhere. It's also hard to jump there because Earth pulls you down," said Dad.

"What ____ⓐ____?" asked Rada.

"There are hills, and they are covered with soft green grass. You can roll down the hills," answered Mom.

"Dad, ⓑ언덕을 굴러 내려가 본 적 있어요?" asked Rada.

"Yes, it's really amazing!" answered Dad.

Jonny was thirsty, so he opened a milk container and shook it. The milk floated in the air and formed balls. Jonny swallowed the balls.

"Jonny, if you drink milk that way on Earth, you'll get wet," said Mom.

19 주어진 영영풀이를 참고하여 빈칸 ⓐ에 철자 e로 시작하는 단어를 쓰시오.

in addition; besides

➡ e_____

20 위 글의 밑줄 친 ⓑ의 우리말에 맞게 한 단어를 보충하여, 주어진 어휘를 알맞게 배열하시오.

a hill / ever / you / rolled / have / ?

➡ _____

21 다음 중 위 글의 내용을 올바르게 이해하지 <u>못한</u> 사람을 고르시오.

혜수: It's not necessary for Rada and Jonny to wear their big heavy space suits on Earth.
정미: Unlike in space, there is air everywhere on Earth and there is gravity, too.
수민: It's not easy to jump on Earth because of gravity.
규식: It will be easy to jump on Earth if Rada and Jonny wear their space suits.
나윤: Rada and Jonny will be able to roll down the hills.

① 혜수   ② 정미   ③ 수민
④ 규식   ⑤ 나윤

Lesson 8

Pride of Korea

🎤 의사소통 기능

- 허가 여부 묻기
  A: Is it OK to sit here?
  B: Sure. Go ahead. / I'm afraid not.

- 금지하기
  Sitting is not allowed here.

🎤 언어 형식

- 간접의문문
  Please tell me **how you found them**.

- because of
  Many Koreans became interested in *Uigwe* **because of** your book.

Words & Expressions

Key Words

- **abroad**[əbrɔ́ːd] 부 해외에서, 해외로
- **allow**[əláu] 동 허락하다, 허용하다
- **army**[áːrmi] 명 군대, 육군
- **behind**[biháind] 전 ~ 뒤에, ~ 배후에
- **college**[kálidʒ] 명 대학
- **continue**[kəntínju] 동 계속하다
- **delicious**[dilíʃəs] 형 맛있는
- **dessert**[dizə́ːrt] 명 디저트, 후식
- **difficulty**[dífikʌlti] 명 어려움
- **display**[displéi] 명 전시
- **exhibition**[èksəbíʃən] 명 박람회, 전시회
- **fan dance** 부채춤
- **finally**[fáinəli] 부 마침내, 결국
- **find**[faind] 동 발견하다, 찾다 (-found-found)
- **fire**[faiər] 동 해고하다
- **fitting room** 탈의실
- **flash**[flæʃ] 명 (카메라) 플래시
- **government**[gʌ́vərnmənt] 명 정부
- **grass**[græs] 명 잔디, 풀
- **historian**[histɔ́ːriən] 명 역사학자
- **however**[hauévər] 부 하지만, 그러나
- **instrument**[ínstrəmənt] 명 악기
- **interesting**[íntərəstiŋ] 형 흥미로운
- **knee**[niː] 명 무릎
- **metal**[métl] 명 금속
- **movable metal type** 금속활자
- **million**[míljən] 명 100만, 수많은

- **museum**[mjuːzíːəm] 명 박물관
- **noise**[nɔiz] 명 소리, 소음
- **printing**[príntiŋ] 명 인쇄
- **pride**[praid] 명 자부심, 긍지
- **prove**[pruːv] 동 입증하다, 증명하다
- **publish**[pʌ́bliʃ] 동 출판하다, 발행하다
- **research**[risə́ːrtʃ] 명 연구, 조사
- **researcher**[risə́ːrtʃər] 명 연구가
- **result**[rizʌ́lt] 명 결과, 결실
- **return**[ritə́ːrn] 명 반환
- **royal**[rɔ́iəl] 형 왕실의
- **search**[səːrtʃ] 동 찾아보다
- **silver**[sílvər] 명 은, 은색
- **special**[spéʃəl] 형 특별한
- **spend**[spend] 동 (돈을) 쓰다, (시간을) 보내다 (-spent-spent)
- **spy**[spai] 명 스파이, 첩자
- **steal**[stiːl] 동 도둑질하다, 훔치다 (-stole-stolen)
- **storm**[stɔːrm] 명 폭풍
- **succeed**[səksíːd] 동 성공하다
- **thief**[θiːf] 명 도둑
- **traditional**[trədíʃənl] 형 전통적인
- **treasure**[tréʒər] 명 보물
- **value**[vǽljuː] 명 가치
- **wedding**[wédiŋ] 명 결혼식
- **while**[hwail] 접 ~하는 동안
- **whole**[houl] 형 전부의, 전체의

Key Expressions

- **as soon as+주어+동사** ~하자마자
- **because+주어+동사** ~ 때문에
- **because of+명사** ~ 때문에
- **be full of** ~로 가득 차 있다
- **become interested in** ~에 관심을 가지다
- **give up** 포기하다
- **Is it OK to+동사원형~?** ~해도 되나요?
- **look at** ~을 보다

- **look for** ~을 찾다
- **right away** 바로, 즉시
- **spend+시간+-ing** ~하면서 시간을 보내다
- **take pictures** 사진을 찍다
- **thanks to** ~ 덕분에
- **try on** ~을 입어 보다
- **Why don't you+동사원형 ~?** ~하는 게 어때?
- **would like to+동사원형** ~하고 싶다

Word Power

※ 동사와 명사의 뜻을 둘 다 가지는 어휘

☐ **display** (동) 전시하다 (명) 전시

☐ **return** (동) 돌려주다 (명) 반환

☐ **fire** (동) 해고하다 (명) 불, 화재

☐ **result** (동) 발생하다 (명) 결과

☐ **value** (동) 소중히 여기다 (명) 가치

☐ **flash** (동) 비추다 (명) 플래시 번쩍임

☐ **search** (동) 찾아보다 (명) 수색

☐ **research** (동) 조사하다 (명) 조사, 연구

※ 형태가 유사한 어휘

☐ **royal** (형) 왕실의 : **loyal** (형) 충실한

☐ **find** (동) 발견하다, 찾다 : **found** (동) 설립하다

☐ **dessert** (명) 디저트, 후식 : **desert** (명) 사막

☐ **abroad** (부) 해외에서 : **aboard** (부) 배를 타고, 승차하여

☐ **grass** (명) 잔디, 풀 : **glass** (명) 유리

☐ **metal** (명) 금속 : **mental** (형) 정신의

English Dictionary

☐ **abroad** 해외로, 해외에서
→ in or to a foreign country
외국에서 또는 외국으로

☐ **allow** 허락하다
→ to say that someone can do something
누군가가 무엇을 할 수 있다고 말하다

☐ **fitting room** 탈의실
→ a room in a clothes shop where you can put on clothes before you buy them
옷 가게에 있는 방으로 옷을 사기 전에 입을 수 있는 곳

☐ **flash** 플래시
→ a bright light on a camera that flashes as you take a photograph in order to provide enough light
사진을 찍을 때 충분한 빛을 제공하기 위해 번쩍이는 카메라의 밝은 빛

☐ **government** 정부
→ the group of people who are responsible for controlling a country or state
나라나 주를 통제하는 데 책임이 있는 사람들의 무리

☐ **pride** 자부심, 긍지
→ a feeling of satisfaction and pleasure in what you have done
당신이 한 일에 대한 만족감과 즐거움

☐ **prove** 입증하다
→ to show that something is true
어떤 일이 사실이라는 것을 보여주다

☐ **publish** 출판하다
→ to print a book, magazine, or newspaper for people to buy
사람들이 구입하도록 책이나 잡지, 신문을 인쇄하다

☐ **research** 조사
→ the work of finding out facts about something
어떤 것에 관한 사실을 알아내는 일

☐ **result** 결과
→ something that happens because of something else
다른 어떤 것 때문에 발생하는 것

☐ **royal** 왕실의
→ relating to or belonging to a king or queen
왕이나 여왕과 관련되거나 속해 있는

☐ **search** 찾아보다
→ to try to find someone or something by looking very carefully
주의 깊게 봄으로써 누군가나 무언가를 찾으려고 하다

☐ **silver** 은, 은빛
→ a shiny white metal that people use for making jewelry and other valuable things
보석이나 다른 귀중품을 만들기 위해 사용하는 반짝이는 흰 금속

☐ **spend** (시간을) 보내다
→ to use time doing something
어떤 일을 하면서 시간을 사용하다

☐ **steal** 훔치다
→ to take something that belongs to someone else
다른 누군가에게 속해 있는 물건을 가져가다

☐ **succeed** 성공하다
→ to do something that you tried or aimed to do
당신이 시도하거나 목표로 하는 일을 해내다

☐ **thanks to** ~ 덕분에
→ used for saying that someone or something is responsible for something good that happened
누군가나 무언가가 일어난 좋은 일에 책임이 있다고 말하는 데 사용되는

☐ **treasure** 보물
→ a group of valuable things, especially gold, silver, or jewels
금, 은, 또는 보석과 같은 귀중한 물건의 집합

 중요

01 다음 빈칸에 들어갈 말이 알맞게 짝지어진 것은?

> • The box was full of _____ such as gold and silver.
> • The _____ of this painting is about one million dollars.

① trash – result   ② army – display

③ trash – value   ④ treasures – value

⑤ treasures – display

서답형

02 〈영어 설명〉을 읽고 빈칸에 알맞은 말을 쓰시오. (주어진 철자로 시작할 것)

> to keep doing something without stopping

> I studied history in college. I went to France to c_____ my studies in 1955.

[03~04] 다음 설명에 해당하는 단어를 고르시오.

03
> to say that someone can do something

① search   ② allow

③ spend   ④ publish

⑤ fire

중요

04
> a feeling of satisfaction and pleasure in what you have done

① confidence   ② happiness

③ glory   ④ result

⑤ pride

서답형

05 다음 우리말에 맞게 빈칸에 알맞은 단어를 쓰시오.

> 1967년에 국립도서관의 연구원이 되자마자, 저는 "의궤"를 찾기 시작했어요.
> ➡ _____ _____ _____ I became a researcher at the National Library in 1967, I began to look for *Uigwe*.

06 다음 글의 흐름상 빈칸에 들어갈 말로 알맞은 것은?

> I thought that *Uigwe*, a collection of royal books, should be returned to Korea, but my bosses at the library didn't like that idea. They even thought that I was a Korean spy and _____ me.

① promoted   ② valued

③ fired   ④ missed

⑤ proved

서답형

07 다음 짝지어진 단어의 관계가 같도록 빈칸에 알맞은 말을 쓰시오.

> stop : continue – fail : _____

 중요

08 다음 빈칸에 들어갈 말이 알맞게 짝지어진 것은?

> I hope people will become more _____ our national treasures abroad and work for their _____.

① indifferent to – value

② indifferent to – return

③ interested in – government

④ interested in – return

⑤ interested in – value

01 다음 빈칸에 들어갈 말을 〈보기〉에서 찾아 쓰시오. (필요하면 변형하여 쓰시오.)

┌─ 보기 ─┐

abroad   allow   prove
tradition   research

(1) I went to the library every day to finish my _____ .

(2) That's a *haegeum*, a _____ Korean musical instrument.

(3) He is _____ now, but he will go back to his country soon.

(4) Sitting on the grass is not _____ .

02 다음 우리말과 같은 표현이 되도록 문장의 빈칸을 채우시오.

(1) 박 박사님, 당신의 노고 덕분에 "직지"와 "의궤"가 발견되었고, 모든 한국인들이 그 점을 당신에게 감사하고 있어요.

➡ Dr. Park, _____ _____ your hard work, *Jikji* and *Uigwe* were _____, and all Koreans thank you for that.

(2) 1992년에 한국 정부는 프랑스 정부에 그것의 반환을 요청했다.

➡ In 1992, the Korean _____ asked the French _____ for its _____ .

03 다음 빈칸에 공통으로 알맞은 단어를 주어진 철자로 시작하여 쓰시오.

(1) • Most animals are afraid of f_____ .
   • We had to f_____ him for dishonesty.

(2) • How do you s_____ your spare time?
   • My parents s_____ a lot of money on books every month.

(3) • He has carried out r_____ into renewable energy sources.
   • Many researchers r_____ into the matter thoroughly.

(4) • We have to work hard to s_____ in life.
   • After many failures, the scientists finally s_____ed in proving their theory.

         * renewable: 재생 가능한

         * thoroughly: 철저히

04 다음 영영풀이에 해당하는 단어를 〈보기〉에서 찾아 첫 번째 칸에 쓰고, 두 번째 칸에는 우리말 뜻을 쓰시오.

┌─ 보기 ─┐

royal   steal   skip   prove   metal

(1) _____ : to show that something is true: _____

(2) _____ : to take something that belongs to someone else: _____

(3) _____ : relating to or belonging to a king or queen: _____

(4) _____ : a hard substance, such as iron, gold, or steel, that is good at conducting electricity and heat: _____

Conversation

① 허가 여부 묻기

> **A** Is it OK to sit here? 여기에 앉아도 되나요?
>
> **B** Sure. Go ahead. / I'm afraid not. 물론이죠. 그렇게 하세요. / 안 될 것 같아요.

- 'Is it OK to ~?'는 '~해도 될까요?'라는 의미로 허가 여부를 묻는 표현이다. 'to+동사원형' 대신 'if+주어+동사'를 써서 말할 수도 있다.

- 허가 여부를 묻는 표현
  - May[Can] I use your cellphone? / Is it okay if I use your cellphone? / Would it be all right if I use your cellphone? / Do you mind if I use your cellphone?

- 허락을 할 때
  - Sure. / Go ahead. / Yes, you can[may]. / Of course. 등으로 답한다.

- 허락을 하지 않을 때
  - I'm sorry, but you can't. / I'm afraid not. / You are not allowed to do that. / You can't do that.

※ 주의할 점

- 'Do you mind if I ~?'로 물을 때는 mind가 '꺼리다, 싫어하다'라는 뜻이기 때문에, 허락의 의미로 Of course not. / No, go ahead. / No, I don't. / Not at all. / No problem. 등 부정문을 사용하고, 허락을 하지 않을 때는 Yes, I do. / Of course. 등을 사용한다.
  - A: Is it OK to take a picture here? 여기서 사진을 찍어도 되나요?
    B: Yes, you can. 네. 찍어도 됩니다.
  - A: Is it okay if I turn on the TV? TV를 켜도 괜찮겠니?
    B: Sure. / I'm afraid not. I'm doing my homework. 물론이야. / 안 될 것 같아. 나는 숙제를 하는 중이야.

핵심 Check

1. 다음 대화의 빈칸에 들어갈 말로 <u>어색한</u> 것은?

   A: _____ ride your bike?
   B: Yes, it's OK.

   ① Can I
   ② May I
   ③ Is it OK to
   ④ Is it OK if I
   ⑤ Do you mind

② 금지하기

Sitting is not allowed here. 여기에 앉는 것은 허용되지 않습니다.

■ '~ is not allowed'는 '~하는 것이 허락되지 않는다'라는 뜻으로, 금지를 나타낼 때 쓰는 표현이다. 비슷한 표현으로는 'You must not ~'이 있다.

금지하는 표현

- You shouldn't ~. (~하면 안 돼요.)
- 명령문을 이용하여 'Do not[Don't] ~. (~하지 마.)'라고 말하거나 허락의 의미를 나타내는 조동사 can을 이용하여 'You cannot ~. (~해서는 안 돼.)'라고 말할 수도 있다.
- 강력한 금지의 표현은 'You must not ~. (~하면 안 됩니다.)'을 사용한다.
- 경고의 의미가 섞인 'You'd better not ~. (~하지 않는 편이 나을 거예요.)'이라는 표현을 쓰기도 한다.

- A: Excuse me. You shouldn't use your cell phone here.
  실례합니다. 당신은 여기서 휴대전화를 사용하시면 안 됩니다.
  B: Oh, I'm sorry. 오, 미안합니다.

- A: You are not allowed to use your smartphone in class.
  수업 중에 휴대폰을 사용하는 것이 허락되어 있지 않아.
  B: I see. 알았습니다.

- A: Do not play the piano at night. 밤에 피아노를 치면 안 돼.
  B: Oh, I'm sorry. 아, 죄송해요.

핵심 Check

2. 다음 대화의 밑줄 친 부분과 바꿔 쓸 수 <u>없는</u> 것은?

A: <u>You must not park here.</u>

B: Oh, I'm sorry.

① You are not allowed to park here.

② Don't park here.

③ You'd better not park here.

④ You shouldn't park here.

⑤ You don't have to park here.

Listen and Talk A-1

B: Excuse me. What's this? ❶I've never seen any food like this.

W: Oh, ❷it's Tteok, a Korean dessert.

B: ❸Is it OK to try some?

W: ❹Sure. Go ahead. It's really delicious.

B: 실례합니다. 이것이 무엇인가요? 저는 이런 음식을 본 적이 없어요.

W: 오, 그것은 한국의 후식인 떡이에요.

B: 먹어 봐도 될까요?

W: 물론이죠. 그렇게 하세요. 정말 맛있답니다.

❶ 현재완료를 사용하여 이전에 한 일에 대한 경험을 표현하는 말이다.

❷ 동격의 콤마로 앞의 명사를 설명하는 역할을 한다.

❸ Is it OK to ~?는 '~해도 될까요?'라는 의미로 허가 여부를 묻는 표현이다.

❹ 허가를 묻는 표현에 대한 허락의 답으로 Sure. Go ahead. / Yes, you can[may]. / Of course. 등으로 답한다.

Check(√) True or False

(1) The boy hasn't eaten Tteok before.　　T ☐ F ☐

(2) The boy is allowed to eat Tteok.　　T ☐ F ☐

Listen and Talk A-2

G: Excuse me. ❶Is it OK to sit over there?

M: You mean, on the grass?

G: Yes. Is it all right?

M: ❷I'm sorry, but sitting on the grass is not allowed.

G: OK, I understand.

G: 실례합니다. 저기에 앉아도 되나요?

M: 잔디 위를 말하는 건가요?

G: 네. 괜찮은가요?

M: 미안하지만, 잔디 위에 앉는 것은 허락되지 않습니다.

G: 알겠습니다, 이해합니다.

❶ 'Is it OK to ~?'는 '~해도 될까요?'라는 의미로 허가 여부를 묻는 표현이다. 'Is it OK if I sit over there?'로 바꾸어 쓸 수 있다.

❷ 'be not allowed'는 허가를 묻는 표현에 대해 허락을 하지 않을 때 사용하는 표현으로 'You can't do that.'으로 표현할 수 있다.

Check(√) True or False

(3) The girl wants to sit on the grass.　　T ☐ F ☐

(4) The girl is not allowed to sit on the grass.　　T ☐ F ☐

Listen and Talk A-3

B: Excuse me. What's this? It looks interesting.
W: Oh, that's a haegeum, a traditional Korean musical instrument.
B: ❶Is it OK to play it?
W: ❷I'm sorry, but it's only for display. Playing it is not allowed.
B: I see.

❶ 'Is it OK to ~?'는 '~해도 될까요?'라는 의미로 허가 여부를 묻는 표현이다. Is it OK if I play it?과 같은 표현이다.
❷ 허가를 묻는 표현에 대해 허락을 하지 않을 때 사용하는 표현이다.

Listen and Talk A-4

G: Excuse me. ❶Is it OK to take pictures here?
M: Yes, it's all right.
G: ❷How about using a flash? Can I use it, too?
M: I'm afraid not. ❸Using a flash is not allowed here.
G: Oh, I see. Thank you.

❶ 'Is it OK to ~?'는 '~해도 될까요?'라는 의미로 허가 여부를 묻는 표현이다.
❷ 'How about -ing?'는 '~는 어때요?'의 뜻이다.
❸ 'Using a flash'는 동명사 주어이고 'is not allowed'는 허락을 하지 않을 때 사용하는 표현이다.

Listen and Talk B

A: ❶Is it OK to sit here?
B: I'm afraid not. Sitting is not allowed here.
A: Oh, I see.

❶ 'Is it OK to ~?'는 '~해도 될까요?'라는 의미로 허가 여부를 묻는 표현이다. 'Is it OK if I sit here?'로 바꾸어 쓸 수 있다.

Listen and Talk C

G: Excuse me, but ❶is it OK to try on this hanbok?
M: Sure. The fitting room is over there.
G: Thanks. Wait a minute. ❷That's also very pretty.
M: Oh, the little hat over there?
G: Yes. What is it?
M: It's a jokduri, ❸a traditional Korean hat for women. It's usually worn on a wedding day.
G: Really? ❹Is it OK to try it on, too?
M: ❺I'm sorry, but it's only for display. Trying it on is not allowed.
G: Oh. Then, I'll just try on this hanbok.

❶ 'Is it OK to ~?'는 '~해도 될까요?'라는 의미로 허가 여부를 묻는 표현이다.
❷ That은 'the little hat over there'를 가리키는 지시대명사다.
❸ 콤마 뒤의 말은 앞의 명사 'jokduri'를 설명하는 동격어다.
❹ 'Is it OK to ~?'는 '~해도 될까요?'라는 의미로 허가 여부를 묻는 표현이고, 'try on'은 이어 동사다. 인칭대명사가 목적어일 때는 반드시 '동사+대명사+부사' 어순으로 사용한다.
❺ 허가를 묻는 표현에 대해 허락을 하지 않을 때 사용하는 표현이다.

Talk and Play

A: ❶Which place do you want to go first in the museum?
B: ❷Why don't you guess?
A: OK. ❸Is it OK to eat food there?
B: Yes. Eating food is allowed.
A: Is it OK to take pictures?
B: No. ❹Taking pictures is not allowed.
A: ❺I got it. You're thinking of going to the Video Room.
B: You're right.

❶ which는 '어떤, 무슨'의 의미의 의문형용사로 명사 place를 수식하는 역할을 한다.
❷ 'Why don't you+동사원형 ~? '은 '~하는 게 어때?'의 뜻이다.
❸ 'Is it OK to ~?'는 '~해도 될까요?'라는 의미로 허가 여부를 묻는 표현이다.
❹ 'Taking pictures'는 동명사 주어로 '사진을 찍는 것은'의 뜻이다. 'is not allowed'는 '허락되지 않는다'라는 뜻으로 허가를 묻는 말에 대한 부정의 답이다.
❺ 'I got it.'은 '알겠어.'라는 뜻이다.

Review 1

G: Excuse me. What's this? It looks interesting.
B: Oh, that's a janggu, a traditional Korean musical instrument.
G: Is it OK to play it?
B: I'm sorry, but ❶it's only for display. Playing it is not allowed.
G: I see.

❶ for display는 '전시를 위한'의 뜻으로, display는 명사로 사용되었다.

Review 2

G: Excuse me, but is it OK to take pictures here?
M: Yes. Go ahead.
G: Can I use a flash, too?
M: Yes. That's also OK.
G: I'm sorry, but I have one more question. Can I eat food here?
M: I'm sorry, but ❶that's not allowed.

❶ that은 'Eating food here'을 나타내는 대명사다.

다음 우리말과 일치하도록 빈칸에 알맞은 말을 쓰시오.

Listen and Talk A-1

B: Excuse me. What's this? _____ _____ _____ any food _____ this.

W: Oh, it's Tteok, a Korean _____.

B: _____ _____ _____ _____ try some?

W: Sure. Go _____. It's really _____.

Listen and Talk A-2

G: Excuse me. Is it OK _____ _____ over there?

M: You _____, on the grass?

G: Yes. Is it all right?

M: I'm sorry, but _____ on the grass _____ _____ _____.

G: OK, I understand.

Listen and Talk A-3

B: Excuse me. What's this? It _____ _____.

W: Oh, that's a haegeum, a _____ Korean musical _____.

B: _____ _____ _____ _____ _____ it?

W: _____ _____, but it's only _____ _____. Playing it is not _____.

B: I see.

Listen and Talk A-4

G: _____ me. _____ _____ _____ _____ _____ pictures here?

M: Yes, it's all right.

G: _____ _____ _____ a flash? Can I use it, too?

M: I'm _____ not. _____ a flash is _____ _____ here.

G: Oh, I see. Thank you.

Listen and Talk B

A: _____ _____ _____ _____ _____?

B: I'm _____. _____ is _____ here.

A: Oh, I see.

해석

B: 실례합니다. 이것이 무엇인가요? 저는 이런 음식을 본 적이 없어요.
W: 오, 그것은 한국의 후식인 떡이에요.
B: 먹어 봐도 될까요?
W: 물론이죠. 그렇게 하세요. 정말 맛있답니다.

G: 실례합니다. 저기에 앉아도 되나요?
M: 잔디 위를 말하는 건가요?
G: 네. 괜찮은가요?
M: 미안하지만, 잔디 위에 앉는 것은 허락되지 않습니다.
G: 알겠습니다, 이해합니다.

B: 실례합니다. 이것은 무엇인가요? 흥미롭게 생겼네요.
W: 오, 그것은 한국의 전통 악기인 해금이에요.
B: 연주를 해 봐도 될까요?
W: 미안하지만, 전시용입니다. 연주를 하는 것은 허락되지 않습니다.
B: 알겠습니다.

G: 실례합니다. 여기서 사진을 찍어도 되나요?
M: 네, 괜찮습니다.
G: 플래시를 사용하는 것은 어떤가요? 사용해도 되나요?
M: 안 될 것 같아요. 플래시를 사용하는 것은 여기서 허용되지 않습니다.
G: 오, 알겠어요. 감사합니다.

A: 여기 앉아도 될까요?
B: 안 될 것 같아요. 여기에 앉는 것은 허용되지 않습니다.
A: 오, 알겠습니다.

Talk and Play

A: _____ place do you want _____ _____ first in the museum?
B: _____ _____ _____ guess?
A: OK. _____ _____ _____ _____ _____ food there?
B: Yes. _____ food is _____.
A: _____ _____ _____ _____ _____ pictures?
B: No. Taking pictures _____ _____ _____.
A: I _____ _____. You're thinking of going to the Video Room.
B: You're right.

Listen and Talk C

G: Excuse me, but _____ _____ _____ to try on this hanbok?
M: Sure. The _____ _____ is over there.
G: Thanks. Wait a minute. That's also very pretty.
M: Oh, the little hat _____ _____?
G: Yes. What is it?
M: It's a jokduri, a _____ Korean hat _____ women. It's usually _____ on a _____ day.
G: Really? _____ _____ _____ _____ _____ _____ _____, too?
M: I'm sorry, but it's only _____ _____. Trying it _____ is not _____.
G: Oh. Then, I'll just _____ _____ this hanbok.

Review 1

G: Excuse me. What's this? It _____ _____.
B: Oh, that's a janggu, a _____ Korean _____ _____.
G: _____ _____ _____ _____ play it?
B: I'm sorry, but it's only _____ _____. Playing it is not _____.
G: I see.

Review 2

G: Excuse me, but _____ _____ _____ to take pictures here?
M: Yes. Go _____.
G: _____ _____ use a flash, too?
M: Yes. That's also OK.
G: I'm sorry, _____ I have _____ _____ question. Can I eat food here?
M: I'm sorry, but that's _____ _____.

해석

A: 박물관에서 어떤 장소를 먼저 가고 싶니?
B: 알아맞혀 볼래?
A: 좋아. 거기에서 음식을 먹어도 되니?
B: 응. 음식을 먹는 것은 허용돼.
A: 사진을 찍어도 되니?
B: 아니. 사진을 찍는 것은 허용되지 않아.
A: 알겠다. 너는 Video Room에 갈 생각이구나.
B: 맞아.

G: 실례지만, 이 한복을 입어 봐도 될까요?
M: 물론이죠. 탈의실은 저쪽입니다.
G: 고마워요. 잠깐만요. 저것도 매우 예쁘네요.
M: 오, 저기 있는 작은 모자요?
G: 네. 그건 뭔가요?
M: 그것은 여자들이 쓰는 한국 전통 모자인 족두리예요. 주로 결혼식 날 쓰죠.
G: 정말요? 그것도 써 봐도 될까요?
M: 죄송하지만, 그것은 전시만 하는 거예요. 써 보시는 건 안 돼요.
G: 오. 그럼, 그냥 이 한복만 입어 볼게요.

G: 실례합니다. 이것은 무엇인가요? 흥미로워 보이네요.
B: 오, 저것은 한국의 전통 악기인 장구예요.
G: 연주해 봐도 되나요?
B: 미안하지만, 전시용이에요. 연주하는 것은 허용되지 않아요.
G: 알겠어요.

G: 실례합니다만, 여기서 사진을 찍어도 되나요?
M: 네. 그렇게 하세요.
G: 플래시를 사용해도 되나요?
M: 네. 그것도 괜찮습니다.
G: 죄송하지만, 질문이 하나 더 있어요. 여기서 음식을 먹어도 되나요?
M: 미안하지만, 그것은 허용되지 않습니다.

01 다음 우리말에 맞게 주어진 단어를 이용하여 빈칸에 알맞은 말을 쓰시오.

> 플래시를 사용하는 것은 여기서 허용되지 않습니다. (allow)
> ➡ _____ a flash _____ not _____ here.

[02~03] 다음 대화의 빈칸에 들어갈 말로 알맞은 것을 고르시오.

02

> A: Is it OK _____ I use your pencil?
> B: No problem.

① that   ② if   ③ whether
④ who   ⑤ why

03

> A: Is it OK to sit here?
> B: _____ Sitting is not allowed here.
> A: Oh, I see.

① Sure.   ② No problem.   ③ Of course.
④ Yes. Go ahead.   ⑤ I'm afraid not.

04 다음 대화의 밑줄 친 부분과 바꿔 쓸 수 없는 것은?

> A: You are not allowed to smoke here.
> B: Oh, I'm sorry. I'll never do that again.

① You cannot smoke here.
② You don't have to smoke here.
③ You'd better not smoke here.
④ You shouldn't smoke here.
⑤ You must not smoke here.

05 다음 대화의 밑줄 친 부분의 의도로 알맞은 것은?

> A: Is it OK to play it?
> B: I'm sorry, but it's only for display. Playing it is not allowed.

① 금지하기   ② 좋아하는 것 묻기
③ 허가 여부 묻기   ④ 부탁하기
⑤ 예정된 것 말하기

[01~02] 다음 대화를 읽고 물음에 답하시오.

> A: Excuse me. What's this? (a)저는 이런 음식을 본 적이 없어요.
> B: Oh, it's Tteok, a Korean dessert.
> A: _____ (A) _____
> B: Sure. Go ahead. It's really delicious.

01 위 대화의 빈칸 (A)에 들어갈 말로 어색한 것은?

① Can I try some?
② Is it OK to try some?
③ May I try some?
④ Must I try some?
⑤ Is it OK if I try some?

서답형

02 위 대화의 밑줄 친 (a)의 우리말에 맞게 주어진 어구를 이용하여 영어로 쓰시오. (현재완료를 이용하여 쓸 것)

> never / see / any food / like

➡ _____

03 자연스러운 대화가 되도록 (A)~(D)를 바르게 배열한 것은?

> (A) I'm sorry, but sitting on the grass is not allowed.
> (B) You mean, on the grass?
> (C) Excuse me. Is it OK to sit over there?
> (D) Yes. Is it all right?

> OK, I understand.

① (A) – (B) – (C) – (D)
② (B) – (A) – (C) – (D)
③ (B) – (C) – (A) – (D)
④ (C) – (B) – (D) – (A)
⑤ (D) – (B) – (A) – (C)

서답형

04 밑줄 친 (A)의 우리말에 맞게 주어진 단어를 이용하여 영어로 쓰시오. (주어진 단어를 포함하여 다섯 단어로 쓸 것 / 어형 변화 필수)

> (sit / not / allow)

> A: Is it OK to sit here?
> B: I'm afraid not. (A)여기에 앉는 것은 허용되지 않습니다.
> A: Oh, I see.

➡ _____ here.

05 다음 대화의 빈칸에 들어갈 말로 어색한 것은?

> G: Excuse me. Is it OK to take pictures here?
> M: Yes, it's all right.
> G: How about using a flash? _____, too?
> M: I'm afraid not. Using a flash is not allowed here.
> G: Oh, I see. Thank you.

① Is it OK if I use it
② Can I use it
③ Should I use it
④ Would it be all right if I use it
⑤ May I use it

[06~07] 다음 대화를 읽고 물음에 답하시오.

> B: Excuse me. What's this? It ⓐlooks interesting.
> W: Oh, that's ⓑa haegeum, a traditional Korean musical instrument.
> B: Is it OK ⓒto play it?
> W: I'm sorry, but it's only ⓓfor display. Playing it ⓔis not allow.
> B: I see.

06 위 대화의 밑줄 친 ⓐ~ⓔ 중 어법상 어색한 것은?

① ⓐ   ② ⓑ   ③ ⓒ   ④ ⓓ   ⑤ ⓔ

서답형
07 다음 물음의 답을 위 대화에서 찾아 쓰시오.

> Q: What isn't allowed?

➡ _____

[08~09] 다음 대화를 읽고 물음에 답하시오.

> G: Excuse me, but (A)여기서 사진을 찍어도 되나요?
> M: Yes. Go ahead.
> G: Can I use a flash, too?
> M: Yes. That's also OK.
> G: I'm sorry, but I have one more question. Can I eat food here?
> M: I'm sorry, but _____(B)_____.

서답형
08 위 대화의 밑줄 친 (A)의 우리말에 맞게 주어진 단어를 이용하여 영어로 쓰시오.

> it / OK / take pictures / here

➡ _____
➡ _____

09 위 대화의 빈칸 (B)에 들어갈 말로 알맞은 것은?

① it's possible   ② that's not allowed
③ no problem   ④ eat food here
⑤ that's allowed

[10~12] 다음 대화를 읽고 물음에 답하시오.

> Kate: Excuse me, but ⓐis it OK to try on this hanbok?
> Man: Sure. The fitting room is over there. (①)
> Kate: Thanks. Wait a minute. That's also very pretty. (②)
> Man: Oh, the little hat over there?
> Kate: Yes. What is it? (③)
> Man: It's a jokduri, ⓑa traditional Korean hat for women. (④)
> Kate: Really? Is it OK to ⓒtry on it, too?
> Man: I'm sorry, but it's only for display. (⑤) ⓓTrying it on is not allowed.
> Kate: Oh. Then, I'll just ⓔtry on this hanbok.

10 위 대화의 (①)~(⑤) 중 다음 문장이 들어갈 위치로 알맞은 것은?

> It's usually worn on a wedding day.

①   ②   ③   ④   ⑤

11 위 대화의 밑줄 친 ⓐ~ⓔ 중 어법상 어색한 것은?

① ⓐ   ② ⓑ   ③ ⓒ   ④ ⓓ   ⑤ ⓔ

12 위 대화의 내용과 일치하지 않는 것은?

① Kate is going to try on the hanbok.
② A jokduri is a traditional Korean hat for women.
③ Kate is not allowed to wear a jokduri.
④ A jokduri is usually worn on a wedding day.
⑤ Both the hanbok and the jokduri are only for display.

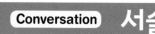
01 다음 대화의 (A)와 (B)에 들어갈 표현을 주어진 조건에 맞게 영어로 쓰시오.

A: Which place do you want to go first in the museum?
B: Why don't you guess?
A: OK. Is it OK to eat food there?
B: Yes. _____(A)_____
A: Is it OK to take pictures?
B: No. _____(B)_____
A: I got it. You're thinking of going to the Video Room.
B: You're right.

┤ 보기 ├
• (A)와 (B) 모두 동명사로 문장을 시작할 것.
• allow를 사용하여 (A)는 허락의 표현을, (B)는 금지의 표현을 사용할 것.

(A) _____
(B) _____

02 다음 대화의 밑줄 친 물음에 대한 답을 주어진 〈조건〉에 맞게 빈칸을 완성하시오.

G: Excuse me. Is it OK to take pictures here?
M: Yes, it's all right.
G: How about using a flash? <u>Can I use it, too?</u>
M: I'm afraid not. _____
G: Oh, I see. Thank you.

┤ 조건 ├
• 동명사를 주어로 쓸 것.
• allow를 사용할 것.
• here를 포함시킬 것.

➡ _____.

03 다음 대화의 빈칸에 들어갈 문장을 주어진 〈조건〉대로 완성하시오.

G: Excuse me. What's this? It looks interesting.
B: Oh, that's a janggu, a traditional Korean musical instrument.
G: _____
B: I'm sorry, but it's only for display. Playing it is not allowed.
G: I see.

┤ 조건 ├
• 장구를 연주해도 되는지 허가 여부를 묻는 표현을 쓸 것.
• OK와 it을 사용하고, 부정사를 이용할 것.

➡ _____.

04 다음 대화의 빈칸에 들어갈 알맞은 표현을 〈보기〉에서 찾아 쓰시오.

G: Excuse me, but _____(A)_____
M: Yes. Go ahead.
G: _____(B)_____
M: Yes. That's also OK.
G: I'm sorry, but ____(C)____ Can I eat food here?
M: I'm sorry, but _____(D)_____

┤ 조건 ├
• I have one more question.
• is it OK to take pictures here?
• Can I use a flash, too?
• that's not allowed.

(A) _____
(B) _____
(C) _____
(D) _____

Grammar

1 간접의문문

> • Please tell me **how you found them**. 그것들을 어떻게 발견하셨는지 말씀해 주세요.

■ 의문문이 동사의 목적절 등과 같이 다른 문장의 일부로 쓰일 때 간접의문문이라고 하며, 직접의문문과 달리 주어와 동사의 도치 현상이 일어나지 않는다. 의문사가 있는 간접의문문의 경우 '의문사＋주어＋동사'의 어순이 된다. 다른 문장 안에서 주어, 목적어, 보어 역할을 하며 동사의 목적어로 주로 쓰인다. 명사처럼 쓰이므로 주로 '…가 ~하는지'로 해석한다.

- **When he left here** was unknown. 〈주어〉 그가 언제 이곳을 떠났는지는 알려지지 않았다.
- I want to know **what his name is**. 〈목적어〉 나는 그 사람의 이름이 무엇인지 알고 싶다.
- This was **when Gandhi stood up for his nation**. 〈보어〉 이때가 간디가 그의 국가를 지지한 때예요.

■ 의문사가 없는 경우에는 의문사 대신에 if나 whether를 쓴다.

- I don't know. + Does he have a brother or a sister?
  → I don't know **if[whether] he has a brother or a sister.** 나는 그에게 남자 형제나 여자 형제가 있는지 모른다.

■ 의문사가 주어인 경우에는 의문사가 주어 역할을 하므로 직접의문문처럼 '의문사＋동사'의 어순임에 유의한다.

- Do you know **who is over there**? 저기 누가 있는지 아십니까?

■ 간접의문문으로 바꾸어 쓸 때에는 의문문에 쓰이는 조동사 do, does, did가 쓰이지 않는 대신, 조동사 do의 시제를 간접의문문의 동사에 반영해야 한다.

- He asked me. + When does the next bus come?
  → He asked me **when the next bus came**. 그는 내게 다음 버스가 언제 오는지 물었다.

■ believe, imagine, suppose, consider, think, guess 등과 같은 동사가 주절에 있을 경우 간접의문문의 의문사를 문장 맨 앞으로 배치한다.

- Do you think? + What did the thief steal?
  → Do you think **what the thief stole**? (✕)
  → **What** do you think **the thief stole**? (○) 너는 도둑이 무엇을 훔쳤다고 생각하니?

핵심 Check

1. 다음 우리말과 일치하도록 빈칸에 알맞은 말을 쓰시오.
   (1) 네가 무슨 걱정을 하고 있는지 말해 줄 수 있니?
      ➡ Can you tell me _____ _____ _____ worried about?
   (2) 그는 내게 밖이 추운지 물었다.
      ➡ He asked me _____ _____ _____ cold outside.

② because of

- Many Koreans became interested in *Uigwe* **because of** your book.
  많은 한국인들이 당신의 책 때문에 "의궤"에 관심을 갖게 되었어요.

- I couldn't sleep last night **because** I was so afraid. 간밤에 너무 무서워서 잠을 잘 수 없었다.

■ because와 because of는 둘 다 '~ 때문에'라는 뜻으로 뒤에 나오는 말이 원인을 나타낸다.

  • I couldn't arrive on time **because** I missed the bus. 버스를 놓쳐서 정각에 올 수가 없었어.

  • His absence from work was **because of** his illness. 그가 결근한 것은 아파서였다.

■ because는 이유를 나타내는 접속사이고, because of는 부사구이다. 접속사 because 뒤에는 주어와 동사가 있는 절이, 부사구 because of 뒤에는 명사 또는 명사구가 온다.

  • They cancelled the game **because** there was a storm.

  • They cancelled the game **because of** a storm. 그들은 폭풍 때문에 시합을 취소했다.

■ because는 '이유'를 나타내는 as, since 등의 접속사와 바꿔 쓸 수 있으며, because of는 on account of, due to, thanks to 등과 바꿔 쓸 수 있다.

  • I came here a bit early **because** my watch gained time.
    = I came here a bit early **since[as]** my watch gained time. 내 시계가 빨라서 나는 이곳에 조금 일찍 왔다.

  • **Because of** bad weather, the school outing was cancelled.
    = **On account of[Due to]** bad weather, the school outing was cancelled.
    악천후 때문에, 학교 소풍은 취소되었다.

핵심 Check

2. 다음 우리말과 일치하도록 빈칸에 알맞은 말을 쓰시오.

(1) 그는 아파서 학교에 오지 않았다.

➡ He didn't come to school _____ he was sick.

(2) 나는 교통 체증 때문에 늦었어.

➡ I was late _____ _____ the heavy traffic.

Grammar 시험대비 기본평가

01 다음 두 문장을 한 문장으로 연결할 때 올바른 것은?

> Can you tell me? What time is it now?

① Can you tell me what time is it now?
② Can you tell me what time it is now?
③ Can you tell me it is what time now?
④ What can you tell me it is time now?
⑤ What can you tell me is it time now?

02 다음 빈칸에 알맞은 것을 고르시오.

> A: Do you know _____?
> B: She is my sister.

① if who is she   ② if who she is
③ that she is   ④ who is she
⑤ who she is

03 다음 빈칸 ⓐ와 ⓑ에 들어갈 말이 알맞게 짝지어진 것을 고르시오.

> • I didn't go to school ___ⓐ___ I had a bad cold.
> • I didn't go to school ___ⓑ___ a bad cold.

① because – because   ② because – because of
③ because of – because for   ④ because of – because
⑤ because for – because

04 다음 주어진 단어를 바르게 배열하여 다음 우리말을 영어로 쓰시오. 필요하다면 단어를 추가하시오.

> 그는 건강상의 이유로 직장을 그만두었다.
> (he, his, the job, health, quit, because)

➡ _____

01 다음 빈칸에 들어갈 말로 가장 적절한 것은?

> Can you tell me _____ ?

① you became a director why
② why did you become a director
③ did why you become a director
④ why you became a director
⑤ why became you a director

02 다음 중 어법상 바르지 <u>않은</u> 것은?

① I couldn't sleep last night because of the loud noise.
② I stayed home because of it snowed too much.
③ She didn't buy it because it looked too small for him.
④ I stayed home because of a bad cold.
⑤ Tom had to leave early because of a traffic jam.

03 다음 중 어법상 옳은 것은?

① Can you tell me where were you born?
② Minho doesn't know where does Kevin live.
③ I stayed home because of I had a high fever.
④ The picnic was canceled because the bad weather.
⑤ I don't remember what time it was.

04 다음 괄호 안에서 알맞은 말을 고르시오.

(1) I didn't sleep well (because / because of) the loud noise.
(2) Sujin studied hard (because / because of) the exam.
(3) She was fired from the National Library of France (because / because of) her bosses thought that she was a spy.
(4) I don't remember what (was his name / his name was).
(5) I want to know what (are you / you are) interested in.
(6) Tell me (that / if) you enjoyed the movie.

05 다음 중 밑줄 친 부분의 쓰임이 <u>다른</u> 하나는?

① <u>If</u> you're finished, may I use the phone?
② <u>If</u> my guess is right, he must be about forty.
③ I want to know <u>if</u> he saw the movie.
④ Do you mind <u>if</u> I speak frankly?
⑤ I can do the shopping for you <u>if</u> you're tired.

06 주어진 단어를 이용하여 영작하시오.

> 너는 언제 영화가 시작하는지 아니? (start)

➡ _____

07 다음 두 문장을 한 문장으로 연결할 때 빈칸에 알맞은 것은?

> She has a test tomorrow. So, she is studying.
> → She's studying _____ she has a test tomorrow.

① because   ② because of
③ so   ④ and
⑤ but

08 다음 우리말을 영어로 바르게 옮긴 것은?

> 그가 그 상점에서 무엇을 샀는지 내게 묻지 마.

① Don't ask me whether he bought at the store.
② Don't ask me he bought what at the store.
③ Don't ask me what did he buy at the store.
④ Don't ask me he bought at the store what.
⑤ Don't ask me what he bought at the store.

09 다음 중 빈칸에 들어갈 말이 나머지 넷과 다른 것은?

① I am nervous _____ I have an exam tomorrow.
② _____ I was hungry, I had a hamburger.
③ Minho was tired, _____ he went to bed early.
④ Kevin got upset _____ his young brother went out with his jacket on.
⑤ Jane didn't go for a walk _____ it was too cold.

10 다음 중 밑줄 친 부분의 어순이 올바르지 <u>않은</u> 것은?

① I want to know <u>what your favorite subject is</u>.
② <u>How he solved the problem</u> is unknown.
③ He wondered <u>if something was wrong with him</u>.
④ The man asked me <u>if or not he could borrow some money</u>.
⑤ The woman was not sure <u>whether the thief was a man</u>.

서답형

11 다음 두 문장을 because를 이용하여 한 문장으로 다시 쓰시오.

(1) It was getting dark. We had to hurry.
　➡ _____

(2) Jim couldn't take a nap. His little sister cried a lot.
　➡ _____
　_____

(3) We didn't go camping. It was because of the bad weather.
　➡ _____

12 다음 중 어법상 바르지 <u>않은</u> 문장의 개수는?

> ⓐ I want to know where is she.
> ⓑ Jim couldn't take a nap because he had to study for the exam.
> ⓒ I wonder if is he at home.
> ⓓ Tell me when the guests will arrive.
> ⓔ We ran away because we were afraid.
> ⓕ Peter couldn't play soccer because the rain.

① 1개   ② 2개   ③ 3개
④ 4개   ⑤ 5개

서답형

13 다음 문장에서 어법상 어색한 것을 바르게 고쳐 다시 쓰시오.

(1) Can I ask you why did you decide to become a teacher?

➡ _____

(2) I want to know you were born where.

➡ _____

(3) Do you think who the girl is?

➡ _____

(4) He asked me that I am Simon's sister.

➡ _____

(5) I took some medicine because a bad cold.

➡ _____

(6) You can't watch the movie because of you're not old enough.

➡ _____
_____

중요

14 다음 두 문장을 간접의문문으로 바르게 바꾼 것은?

• Can you tell me?
• When did you become a teacher?

① When you became a teacher can you tell me?

② When can you tell me did you become a teacher?

③ When can you tell me you became a teacher?

④ Can you tell me when did you become a teacher?

⑤ Can you tell me when you became a teacher?

15 다음 중 어법상 바르지 않은 것은?

I ①missed the airplane ②to New York ③because ④a ⑤heavy traffic jam.

①   ②   ③   ④   ⑤

중요

16 우리말과 의미가 같도록 빈칸에 들어갈 말로 알맞은 것을 고르시오.

나는 그녀가 내 선물을 좋아할지 잘 모르겠다.
→ I'm not sure _____.

① if she will like my present

② she will like my present

③ will she like my present

④ that she likes my present

⑤ whether she likes my present

[17~18] 다음 빈칸에 가장 알맞은 것을 고르시오.

17

I want to go to Hawaii _____ it's warm and beautiful.

① and   ② but   ③ so
④ though   ⑤ because

중요

18

I forgot to ask you _____ you are hungry.

① because   ② because of
③ as   ④ that
⑤ if

서답형

19 다음 두 문장을 하나의 문장으로 바꿔 쓰시오.

• Please tell me.
• What did the thief steal?

➡ _____

01 다음 두 문장을 하나의 문장으로 바꿔 쓰시오.

(1) I'd like to know. + What did you want to be when you were young?

➡ _____
_____

(2) Can you tell me? + When and where were you born?

➡ _____

(3) I don't know. + Who borrowed your book?

➡ _____

(4) I wonder. + Does my child express himself well in English?

➡ _____
_____

(5) Do you know? + Will it rain today?

➡ _____

(6) Do you believe? + What were you in a previous life?

➡ _____

02 because를 이용하여 주어진 문장과 같은 의미가 되도록 한 문장으로 쓰시오.

(1) It's snowing a lot. So, there is no school today.

➡ _____
_____
_____

(2) Jaemin didn't arrive. So, we couldn't start the meeting.

➡ _____
_____
_____

03 다음 그림을 참고하여 주어진 대화의 빈칸을 완성하시오.

A: Please tell us (1)_____ 297 books of *Uigwe*?
B: Oh, I found them in 1977.
A: Could you tell us (2)_____?
B: I found them in the National Library of France.

04 다음 그림을 참고하여 다음 빈칸에 알맞은 말을 7 단어로 쓰시오.

A: Why can't he enter the zoo?
B: He can't enter the zoo _____
_____.

05 다음 문장은 두 개의 문장을 한 문장으로 쓴 것이다. 원래의 두 문장을 쓰시오.

(1) I'd like to know who your best friend is.

➡ _____

(2) She didn't tell me whom she met yesterday.

➡ _____

(3) He wondered if something was wrong with him.

➡ _____

(4) What do you think you will wear on Monday?

➡ _____

06 괄호 안에 주어진 어휘를 이용하여 다음 우리말을 영작하시오.

(1) Jessie한테 무슨 일이 생겼는지 내게 말해 줄 수 있니? (tell, happen, to, 8 단어)

➡ _____

(2) 그는 내게 돈이 좀 있는지 물었다.
(ask, have, any money, 8 단어)

➡ _____

(3) 나는 누가 이 책을 썼는지 알고 싶다.
(want, write, 8 단어)

➡ _____

(4) 건강의 비결이 뭐라고 생각하십니까?
(the secret, your health, think, 10 단어)

➡ _____

(5) 나는 감기 때문에 그의 생일 파티에 가지 않았다.
(a cold, because, 11 단어)

➡ _____

(6) 나는 어지러워서 앉았다.
(sit down, feeling dizzy, 8 단어)

➡ _____

(7) Michael과 Jane이 다투는 바람에 모두 일찍 떠났다.
(everyone, leave, have an argument, 10 단어)

➡ _____
_____

07 다음 문장을 어법에 맞게 고쳐 쓰시오.

(1) I don't remember what was the thief wearing.

➡ _____

(2) I don't know did who steal my camera.

➡ _____

(3) Can you tell me how did you become interested in *Uigwe*?

➡ _____
_____

(4) I asked her that she was ready to go.

➡ _____

(5) Do you suppose what most American teenagers seek help for?

➡ _____
_____

(6) Jane woke up in the middle of the night because a bad dream.

➡ _____
_____

(7) Yesterday Mary went shopping because of she wanted to buy a gift for her dad.

➡ _____
_____

08 다음 빈칸에 알맞은 말을 쓰시오.

It snowed a lot. So I couldn't go outside.
➡ I couldn't go outside _____ it snowed a lot.

Reading

An Interview with Dr. Park Byeong-seon

On May 27, 2011, 297 books of *Uigwe*, a collection of royal books
<small>날이나 요일 앞에 전치사 on</small> <small>동격 관계</small>
the French army took in 1866, came back to Korea. The person behind
<small>books와 the French army 사이에 목적격 관계대명사 which 또는 that 생략</small>
this return is Dr. Park Byeong-seon, a historian who spent her whole
<small>Dr. Park Byeong-seon과 a historian은 동격 관계</small> <small>주격 관계대명사</small>
life searching for Korean national treasures abroad.
<small>spend+시간+-ing: ~하는 데 시간을 보내다</small>

Q: Can you tell me how you became interested in *Uigwe*?
<small>의문문이 다른 문장의 일부로 쓰이면 '의문사＋주어＋동사' 어순의 간접의문문이 된다.</small>

Dr. Park: I studied history in college. I went to France to continue
<small>부사적 용법(목적)</small>
my studies in 1955. As you know, the French army took many of
<small>~ 처럼</small>
our national treasures in 1866. I wanted to find them while I was
<small>1866년에 프랑스군이 가져간 우리 문화재</small>
studying there. *Uigwe* was one of them.

Q: You found 297 books of *Uigwe* in the National Library of France, in
Paris. Please tell me how you found them.
<small>의문문이 다른 문장의 일부로 쓰이면 '의문사＋주어＋동사' 어순의 간접의문문이 된다.</small>

Dr. Park: As soon as I became a researcher at the National Library in
<small>'~하자마자'</small>
1967, I began to look for *Uigwe*. After 10 years, in 1977, I finally
<small>begin은 목적어로 to부정사와 동명사를 모두 취할 수 있다.</small>
found the books. I think I looked at more than 30 million books.
<small>~ 이상</small>

Q: I'm sure you were very excited when you found the books.

Dr. Park: Yes, I was, but more difficulties were waiting for me. I thought
that the books should be returned to Korea, but my bosses at the
<small>조동사가 있는 문장의 수동태: 조동사＋be동사＋과거분사</small>
library didn't like that idea. They even thought that I was a Korean
<small>'그 책들이 한국에 반환되어야 한다는 박병선 박사의 생각</small>
spy and fired me.
<small>fire: 해고하다</small>

 확인문제

● 다음 문장이 본문의 내용과 일치하면 T, 일치하지 <u>않으면</u> F를 쓰시오.

1   *Uigwe* is a collection of royal books the French army took in 1866. ☐

2   When Dr. Park became a researcher, she looked at *Uigwe*. ☐

3   Dr. Park thinks she looked at less than 30 million books. ☐

4   Dr. Park was very excited when she found *Uigwe*. ☐

royal 왕의, 왕실의
army 군대, 육군
spend (시간을) 보내다
search ~을 찾다
treasure 보물
abroad 해외에서
continue 계속하다
million 100만
research 연구
value 가치
result 결과
publish 출판하다, 발행하다
government 정부

After that, I had to go to the library as a visitor, so it was not easy to
도서관의 상사들이 박병선 박사를 해고한 것　　　　　　　'～로(서)'(자격)　　　가주어

do research on *Uigwe*. However, I didn't give up. For more than ten
진주어　　　　　　　　　　　　　　포기하다

years, I went to the library every day to finish my research. I wanted to
목적을 나타내는 to부정사의 부사적 용법

show people the value of *Uigwe*.
3형식: show the value of *Uigwe* to people

Q: The results of your research were published as a book in Korea in 1990.
수동태　　　～으로

Many Koreans became interested in *Uigwe* because of your book.
'～에 관심을 갖게 되다'　　　because of+명사(구)

Dr. Park: Yes. In 1992, the Korean government asked the French
ask A for B: A에게 B를 요청하다

government for its return and, finally, the 297 books are here now.

Q: Before I finish this interview, I'd like to ask you about *Jikji*, a book
*Jikji*와 a book은 동격 관계

that changed the history of printing.
주격 관계대명사

Dr. Park: I found it in my first year at the library. I knew right away that it
= *Jikji*　　　　　　　　= immediately

was very special. I worked hard to prove its value and finally succeeded.
목적을 나타내는 to부정사의 부사적 용법

At a book exhibition in Paris in 1972, *Jikji* was displayed as the oldest
be동사+과거분사: (수동태) '전시되었다'

book in the world that was printed with movable metal type.
주격 관계대명사　　　～으로(도구)

Q: Dr. Park, thanks to your hard work, *Jikji* and *Uigwe* were found, and
'～ 덕택에, ～ 덕분에'　　　　　　수동태

all Koreans thank you for that.
thank A for B: B에 대해 A에게 감사하다

Dr. Park: I hope people will become more interested in our national

treasures abroad and work for their return.
해외에 있는 우리의 문화재

---

visitor 손님, 방문객

prove 입증하다, 증명하다

succeed 성공하다

metal 금속

printing 인쇄

thanks to ～ 덕분에

📎 **확인문제**

● 다음 문장이 본문의 내용과 일치하면 T, 일치하지 않으면 F를 쓰시오.

1　It was not easy for Dr. Park to do research on *Uigwe*. ☐

2　The results of Dr. Park's research were published as a book in France in 1990. ☐

3　Many Koreans became interested in *Uigwe* because of Dr. Park's book. ☐

4　*Jikji* is a book that changed the history of printing. ☐

5　Dr. Park found *Jikji* in 1972. ☐

우리말을 참고하여 빈칸에 알맞은 말을 쓰시오.

1 An _____ _____ Dr. Park Byeong-seon

2 _____ May 27, 2011, 297 books of *Uigwe*, _____ _____ _____ royal books the French army took in 1866, _____ _____ _____ Korea.

3 The person _____ _____ _____ is Dr. Park Byeong-seon, a historian who spent her whole life _____ Korean national treasures _____.

4 Q: Can you tell me _____ you _____ _____ *Uigwe*?

5 Dr. Park: I _____ _____ in college.

6 I went to France _____ _____ my studies in 1955.

7 _____ _____ _____, the French army took many of our national treasures in 1866.

8 I wanted to find them _____ I was studying there.

9 *Uigwe* was _____ _____ _____.

10 Q: You found _____ _____ _____ _____ in the National Library of France, in Paris.

11 Please tell me _____ you found them.

12 Dr. Park: _____ _____ _____ I became a researcher at the National Library in 1967, I began to _____ _____ *Uigwe*.

13 After 10 years, in 1977, I _____ found the books.

14 I think I _____ _____ more than _____ _____ books.

15 Q: _____ _____ you were very excited when you found the books.

16 Dr. Park: Yes, I was, but _____ _____ were waiting for me.

17 I thought that the books _____ _____ _____ Korea, but my bosses at the library didn't like _____ _____.

18 They _____ _____ that I was a Korean spy and _____ me.

19 After that, I had to go to the library _____ _____ _____, so it was not easy to _____ _____ _____ Uigwe.

20 _____, I didn't give up.

21 _____ _____ _____ ten years, I went to the library every day to finish my research.

22 I wanted to show people _____ _____ _____ _____.

23 Q: The results of your research _____ _____ _____ a book in Korea in 1990.

24 Many Koreans became interested in Uigwe _____ _____ your book.

25 Dr. Park: Yes. In 1992, the Korean government _____ the French government _____ its return and, finally, the 297 books _____ _____ _____.

26 Q: Before I finish this interview, _____ _____ _____ you about Jikji, a book that changed the history of _____.

27 Dr. Park: I found it _____ _____ _____ _____ at the library.

28 I knew _____ _____ that it was very special.

29 I worked hard _____ _____ _____ _____ and finally succeeded.

30 At a book exhibition in Paris in 1972, Jikji _____ _____ _____ the oldest book in the world that was printed with _____ _____ _____.

31 Q: Dr. Park, _____ _____ your hard work, Jikji and Uigwe were found, and all Koreans _____ you _____ that.

32 Dr. Park: I hope people will become more interested in _____ _____ _____ _____ and work for their _____.

18 그들은 심지어 제가 한국의 스파이라고 생각했고 저를 해고했죠.

19 그 후에, 저는 방문객으로 도서관에 가야만 했고, 그래서 "의궤"를 연구하는 것이 쉽지 않았어요.

20 하지만 저는 포기하지 않았죠.

21 10년 넘게, 연구를 끝마치기 위해 매일 도서관에 갔어요.

22 저는 사람들에게 "의궤"의 가치를 보여 주고 싶었어요.

23 Q: 당신의 연구 결과가 1990년 한국에서 책으로 출판되었죠.

24 많은 한국인들이 당신의 책 때문에 "의궤"에 관심을 갖게 되었어요.

25 Dr. Park: 네. 1992년에 한국 정부는 프랑스 정부에 그것의 반환을 요청했고, 마침내 297권의 책이 지금 여기 있게 된 거죠.

26 Q: 인터뷰를 마치기 전에, 인쇄의 역사를 바꾼 책인 "직지"에 대해 여쭙고 싶어요.

27 Dr. Park: 저는 도서관에서 근무한 첫해에 그것을 발견했어요.

28 그것이 아주 특별하다는 것을 바로 알았어요.

29 저는 그것의 가치를 증명하기 위해 열심히 연구했고 마침내 성공했죠.

30 1972년에 파리 도서 박람회에서 "직지"는 금속 활자로 인쇄된 세계에서 가장 오래된 책으로 전시되었죠.

31 Q: 박 박사님, 당신의 노고 덕분에 "직지"와 "의궤"가 발견되었고, 모든 한국인이 그 점을 당신에게 감사하고 있어요.

32 Dr. Park: 저는 사람들이 해외에 있는 우리의 문화재에 더 많은 관심을 갖고 그것의 반환을 위해 애써 주시기를 바랍니다.

● 우리말을 참고하여 본문을 영작하시오.

1 박병선 박사와의 인터뷰
➡ _____

2 2011년 5월 27일에 프랑스군이 1866년에 가져갔던 왕실 서적인 "의궤" 297권이 한국으로 돌아왔다.
➡ _____

3 이 반환 뒤에 있는 인물이 해외에 있는 한국의 문화재를 찾기 위해 전 생애를 바친 역사학자 박병선 박사이다.
➡ _____
_____

4 Q: "의궤"에 어떻게 관심을 갖게 되셨는지 말씀해 주시겠어요?
➡ _____

5 Dr. Park: 저는 대학에서 역사를 공부했어요.
➡ _____

6 저는 1955년에 학업을 계속하기 위해 프랑스에 갔습니다.
➡ _____

7 아시다시피, 프랑스군은 1866년에 우리 문화재를 많이 가져갔어요.
➡ _____

8 저는 그곳에서 공부하는 동안 그것들을 찾고 싶었어요.
➡ _____

9 "의궤"는 그것들 중의 하나였어요.
➡ _____

10 Q: 당신은 파리에 있는 프랑스 국립도서관에서 297권의 "의궤"를 발견하셨어요.
➡ _____

11 그것들을 어떻게 발견하셨는지 말씀해 주세요.
➡ _____

12 Dr. Park: 1967년에 국립도서관의 연구원이 되자마자, 저는 "의궤"를 찾기 시작했어요.
➡ _____
_____

13 10년 후인 1977년에 마침내 그 책들을 발견했죠.
➡ _____

14 제 생각에 3천만 권 이상의 책을 본 것 같아요.
➡ _____

15 Q: 그 책들을 발견했을 때 무척 흥분하셨겠어요.
➡ _____

16 Dr. Park: 네, 하지만 더 큰 어려움이 저를 기다리고 있었어요.
➡ _____

17 저는 그 책들이 한국에 반환되어야 한다고 생각했지만, 도서관의 제 상사들은 그 생각을 좋아하지 않았어요.
➡ _____
_____

18 그들은 심지어 제가 한국의 스파이라고 생각했고 저를 해고했죠.

➡ _____

19 그 후에, 저는 방문객으로 도서관에 가야만 했고, 그래서 "의궤"를 연구하는 것이 쉽지 않았어요.

➡ _____

20 하지만 저는 포기하지 않았죠.

➡ _____

21 10년 넘게, 연구를 끝마치기 위해 매일 도서관에 갔어요.

➡ _____

22 저는 사람들에게 "의궤"의 가치를 보여 주고 싶었어요.

➡ _____

23 Q: 당신의 연구 결과가 1990년 한국에서 책으로 출판되었죠.

➡ _____

24 많은 한국인들이 당신의 책 때문에 "의궤"에 관심을 갖게 되었어요.

➡ _____

25 Dr. Park: 네. 1992년에 한국 정부는 프랑스 정부에 그것의 반환을 요청했고, 마침내 297권의 책이
지금 여기 있게 된 거죠.

➡ _____

_____

26 Q: 인터뷰를 마치기 전에, 인쇄의 역사를 바꾼 책인 "직지"에 대해 여쭙고 싶어요.

➡ _____

_____

27 Dr. Park: 저는 도서관에서 근무한 첫해에 그것을 발견했어요.

➡ _____

28 그것이 아주 특별하다는 것을 바로 알았어요.

➡ _____

29 저는 그것의 가치를 증명하기 위해 열심히 연구했고 마침내 성공했죠.

➡ _____

30 1972년에 파리 도서 박람회에서 "직지"는 금속 활자로 인쇄된 세계에서 가장 오래된 책으로 전시되었죠.

➡ _____

_____

31 Q: 박 박사님, 당신의 노고 덕분에 "직지"와 "의궤"가 발견되었고, 모든 한국인들이 그 점을 당신에게
감사하고 있어요.

➡ _____

_____

32 Dr. Park: 저는 사람들이 해외에 있는 우리의 문화재에 더 많은 관심을 갖고 그것의 반환을 위해 애써
주시기를 바랍니다.

➡ _____

_____

[01~03] 다음 글을 읽고 물음에 답하시오.

①In May 27, 2011, 297 books ②of *Uigwe*, a collection of royal books the French army took ③in 1866, came back to Korea. The person behind this return is Dr. Park Byeong-seon, a historian who spent her whole life searching ④for Korean national treasures abroad.

Q: Can you tell me how you became interested ⑤in *Uigwe*?

Dr. Park: I studied history in college. I went to France to continue my studies in 1955. ⓐ 아시다시피, the French army took many of our national treasures in 1866. I wanted to find them while I was studying there. *Uigwe* was one of them.

서답형

01 위 글의 밑줄 친 전치사 ①~⑤ 중에서 옳지 않은 것을 찾아 고치시오.

_____ ➡ _____

서답형

02 위 글의 밑줄 친 ⓐ의 우리말을 세 단어로 쓰시오.

➡ _____

03 위 글의 내용과 일치하지 않는 것은?

① In 2011, *Uigwe* came back to Korea.
② The French army took *Uigwe* from Korea in 1866.
③ Dr. Park spent her whole life searching for Korean national treasures abroad.
④ In 1955, Dr. Park went to France to continue her studies.
⑤ Dr. Park wanted to introduce *Uigwe* while she was studying in France.

[04~07] 다음 글을 읽고 물음에 답하시오.

Q: You found 297 books of *Uigwe* in the National Library of France, in Paris.

_____ⓐ_____

Dr. Park: As soon as I became a researcher at the National Library in 1967, I began to look for *Uigwe*. After 10 years, in 1977, I ⓑfinally found the books. I think I looked at more than 30 million books.

Q: I'm sure you were very excited when you found the books.

Dr. Park: Yes, I was, but more difficulties were waiting for me. I thought that the books should be returned to Korea, but my bosses at the library didn't like that idea. They even thought that I was a Korean spy and fired me. After that, I had to go to the library as a visitor, so it was not easy to do research on *Uigwe*. However, I didn't give up. For more than ten years, I went to the library every day to finish my research. I wanted to show people the value of *Uigwe*.

서답형

04 다음 두 문장을 합쳐서 위 글의 빈칸 ⓐ에 알맞은 형태로 쓰시오.

> • Please tell me.
> • How did you find them?

➡ _____

05 위 글의 밑줄 친 ⓑfinally와 바꿔 쓸 수 없는 말을 모두 고르시오.

① at least   ② in the end
③ lastly   ④ at last
⑤ in the long run

서답형

06 Why was Dr. Park fired? Fill in the blanks with the suitable words.

> Because her bosses at the library didn't like _____ _____ and they even thought that she was _____ _____ _____.

중요

07 위 글의 마지막 부분에서 알 수 있는 Dr. Park의 성격으로 가장 알맞은 것을 고르시오.

① friendly   ② strong-willed

③ polite   ④ creative

⑤ curious

[08~11] 다음 글을 읽고 물음에 답하시오.

Q: Before I finish this interview, I'd like to ask you about *Jikji*, a book ⓐthat changed the history of printing.

Dr. Park: I found it in my first year at the library. I knew right away that it was very special. I worked hard to prove its value and finally succeeded. At a book exhibition in Paris in 1972, *Jikji* was displayed as the oldest book in the world that was printed with movable ⓑ금속 활자.

Q: ⓒDr. Park, in spite of your hard work, *Jikji* and *Uigwe* were found, and all Koreans thank you for that.

Dr. Park: I hope people will become more interested in our national treasures abroad and work for their return.

08 위 글의 밑줄 친 ⓐthat과 문법적 쓰임이 같은 것을 모두 고르시오.

① Look at the boy and the dog that are running there.

② I can't walk that far.

③ She said that the story was true.

④ Which would you prefer, this or that?

⑤ It's the best novel that I've ever read.

서답형

09 위 글의 밑줄 친 ⓑ의 우리말을 두 단어로 쓰시오.

➡ _____

서답형

10 위 글의 밑줄 친 ⓒ에서 흐름상 어색한 부분을 찾아 고치시오.

_____ ➡ _____

11 위 글의 제목으로 알맞은 것을 고르시오.

① Let Me Ask You a Final Question

② What Is *Jikji*?

③ Dr. Park Proved the Value of *Jikji*

④ *Jikji* Was Displayed at a Book Exhibition

⑤ Our National Treasures Abroad Must Be Returned

[12~14] 다음 글을 읽고 물음에 답하시오.

On May 27, 2011, ⓐ297 books of *Uigwe*, a collection of royal books the French army took in 1866, came back to Korea. The person behind this return is Dr. Park Byeong-seon, a historian who spent her whole life searching for Korean national treasures abroad.

Q: Can you tell me how you became interested in *Uigwe*?

Dr. Park: I studied history in college. I went to France to continue my studies in 1955. ⓑ As you know, the French army took many of our national treasures in 1866. I wanted to find them while I was studying there. *Uigwe* was one of them.

12 위 글의 밑줄 친 ⓐ에서 royal books와 the French army 사이에 생략된 말로 옳은 것을 모두 고르시오.

① that   ② who   ③ whom
④ which   ⑤ what

13 위 글의 밑줄 친 ⓑAs와 같은 의미로 쓰인 것을 고르시오.

① He came up to me as I was speaking.
② As you see, he is a genius.
③ As I was tired, I soon fell asleep.
④ He treats me as a child.
⑤ As we go up, the air grows colder.

14 위 글을 읽고 "의궤"에 대해 대답할 수 없는 것을 고르시오.

① What is *Uigwe*?
② How many books does it have in all?
③ Who made it and what is recorded in it?
④ Who took it from Korea?
⑤ When did it come back to Korea?

[15~18] 다음 글을 읽고 물음에 답하시오.

Q: You found 297 books of *Uigwe* in the National Library of France, in Paris. Please tell me how you found ①them.

Dr. Park: As soon as I became a researcher at the National Library in 1967, I began to look for *Uigwe*. After 10 years, in 1977, I finally found ②the books. I think I looked at ③more than 30 million books.

Q: I'm sure you were very excited when you found ④the books.

Dr. Park: Yes, I was, but more difficulties were waiting for me. I thought that ⑤ the books should be returned to Korea, but my bosses at the library didn't like that idea. They even thought that I was a Korean spy and fired me. After that, I had to go to the library as a visitor, so it was not easy to do research on *Uigwe*. ___ⓐ___, I didn't give up. For more than ten years, I went to the library every day to finish my research. I wanted to show people the value of *Uigwe*.

15 위 글의 빈칸 ⓐ에 들어갈 알맞은 말을 고르시오.

① Therefore ② For example
③ Besides ④ However
⑤ In other words

16 밑줄 친 ①~⑤ 중에서 가리키는 대상이 나머지 넷과 **다른** 것은?

① ② ③ ④ ⑤

17 위 글의 내용과 어울리는 속담을 고르시오. (두 개)

① A stitch in time saves nine.
② Where there is a will, there is a way.
③ It never rains but it pours.
④ Better late than never.
⑤ Many drops make a shower.

18 위 글을 읽고 대답할 수 **없는** 질문은?

① When did Dr. Park begin to look for *Uigwe*?
② How long did it take for Dr. Park to find *Uigwe*?
③ How many books did she look at before finding *Uigwe*?
④ What did she think when she found *Uigwe*?
⑤ What's the value of *Uigwe*?

[19~20] 다음 글을 읽고 물음에 답하시오.

Q: Before I finish this interview, I'd like to ask you about *Jikji*, a book ___①___ changed the history of printing.
Dr. Park: I found it in my first year at the library. I knew right away ___②___ it was very special. I worked hard to prove its value and finally succeeded. At a book exhibition in Paris in 1972, *Jikji* was displayed ___③___ the oldest book in the world ___④___ was printed with movable metal type.
Q: Dr. Park, thanks to your hard work, *Jikji* and *Uigwe* were found, and all Koreans thank you for ___⑤___.
Dr. Park: I hope people will become more interested in our national treasures abroad and work for their return.

19 위 글의 빈칸 ①~⑤에 들어갈 말이 나머지 넷과 **다른** 것은?

① ② ③ ④ ⑤

20 위 글의 내용과 일치하지 <u>않는</u> 것은?

① The last question was about *Jikji*.

② *Jikji* changed the history of printing.

③ Dr. Park succeeded in proving the value of *Jikji*.

④ In 1972, Gutenberg Bible was proved as the oldest book in the world.

⑤ Thanks to Dr. Park's hard work, *Jikji* and *Uigwe* were found.

[21~23] 다음 글을 읽고 물음에 답하시오.

Q: I'm sure you were very excited when you found the books.

Dr. Park: Yes, I was, but more difficulties were waiting for me. (①) They even thought that I was a Korean spy and ⓐfired me. (②) After that, I had to go to the library as a visitor, so it was not easy to do research on *Uigwe*. (③) However, I didn't give up. (④) For more than ten years, I went to the library every day ⓑto finish my research. (⑤) I wanted to show people the value of *Uigwe*.

21 위 글의 흐름으로 보아, 주어진 문장이 들어가기에 가장 적절한 곳은?

I thought that the books should be returned to Korea, but my bosses at the library didn't like that idea.

①   ②   ③   ④   ⑤

22 위 글의 밑줄 친 ⓐfired와 같은 의미로 쓰인 것을 고르시오.

① She <u>fired</u> an arrow at the target.

② They <u>fired</u> questions at him.

③ He was <u>fired</u> because he was lazy.

④ The book <u>fired</u> his imagination.

⑤ He <u>fired</u> the gun into the air.

서답형

23 위 글의 밑줄 친 ⓑ를 다음과 같이 바꿔 쓸 때 빈칸에 들어갈 알맞은 말을 쓰시오.

(1) _____ _____ _____ my research

(2) _____ _____ _____ my research

(3) _____ _____ _____ I _____ my research

(4) _____ _____ I _____ finish my research

[24~26] 다음 글을 읽고 물음에 답하시오.

Q: Before I finish this interview, I'd like to ask you about *Jikji*, a book that changed the history of printing.

Dr. Park: I found it in my first year at the library. I knew right away that it was very (A)[common / special]. I worked hard to prove its value and finally succeeded. At a book (B)[exhibition / explanation] in Paris in 1972, *Jikji* (C)[displayed / was displayed] as the oldest book in the world that was printed with movable metal type.

Q: Dr. Park, thanks to your hard work, *Jikji* and *Uigwe* were found, and all Koreans thank you for ⓐthat.

Dr. Park: I hope people will become more interested in our national treasures abroad and work for ⓑtheir return.

서답형

24 위 글의 괄호 (A)~(C)에서 문맥이나 어법상 알맞은 낱말을 골라 쓰시오.

(A) _____ (B) _____ (C) _____

서답형

25 위 글의 밑줄 친 ⓐthat과 ⓑtheir가 가리키는 내용을 우리말로 쓰시오.

ⓐ _____

ⓑ _____

26 위 글의 두 사람의 관계로 알맞은 것을 고르시오.

① employer – employee

② interviewer – applicant

③ trainer – trainee

④ interviewer – interviewee

⑤ manager – candidate

[27~28] 다음 인터뷰 기사를 읽고 물음에 답하시오.

An Interview with Kim Yubin

The following is the interview I had with Kim Yubin, a local police officer.

Q: Can you tell me ⓐwhen and where were you born?

A: I was born in Seoul on March 11, 1980.

Q: I'd like (A)[to know / knowing] what your goal in life is.

A: My goal in life is (B)[to make / making] a better world.

Q: Can you tell me ⓑwhat do you like about your job?

A: I like (C)[to help / helping] people.

I think that Kim Yubin is a great police officer.

서답형

27 위 글의 밑줄 친 ⓐ와 ⓑ를 어법상 바르게 고쳐 쓰시오.

ⓐ _____

ⓑ _____

서답형

28 위 글의 괄호 (A)~(C)에서 어법상 알맞은 낱말을 골라 쓰시오. (둘 다 가능한 경우에는 둘 다 쓰시오.)

ⓐ _____

ⓑ _____

ⓒ _____

[01~03] 다음 글을 읽고 물음에 답하시오.

On May 27, 2011, 297 books of *Uigwe*, a (A)[collection / correction] of royal books the French army took in 1866, came back to Korea. The person (B)[behind / in front of] ⓐthis return is Dr. Park Byeong-seon, a historian who spent her whole life searching for Korean national treasures (C)[aboard / abroad].

Q: Can you tell me ⓑ"의궤"에 어떻게 관심을 갖게 되셨는지?

Dr. Park: I studied history in college. I went to France to continue my studies in 1955. As you know, the French army took many of our national treasures in 1866. I wanted to find them while I was studying there. *Uigwe* was one of them.

01 위 글의 괄호 (A)~(C)에서 문맥상 알맞은 낱말을 골라 쓰시오.

(A) _____ (B) _____ (C) _____

02 다음 빈칸 (A)와 (B)에 알맞은 단어를 넣어 ⓐthis return에 대한 설명을 완성하시오.

the return of *Uigwe* from (A)_____ to (B)_____

03 위 글의 밑줄 친 ⓑ의 우리말에 맞게 주어진 어휘를 이용하여 6 단어로 영작하시오.

how, became

➡ _____

[04~07] 다음 글을 읽고 물음에 답하시오.

Q: You found 297 books of *Uigwe* in the National Library of France, in Paris. Please tell me how you found them.

Dr. Park: As soon as I became a researcher at the National Library in 1967, ⓐI began to look for *Uigwe*. After 10 years, in 1977, I finally found the books. I think I looked at more than 30 million books.

Q: I'm sure you were very excited when you found the books.

Dr. Park: Yes, I was, but more difficulties were waiting for me. ⓑ저는 그 책들이 한국에 반환되어야 한다고 생각했어요, but my bosses at the library didn't like that idea. ⓒThey even thought that I was a Korean spy and hired me. After that, I had to go to the library as a visitor, so it was not easy to do research on *Uigwe*. However, I didn't give up. For more than ten years, I went to the library every day to finish my research. I wanted to show people the value of *Uigwe*.

04 위 글의 밑줄 친 ⓐ를 다음과 같이 바꿔 쓸 때 빈칸에 들어갈 알맞은 말을 쓰시오.

I began _____ for *Uigwe*.

05 위 글의 밑줄 친 ⓑ의 우리말에 맞게 주어진 어휘를 이용하여 10 단어로 영작하시오.

that, should, return to

➡ _____

06 위 글의 밑줄 친 ⓒ에서 흐름상 어색한 부분을 찾아 고치시오.

_____ ➡ _____

07 위 글의 내용과 일치하도록 다음 빈칸 (A)~(C)에 알맞은 단어를 쓰시오.

> (A)_____ _____ _____ Dr. Park became a researcher at the National Library in 1967, she began to look for *Uigwe*. In spite of many (B)_____, she didn't give up because she wanted to show people the (C)_____ of *Uigwe*, and after 10 years, she found the books.

[08~09] 다음 글을 읽고 물음에 답하시오.

Q: Before I finish this interview, I'd like to ask you about *Jikji*, a book that changed the history of printing.

Dr. Park: I found it in my first year at the library. I knew right away that it was very special. I worked hard to prove its value and finally ⓐsucceeded. At a book exhibition in Paris in 1972, *Jikji* was displayed as the oldest book in the world that was printed with movable metal type.

Q: Dr. Park, thanks to your hard work, *Jikji* and *Uigwe* were found, and all Koreans thank you for that.

Dr. Park: I hope people will become more interested in our national treasures abroad and work for their return.

08 위 글의 밑줄 친 ⓐsucceeded 뒤에 생략된 말을 쓰시오. (전치사 in을 포함하여 4 단어)

➡ _____

09 다음 빈칸 (A)~(C)에 알맞은 단어를 넣어 *Jikji*에 대한 소개를 완성하시오.

> *Jikji* is a book that changed the history of (A)_____ because it turned out that *Jikji* was the (B)_____ book in the world that was printed with (C)_____ _____ _____.

[10~12] 다음 글을 읽고 물음에 답하시오.

On May 27, 2011, 297 books of *Uigwe*, a collection of royal books the French army took in 1866, came back to Korea. ⓐThe person (____) this return is Dr. Park Byeong-seon, a historian who spent her whole life searching for Korean national treasures abroad.

Q: Can you tell me how you became interested in *Uigwe*?

Dr. Park: I studied history in college. I went to France to continue my studies in 1955. As you know, the French army took many of our national treasures in 1866. I wanted to find ⓑthem while I was studying there. *Uigwe* was one of them.

10 다음과 같은 뜻이 되도록 위 글의 밑줄 친 ⓐ의 빈칸에 들어갈 알맞은 한 단어를 쓰시오.

> The person who made this return possible

➡ _____

11 위 글의 밑줄 친 ⓑthem이 가리키는 것을 영어로 쓰시오.

➡ _____
_____

12 다음 빈칸 (A)~(C)에 알맞은 단어를 넣어 *Uigwe*에 대한 소개를 완성하시오.

> It is a collection of (A)_____ _____ of Korea which the French army took in 1866. Thanks to the effort of (B)_____ _____ _____, however, it came back to Korea from France on May 27, 2011.

해석

After You Read C Think and Talk

A: What do you think about Dr. Park?
　　How(x)
B: I think she had a strong will. She had many difficulties, but she didn't give
　　think와 she 사이에 접속사 that 생략
up.

C: I think she had a great passion for her work. As a historian, she was very
　　　　　　　　　　　　　　　　　~에 대한　　　~로서(역할, 자격)
passionate about finding Korean national treasures abroad.
전치사 다음에 동명사를 쓴다.　　　　　　해외에 있는 한국의 문화재

구문해설　• will: 의지　• give up: 포기하다　• passion: 열정　• passionate: 열정적인

A: 박 박사에 대해 어떻게 생각하니?

B: 그녀는 강한 의지를 가졌다고 생각해. 그녀는 많은 어려움을 겪었지만 포기하지 않았어.

C: 그녀는 자신의 일에 대해 강한 열정을 가졌다고 생각해. 역사학자로서, 그녀는 해외에 있는 한국의 문화재를 찾는 것에 대해 매우 열정적이었어.

Think and Write Step 2

An Interview with Kim Yubin

The following is the interview I had with Kim Yubin, a local police officer.
　다음은　　　　　　　　　　　　　　　　　　　　　　Kim Yubin을 설명하는 동격어구다.
Q: Can you tell me when and where you were born?
　　　　　tell의 직접목적어로 '의문사+주어+동사' 어순의 간접의문문
A: I was born in Seoul on March 11, 1980.
　　태어났다
Q: I'd like to know what your goal in life is.
　'~하고 싶다'(= want to) know의 목적어로 '의문사+주어+동사' 어순의 간접의문문
A: My goal in life is to make a better world.
　　　　　　　　보어 자리에 사용된 부정사의 명사적 용법
Q: Can you tell me what you like about your job?
　　　　　tell의 직접목적어로 '의문사+주어+동사' 어순의 간접의문문
A: I like helping people.

I think that Kim Yubin is a great police officer.
　　　명사절을 이끄는 접속사

구문해설　• interview: 인터뷰　• be born: 태어나다　• would like to+동사원형: ~하고 싶다
• goal: 목표

김유빈 씨와의 인터뷰
다음은 제가 지역 경찰관 김유빈 씨와 한 인터뷰입니다.
Q: 당신은 언제, 어디서 태어나셨는지 말씀해 주시겠어요?
A: 저는 1980년 3월 11일에 서울에서 태어났어요.
Q: 당신의 인생의 목표가 무엇인지 알고 싶어요.
A: 저의 인생의 목표는 더 나은 세상을 만드는 것입니다.
Q: 당신의 직업에 관해 당신이 좋아하는 것이 무엇인지 말씀해 주시겠어요?
A: 저는 사람들을 돕는 것이 좋아요.
저는 김유빈 씨가 대단한 경찰관이라고 생각합니다.

Team Project Create

Jikji, South Korea's National Treasure No. 1132

Jikji was printed at Heungdeoksa in 1377. It is now in the National Library of
　　　　　　　수동태
France, in Paris. It is the world's oldest book that was printed with movable
　　　　　　　　　　　　　　　　　　　　최상급　　　　　　　수동태　　　　금속활자
metal type.

구문해설　• treasure: 보물　• National Library: 국립도서관　• movable: 움직일 수 있는, 이동할 수
있는　• metal: 금속

직지, 한국의 국보 1132번
직지는 1377년 흥덕사에서 인쇄되었다. 현재는 파리의 프랑스 국립도서관에 있다. 직지는 금속활자로 인쇄된 세계에서 가장 오래된 책이다.

01 다음 단어 중 나머지 넷과 성격이 <u>다른</u> 하나는?

① fire ② allow ③ return
④ display ⑤ flash

02 다음 빈칸 ⓐ와 ⓑ에 들어갈 단어가 바르게 짝지어진 것은?

• As you know, the French army took many of our national ___ⓐ___ in 1866.
• At a book exhibition in Paris in 1972, *Jikji* was ___ⓑ___ as the oldest book in the world.

① values – displayed
② value – fired
③ treasures – spent
④ treasures – displayed
⑤ treasures – returned

[03~04] 다음 영영 풀이에 해당하는 것을 고르시오.

03

used for saying that someone or something is responsible for something good that happened

① at last ② look for
③ thanks to ④ right away
⑤ give up

04

the work of finding out facts about something

① research ② silver
③ result ④ government
⑤ flash

05 다음 문장의 빈칸에 공통으로 들어갈 알맞은 말을 쓰시오.

• It wasn't easy for him, but he didn't _____ _____.
• They don't _____ _____ easily even though they fail many times.

06 다음 중 밑줄 친 부분의 뜻이 <u>잘못된</u> 것은?

① They even thought that I was a Korean spy and <u>fired</u> me. (해고했다)
② I went to the library every day to finish my <u>research</u>. (연구)
③ The results of your research were <u>published</u> as a book in Korea in 1990. (입증되었다)
④ I knew <u>right away</u> that it was very special. (바로)
⑤ <u>As soon as</u> I became a researcher at the National Library in 1967, I began to look for *Uigwe*. (~하자마자)

07 다음 대화의 밑줄 친 ⓐ의 의도로 알맞은 것은?

W: Excuse me, but ⓐ<u>is it OK if I park my car here?</u>
M: Did you come to Star Theater?
W: No. I came to Tim's Restaurant.
M: I'm sorry, but this parking lot is only for the customers of the theater.
W: Oh. I didn't know that.

① 금지하기 ② 좋아하는 것 묻기
③ 허락 구하기 ④ 부탁하기
⑤ 예정된 것 말하기

[08~10] 다음 대화를 읽고 물음에 답하시오.

G: Excuse me, but is it OK to try on this hanbok? (①)

M: Sure. The fitting room is over there.

G: Thanks. Wait a minute. (②)

M: Oh, the little hat over there? (③)

G: Yes. What is it?

M: It's a jokduri, a traditional Korean hat for women. (④) It's usually worn on a wedding day.

G: Really? Is it OK to try it on, too? (⑤)

M: I'm sorry, but (A)그것은 전시만 하는 거예요. Trying it on is not allowed.

G: Oh. Then, I'll just try on this hanbok.

08 다음 주어진 문장이 들어갈 위치로 알맞은 것은?

> That's also very pretty.

①   ②   ③   ④   ⑤

09 다음 질문에 대한 답을 위 대화에서 찾아 쓰시오.

> Q: What two things does the girl want to try on?

➡ She _____.

10 위 대화의 밑줄 친 (A)의 우리말에 맞게 주어진 단어를 이용하여 영어로 쓰시오. (four words)

> only / display

➡ _____

11 다음 대화의 밑줄 친 (A)~(E) 중 어법상 어색한 것은?

A: (A)Which place do you want to go to first in the museum?

B: (B)Why don't you guess?

A: OK. (C)Is it OK to use smartphones there?

B: Yes. (D)Using smartphones are allowed.

A: Is it OK to take pictures?

B: No. Taking pictures is not allowed.

A: I got it. You're thinking of (E)going to the Gift Shop.

B: You're right.

① (A)   ② (B)   ③ (C)   ④ (D)   ⑤ (E)

12 우리말에 맞게 영어로 바르게 표현하지 <u>않은</u> 것은?

① 알아맞혀 볼래?

   → Why don't you guess?

② 저는 이런 음식을 한번도 본 적이 없어요.

   → I've never seen any food like this.

③ 저기에 앉아도 되나요?

   → Is it OK to sit over there?

④ 그것은 여자들이 쓰는 한국 전통 모자인 족두리예요.

   → It's a jokduri, a traditional Korean hat for women.

⑤ 헬스장은 저쪽입니다.

   → The fitting room is over there.

13 다음에 제시된 단어와 〈조건〉에 맞게 아래 대화의 빈칸을 완성하시오.

┌─ 조건 ├─
(A) • 앉아도 되는지 허가 여부를 묻는 표현을 쓸 것.
　　• to sit / over there
(B) • (A)의 물음에 대한 금지의 답을 쓸 것.
　　• 동명사를 이용할 것.
　　• allow를 이용할 것.

A: Excuse me. _____(A)_____
B: You mean, on the grass?
A: Yes. Is it all right?
B: I'm sorry, but _____(B)_____.
A: OK, I understand.

(A) _____
(B) _____

14 다음 대화를 읽고 아래 물음에 영어로 답하시오.

G: Excuse me, but is it OK to try on this hanbok?
M: Sure. The fitting room is over there.
G: Thanks. Wait a minute. That's also very pretty.
M: Oh, the little hat over there?
G: Yes. What is it?
M: It's a jokduri, a traditional Korean hat for women. It's usually worn on a wedding day.
G: Really? Is it OK to try it on, too?
M: I'm sorry, but it's only for display. Trying it on is not allowed.
G: Oh. Then, I'll just try on this hanbok.

Q: Is trying on a jokduri allowed?
➡ _____, _____ _____. The jokduri is only _____ _____.

15 다음 문장의 빈칸에 공통으로 들어갈 알맞은 말을 쓰시오.

• The game was cancelled _____ of the storm.
• I had to stay home all day _____ I had a bad cold.

16 다음 중 어법상 바르지 않은 것은?

① I'd like to know what color the thief's hair was.
② Can you tell me what you like about your job?
③ I wonder who you danced with at the party.
④ Do you have any idea what is going to happen?
⑤ However, she is not sure she will return in the future.

17 다음 문장을 두 문장으로 나누어 쓰시오.

(1) I'm not sure if my grandfather will like my present.
　➡ _____
(2) Can you tell me where the bathroom is?
　➡ _____
(3) I'd like to know who you met at the party.
　➡ _____
(4) Did you know who was in the classroom?
　➡ _____
(5) What do you think Jane's secret is?
　➡ _____
(6) I'm curious if you can lend me the book.
　➡ _____

18 다음 밑줄 친 if[if]의 쓰임이 나머지 넷과 **다른** 하나를 고르시오.

① She is not sure if it's a great idea.
② I asked her if she knew French.
③ I can't hear you if you don't speak loudly.
④ Please tell me if there's anything I can do to help you.
⑤ We have no idea if they like it or not.

19 다음 우리말을 영어로 바르게 옮긴 것은?

> 얼마나 오래 여기 머물지 내게 말해 줄 수 있니?

① How long can you tell me you will stay here?
② How long will you stay here can you tell me?
③ Can you tell me how long will you stay here?
④ Can you tell me how long you will stay here?
⑤ Can you tell me how you will stay here long?

Reading

[20~22] 다음 글을 읽고 물음에 답하시오.

ⓐOn May 27, 2011, 297 books of *Uigwe*, a collection of royal books the French army took them in 1866, came back to Korea. The person behind this return is Dr. Park Byeong-seon, a historian who spent her whole life searching for Korean national treasures abroad.

Q: Can you tell me how you became interested in *Uigwe*?

Dr. Park: I studied history in college. I went to France to continue my studies in 1955. As you know, the French army took many of our national treasures in 1866. I wanted to find them ⓑwhile I was studying there. *Uigwe* was one of them.

20 위 글의 밑줄 친 ⓐ에서 어법상 틀린 부분을 찾아 고치시오.

_____ ➡ _____

21 위 글의 밑줄 친 ⓑ를 다음과 같이 바꿔 쓸 때 빈칸에 들어갈 알맞은 말을 쓰시오.

> _____ my stay there for study

22 위 글을 읽고 대답할 수 **없는** 질문은?

① When was *Uigwe* returned to Korea?
② What did Dr. Park study in college?
③ When did the French army take *Uigwe*?
④ How long did it take for Dr. Park to find *Uigwe*?
⑤ When did Dr. Park want to find our national treasures abroad?

[23~26] 다음 글을 읽고 물음에 답하시오.

Q: I'm sure you were very excited when you found the books.

Dr. Park: Yes, I was, but more difficulties were waiting for me. I thought that the books should be returned to Korea, but my bosses at the library didn't like that idea. They even thought that I was a Korean spy and fired me. After that, I had to go to the library ⓐas a visitor, so it was not easy to do research on *Uigwe*. However, I didn't give up. For more than ten years, I went to the library every day to finish my research. ⓑI wanted to show people the value of *Uigwe*.

23 위 글의 밑줄 친 ⓐas와 같은 의미로 쓰인 것을 고르시오.

① As the door was open, I walked in.
② Her anger grew as she talked.
③ My sister runs as fast as you.
④ She came up as I was speaking.
⑤ He was famous as a poet.

24 Why did Dr. Park have to go to the library as a visitor? Fill in the blanks with the suitable words.

> Because her _____ at the library thought that she was a Korean spy and _____ her.

25 위 글의 밑줄 친 ⓑ와 같은 뜻이 되도록 빈칸에 알맞은 말을 쓰시오.

> I wanted to show the value of *Uigwe* _____ people.

26 위 글의 내용과 일치하지 <u>않는</u> 것은?

① Dr. Park was very excited when she found the books.
② More difficulties were awaiting her after Dr. Park found the books.
③ Dr. Park's bosses at the library thought that the books should be returned to Korea.
④ It was hard for Dr. Park to do research on *Uigwe*.
⑤ For over ten years, Dr. Park went to the library every day in order that she could finish her research.

[27~29] 다음 글을 읽고 물음에 답하시오.

Q: Before I finish this interview, I'd like to ask you about *Jikji*, ①a book that changed the history of printing.

Dr. Park: I found ②it in my first year at the library. I knew ⓐright away that ③it was very special. I worked hard to prove its value and finally succeeded. At ④a book exhibition in Paris in 1972, *Jikji* was displayed as ⑤the oldest book in the world that was printed with movable metal type.

Q: Dr. Park, thanks to your hard work, *Jikji* and *Uigwe* were found, and all Koreans thank you for that.

Dr. Park: I hope people will become more interested in our national treasures abroad and work for their return.

27 위 글의 밑줄 친 ①~⑤ 중에서 가리키는 대상이 나머지 넷과 다른 것은?

①   ②   ③   ④   ⑤

28 위 글의 밑줄 친 ⓐright away와 바꿔 쓸 수 있는 한 단어를 쓰시오. (i로 시작할 것.)

➡ _____

29 위 글의 주제로 알맞은 것을 고르시오.

① Learn how to finish the interview well.
② Thanks to Dr. Park, the value of *Jikji* was found.
③ Dr. Park found *Jikji* in her first year at the library.
④ Koreans thank Dr. Park for her hard work.
⑤ Dr. Park hopes for the return of our national treasures abroad.

출제율 95%

01 다음 글의 괄호 안에서 알맞은 단어를 선택하시오.

> On May 27, 2011, 297 books of *Uigwe*, a collection of [loyal / royal] books the French army took in 1866, came back to Korea.

출제율 90%

02 다음 영영 풀이에 해당하는 단어는?

> a bright light on a camera that flashes as you take a photograph in order to provide enough light

① silver   ② result   ③ flash

④ success   ⑤ pride

출제율 90%

03 다음 글의 괄호 (A)~(C)에서 알맞은 단어를 고르시오.

> I thought that the books should be (A) [stolen / returned] to Korea, but my bosses at the library didn't like that idea. They even thought that I was a Korean spy and fired me. After that, I had to go to the library as (B)[a visitor / an employee], so it was not easy to do research on *Uigwe*. However, I didn't give up. For more than ten years, I went to the library every day to finish my research. I wanted to show people the (C)[return / value] of *Uigwe*.

① stolen – a visitor – return

② stolen – an employee – value

③ returned – a visitor – return

④ returned – an employee – return

⑤ returned – a visitor – value

출제율 100%

04 다음 대화의 밑줄 친 부분 중 어법상 어색한 것은?

> G: Excuse me. ⓐIs it OK to take pictures here?
> M: Yes, it's all right.
> G: ⓑHow about to use a flash? ⓒCan I use it, too?
> M: ⓓI'm afraid not. ⓔUsing a flash is not allowed here.
> G: Oh, I see. Thank you.

① ⓐ   ② ⓑ   ③ ⓒ   ④ ⓓ   ⑤ ⓔ

출제율 95%

05 다음 글의 밑줄 친 (A)~(E)의 해석으로 틀린 것은?

> Before I (A)finish this interview, I'd like to ask you about *Jikji*, a book that changed the history of (B)printing.
> Dr. Park: I found it in my first year at the library. I knew right away that it was very special. I worked hard to (C)prove its value and finally succeeded. At a book (D)exhibition in Paris in 1972, *Jikji* was displayed as the oldest book in the world that was printed with (E)movable metal type.

① (A) 끝내다   ② (B) 인쇄

③ (C) 발견하다   ④ (D) 박람회

⑤ (E) 금속활자

[06~07] 다음 대화를 읽고 물음에 답하시오.

> A: Which place do you want to go first in the museum?
> B: Why don't you guess?
> A: OK. _____(A)_____
> B: Yes. Eating food is allowed.
> A: Is it OK to take pictures?
> B: No. (B)사진을 찍는 것은 허용되지 않아.
> A: I got it. You're thinking of going to the Video Room.
> B: You're right.

06 위 대화의 (A)에 들어갈 말로 알맞은 것을 고르시오.

① Is it OK to sit over there?

② Is it OK to eat food there?

③ Can I play it?

④ Is it OK to take pictures here?

⑤ Do you mind if I eat food there?

07 위 글의 밑줄 친 (B)의 우리말에 맞게 다음 문장의 빈칸을 채우시오. (allow를 이용할 것.)

_____ pictures _____ not _____ .

[08~09] 다음 대화를 읽고 물음에 답하시오.

G: Excuse me, but is it OK ____ⓐ____ this hanbok?

M: Sure. The fitting room is over there.

G: Thanks. Wait a minute. (A)That is also very pretty.

M: Oh, the little hat over there?

G: Yes. What is it?

M: It's a jokduri, a ____ⓑ____ Korean hat for women. It's usually worn on a wedding day.

G: Really? Is it OK to try it on, too?

M: I'm sorry, but it's only for ____ⓒ____ . Trying it on is not allowed.

G: Oh. Then, I'll just try on this hanbok.

08 위 대화의 ⓐ~ⓒ에 들어갈 말로 알맞은 것은?

① if you – traditional – display

② if you – modern – woman

③ to try on– traditional – display

④ to try on – modern – display

⑤ to try on – traditional – woman

09 위 대화의 밑줄 친 (A)가 가리키는 말을 본문에서 찾아 세 단어로 쓰시오.

➡ _____

10 다음 대화의 빈칸 ⓐ, ⓑ에 'allow'를 알맞은 형태로 바꾸어 쓰시오.

A: Which place do you want to go to first in the museum?

B: Why don't you guess?

A: OK. Is it OK to use smartphones there?

B: Yes. Using smartphones ⓐ_____ _____.

A: Is it OK to eat food?

B: OK. Eating food ⓑ_____ _____.

A: I got it. You're thinking of going to the Restaurant.

B: You're right.

11 다음 중 어법상 옳은 것은?

① I want to know how did you spend your vacation.

② Please tell me where the book is.

③ I wonder if or not she got angry at me.

④ We didn't win the game because my mistake.

⑤ You can't watch the movie because of you're not old enough.

출제율 90%

12 다음 두 문장을 한 문장으로 쓰시오.

(1) Do you think? What is the best way to encourage kids to study more?

➡ _____

_____

(2) Can you tell me? Who is your favorite actor?

➡ _____

(3) The car accident happened. The road was slippery.

➡ _____

_____

(4) Tina ran into the house. It started to rain.

➡ _____

_____

출제율 100%

13 다음 그림을 보고 주어진 어휘를 이용하여 빈칸에 알맞은 말을 쓰시오.

A: Can you tell me _____

_____? (in your free time, like doing, what)?

B: I like riding a horse a lot.

A: Why do you like riding a horse?

B: I enjoy riding a horse _____

_____. (it, fun, really)

출제율 95%

14 because와 because of를 이용하여 두 문장을 한 문장으로 각각 연결하시오.

(1) I went to the school health room.
I had a headache.

➡ _____

_____

(2) He got food poisoning.
He ate undercooked chicken.

➡ _____

_____

[15~18] 다음 글을 읽고 물음에 답하시오.

On May 27, 2011, 297 books of *Uigwe*, a collection of (A)[loyal / royal] books the French army took in 1866, came back to Korea. The person behind this return is Dr. Park Byeong-seon, ⓐ해외에 있는 한국의 문화재를 찾기 위해 전 생애를 바친 역사학자.

Q: Can you tell me how you became (B) [interesting / interested] in *Uigwe*?

Dr. Park: I studied history in college. I went to France ⓑto continue my studies in 1955. As you know, the French army took many of our national treasures in 1866. I wanted to find them (C)[during / while] I was studying there. *Uigwe* was one of them.

출제율 90%

15 위 글의 괄호 (A)~(C)에서 문맥이나 어법상 알맞은 낱말을 골라 쓰시오.

(A) _____ (B) _____ (C) _____

16 위 글의 밑줄 친 ⓐ의 우리말에 맞게 주어진 어휘를 이용하여 13 단어로 영작하시오. *출제율 85%*

> who, searching, Korean national treasures abroad

➡ _____

_____

17 위 글의 밑줄 친 ⓑto continue와 to부정사의 용법이 <u>다른</u> 것을 고르시오. (2개) *출제율 90%*

① Was it possible to continue her studies in France?

② She left for France to continue her studies.

③ She was happy to continue her studies in France.

④ Did she want to continue her studies?

⑤ She must be a woman of strong will to continue her studies abroad.

18 위 글을 읽고 박병선 박사에 대해 알 수 <u>없는</u> 것을 고르시오. *출제율 100%*

① What did Dr. Park Byeong-seon do throughout her lifetime?

② What subject did she study in college?

③ How old was she when she went to France?

④ Why did she go to France?

⑤ What did she want to find while she was studying in France?

[19~22] 다음 글을 읽고 물음에 답하시오.

> **Q:** You found 297 books of *Uigwe* in the National Library of France, in Paris. Please tell me how you found them.
>
> **Dr. Park:** ⓐAs soon as I became a researcher at the National Library in 1967, I began to look ___(A)___ *Uigwe*. After 10 years, in 1977, I finally found the books. I think I looked ___(B)___ ⓑmore than 30 millions books.

19 위 글의 빈칸 (A)와 (B)에 들어갈 전치사가 바르게 짝지어진 것은? *출제율 95%*

① for – after　　② at – for

③ for – at　　④ at – after

⑤ with – for

20 위 글의 밑줄 친 ⓐAs soon as와 바꿔 쓸 수 <u>없는</u> 말을 고르시오. *출제율 90%*

① Directly　　② Exactly

③ The moment　　④ The instant

⑤ Immediately

21 위 글의 밑줄 친 ⓑ에서 어법상 <u>틀린</u> 부분을 찾아 고치시오. *출제율 90%*

_____ ➡ _____

22 다음 문장에서 위 글의 내용과 <u>다른</u> 부분을 찾아서 고치시오. *출제율 95%*

> In 1967, Dr. Park became a researcher at the National Library of France, in Paris, and in 1977, she tried to find 297 books of *Uigwe*.

_____ ➡ _____

서술형 실전문제

01 아래 〈조건〉에 맞게 주어진 단어를 이용하여 빈칸에 알맞은 말을 쓰시오.

> B: Excuse me. What's this? It looks interesting.
> W: Oh, that's a haegeum, a traditional Korean musical instrument.
> B: (A) _____
> W: I'm sorry, but it's only for display.
>   (B) _____
> B: I see.

┤ 조건 ├
> (A) • 해금을 연주해도 되는지 허가 여부를 묻는 표현을 쓸 것.
>   • if절을 쓸 것.
>   • OK, it을 이용할 것.
> (B) • 금지하는 표현을 5 단어로 쓸 것.
>   • must를 이용할 것.

02 다음 그림을 보고 '허락과 금지'의 표현을 사용하여 대화의 빈칸을 완성하시오.

┤ 조건 ├
> • 동명사 주어로 시작할 것.
> • allow를 이용할 것.

> A: Which place do you want to go to first in the museum?
> B: Why don't you guess?
> A: OK. Is it OK to use smartphones there?
> B: Yes. (A)_____.
> A: Is it OK to take pictures?
> B: No. (B)_____.
> A: I got it. You're thinking of going to the Gift Shop.
> B: You're right.

03 두 문장을 한 문장으로 만들었을 때, 나머지 한 문장을 쓰시오.

(1) • I want to ask you.
   • _____
➡ I want to ask you what you like to do.

(2) • I'm not sure.
   • _____
➡ I'm not sure if my boss will accept my idea.

(3) • I was very tired.
   • _____
➡ I was very tired because I worked all day yesterday.

04 because of를 이용하여 두 문장을 연결하시오.

(1) There was a heavy rain. I stayed home.
➡ _____

(2) I had a high fever. I couldn't sleep last night.
➡ _____

05 괄호 안에 주어진 어휘를 이용하여 다음 우리말을 영작하시오.

(1) 그녀는 불편한 신발 때문에 달릴 수 없었다. (her uncomfortable shoes)
➡ _____

(2) Mark는 일을 해야 해서 우리와 함께 하지 않았다. (us, join, work, have to)
➡ _____

(3) 너는 그녀가 어디에 갔는지 알고 있니? (know)
➡ _____

(4) 그녀는 자기가 그 영화를 보았는지 기억할 수 없었다. (remember, watch)
➡ _____
_____

On May 27, 2011, 297 books of *Uigwe*, a collection of royal books the French army took in 1866, ⓐcame back to Korea. The person behind this return is Dr. Park Byeong-seon, ⓑa historian who spent her whole life to search for Korean national treasures abroad.

Q: Can you tell me how you became interested in *Uigwe*?

Dr. Park: I studied history in college. I went to France to continue my studies in 1955. As you know, the French army took many of our national treasures in 1866. I wanted to find them while I was studying there. *Uigwe* was one of them.

06 How did Dr. Park Byeong-seon become interested in *Uigwe*? Fill in the blanks with the suitable words.

> She went to France to continue to study history (A)_____ _____. While she was studying there, she wanted to find many of our (B)_____ _____ that the French army took (C)_____ _____ and *Uigwe* was one of them.

07 위 글의 밑줄 친 ⓐ를 다음과 같이 바꿔 쓸 때 빈칸에 들어갈 알맞은 말을 본문의 한 단어를 변형하여 쓰시오.

> _____ _____ to Korea

08 위 글의 밑줄 친 ⓑ에서 어법상 틀린 부분을 찾아 고치시오.

_____ ➡ _____

Q: I'm sure you were very excited when you (A)[found / founded] the books.

Dr. Park: Yes, I (B)[am / was], but ⓐmore difficulties were waiting for me. I thought that ⓑthe books should be returned to Korea, but my bosses at the library didn't like that idea. They even thought that I was a Korean spy and fired me. After that, I had to go to the library as a (C)[librarian / visitor], so it was not easy to do research on *Uigwe*. However, I didn't give up. For more than ten years, I went to the library every day to finish my research. I wanted to show people the value of *Uigwe*.

09 위 글의 괄호 (A)~(C)에서 문맥이나 어법상 알맞은 낱말을 골라 쓰시오.

(A) _____ (B) _____ (C) _____

10 위 글의 ⓐmore difficulties에 해당하는 것 세 가지를 우리말로 쓰시오.

(1) _____

_____

(2) _____

_____

(3) _____

_____

11 위 글의 밑줄 친 ⓑ를 they로 시작하여 능동태로 고치시오.

➡ _____

01 다음 주어진 정보를 이용하여 대화의 빈칸을 완성하시오.

> allowed: set up a tent / not allowed: fish in the lake

> G: Excuse me. _____?
> M: Yes, it's all right.
> G: _____ fishing in the lake? Can I fish in the lake, too?
> M: I'm _____. Fishing in the lake _____.
> G: Oh, I see. Thank you.

02 주어진 어구를 이용하여 자신의 경우를 생각하여 쓰시오.

> ┌ 보기 ┐
> because … / because of … / I don't know …

(1) _____

(2) _____

(3) _____

03 다음 내용을 바탕으로 박병선 박사에 관한 미니북을 만드시오.

> In 1955: • studied history in college • went to France to continue to study history
> In 1967: • became a researcher at the National Library • began to look for *Uigwe*
> In 1972: • found *Jikji* • worked hard to prove value of *Jikji* • finally, displayed at a book exhibition
> In 1977: • she looked at more than 30 million books • she finally found *Uigwe*
> In 1990: • result of research on *Uigwe* published as a book in Korea
> In 2011: • *Uigwe* came back to Korea • spent whole life for Korean treasure

> Dr. Park Byeong-seon
> In 1955, she studied history and went to France (A)_____ to study histoy.
> In 1967, she became (B)_____ at the National Library and began to look for (C)_____.
> In 1972, she found (D)_____ and worked hard to prove the value of *Jikji*. Finally, *Jikji* was displayed at a book exhibition.
> In 1977, after she looked at (E)_____, she finally found *Uigwe*.
> In 1990, The results of her research on *Uigwe* (F)_____ as a book in Korea.
> In 2011, *Uigwe* came back to Korea. She spent her whole life for Korean national treasures abroad.

단원별 모의고사

01 다음 단어에 대한 영어 설명이 <u>어색한</u> 것은?

① fitting room: a room in a clothes shop where you can put on clothes before you buy them

② silver: a shiny white metal that people use for making jewelry and other valuable things

③ succeed: to do something that you tried or aimed to do

④ government: the group of people who are responsible for controlling a country or state

⑤ aboard: in or to a foreign country

02 다음 글의 빈칸에 공통으로 들어갈 말을 주어진 철자로 쓰시오.

- To get the best r_____, you have to do your best.
- Disease can often r_____ from poverty.

03 다음 영영풀이에 해당하는 단어를 고르시오.

to try to find someone or something by looking very carefully

① search   ② allow
③ spend   ④ prove
⑤ publish

[04~05] 다음 대화의 빈칸에 들어갈 말로 알맞은 것을 고르시오.

04
B: Excuse me. What's this? It looks interesting.
W: Oh, that's a haegeum, a traditional Korean musical instrument.
B: Is it OK to play it?
W: I'm sorry, but it's only for display.
_____
B: I see.

① Playing it is allowed.
② How about playing the haegeum?
③ You can play it.
④ Playing it is not allowed.
⑤ I play it well.

05
A: Which place do you want to go first in the museum?
B: Why don't you guess?
A: OK. _____
B: Yes. Eating food is allowed.
A: Is it OK to take pictures?
B: No. Taking pictures is not allowed.

① Do I have to eat food there?
② Is it OK to eat food there?
③ Where can we eat food?
④ Do you mind if I eat food there?
⑤ When did you eat food there?

06 다음 중 짝지어진 대화가 <u>어색한</u> 것은?

① A: Excuse me, but is it OK to take pictures here?
　 B: Yes. Go ahead.

② A: What's this? It looks interesting.
　 B: Oh, that's a janggu, a traditional Korean musical instrument.

③ A: Excuse me. Is it OK to sit over there?
　 B: I'm sorry, but sitting on the grass is allowed.

④ A: Excuse me, but is it OK if I try on this jacket?
　 B: Sure. The fitting room is over there.

⑤ A: Is it OK to take pictures?
　 B: No. Taking pictures is not allowed.

[07~09] 다음 대화를 읽고 물음에 답하시오.

Kate: Excuse me, but _____(A)_____
Man: Sure. The fitting room is over there.
Kate: Thanks. Wait a minute. That's also very pretty.
Man: Oh, the little hat over there?
Kate: Yes. What is it?
Man: It's a jokduri, a traditional Korean hat for women. It's usually worn on a wedding day.
Kate: Really? Is it OK to try it on, too?
Man: I'm sorry, but it's only for display. Trying it on is not allowed.
Kate: Oh. Then, I'll just try on this hanbok.

07 위 대화의 빈칸 (A)에 들어갈 말로 알맞은 것은?

① is it OK to take pictures here?
② is it OK to eat food there?
③ is it OK to sit here?
④ is it OK to try on this hanbok?
⑤ is it OK to play it?

08 What is Kate going to do?

➡ She is _____.

09 위 대화를 읽고 Kate가 쓴 글을 완성하시오.

Today, I tried on a hanbok. I also wanted to try on a jokduri, a _____ Korean hat for _____, but I could not. It was only for _____, so trying it on was not _____. A jokduri is usually worn on a _____ _____.

10 다음 대화의 빈칸에 들어갈 말은?

G: Excuse me, but is it OK to take pictures here?
M: _____
G: Can I use a flash, too?
M: Yes. That's also OK.
G: I'm sorry, but I have one more question. Can I eat food here?
M: I'm sorry, but that's not allowed.

① I'm sorry, but you can't.
② I'm afraid not.
③ You are not allowed to do that.
④ Yes. Go ahead.
⑤ You can't do that.

11 다음 대화의 빈칸에 들어갈 말은?

> A: Which place do you want to go to first in the museum?
> B: Why don't you guess?
> A: OK. Is it OK to use smartphones there?
> B: Yes. Using smartphones is allowed.
> A: Is it OK to take pictures?
> B: No. _____
> A: I got it. You're thinking of going to the Gift Shop.
> B: You're right.

① Taking pictures is allowed.
② Of course.
③ Taking pictures is not allowed.
④ You can take pictures.
⑤ That's also OK.

12 다음 중 빈칸에 들어갈 말이 나머지 넷과 다른 것은?

① Jim couldn't take a nap _____ the room was too hot.
② There was a heavy snow, _____ the road was closed.
③ The children were hungry _____ there was no food in the house.
④ _____ of her book, many Koreans became interested in *Jikji*.
⑤ Peter couldn't play soccer _____ it rained.

13 다음 밑줄 친 부분의 쓰임이 나머지 넷과 다른 것은?

① I'm not sure <u>if</u> we're going to find her.
② Mariel asked me <u>if</u> I would love her forever.
③ I wonder <u>if</u> the news is true.
④ You may fail <u>if</u> you are lazy.
⑤ Please see <u>if</u> the children are dressed for school.

14 다음 빈칸에 알맞은 표현을 <u>모두</u> 고르시오.

> I was late this morning _____ there was heavy traffic.

① because of ② because ③ so
④ if ⑤ since

15 다음 두 문장을 간접의문문을 이용하여 한 문장으로 쓰시오.

(1) I don't know. + Who broke the window?
　➡ _____

(2) Tell me. + How did you find the key?
　➡ _____

(3) I have no idea. + Does he loves me or not?
　➡ _____

(4) Do you think? + Who will be selected as the best player of the game?
　➡ _____
　_____

16 주어진 어휘를 이용하여 다음 우리말을 영작하시오. (because나 간접의문문을 이용하여 쓸 것.)

(1) 나는 조부모님이 멀리 사시기 때문에 자주 뵙지 못한다. (my grandparents, see, live, often, far away)
　➡ _____
　_____

(2) 그들은 그녀의 일 때문에 일본으로 이사 갔다. (move, job)
　➡ _____

(3) 그의 부주의 때문에 사고가 일어났다. (the accident, his carelessness, happen)
　➡ _____

(4) Minho는 Kevin이 장래에 무엇이 되고 싶은지 알고 있다. (want, be, in the future)
　➡ _____

(5) Daniel은 그가 전화를 어디에 두었는지 확신하지 못한다. (put, sure, his phone)
　➡ _____

(6) 사장님이 지금 당신을 만나실 수 있는지 확인해 보겠습니다. (the president, check, meet)
　➡ _____

[17~18] 다음 글을 읽고 물음에 답하시오.

On May 27, 2011, 297 books of *Uigwe*, a collection of royal books the French army took in 1866, came back to Korea. The person behind this return is Dr. Park Byeong-seon, a historian ___ⓐ___ spent her whole life searching for Korean national treasures abroad.

Q: Can you tell me how you became interested in *Uigwe*?

Dr. Park: I studied history in college. I went to France to continue my studies in 1955. As you know, the French army took many of our national treasures in 1866. I wanted to find them while I was studying there. *Uigwe* was one of them.

my bosses at the library didn't like ⓐthat idea. They even thought that I was a Korean spy and fired me. After that, I had to go to the library as a visitor, so it was not easy ⓑto do research on *Uigwe*. However, I didn't give up. For more than ten years, I went to the library every day to finish my research. I wanted to show people the value of *Uigwe*.

Q: The results of your research were published as a book in Korea in 1990. Many Koreans became interested in *Uigwe* ⓒbecause of your book.

Dr. Park: Yes. In 1992, the Korean government asked the French government for its return and, finally, the 297 books are here now.

17 위 글의 빈칸 ⓐ에 들어갈 알맞은 말을 쓰시오.

➡ _____

18 다음 빈칸 (A)와 (B)에 알맞은 단어를 넣어 박병선 박사에 대한 소개를 완성하시오.

> Dr. Park Byeong-seon was (A)_____
> _____ who spent her whole life searching for Korean national treasures (B)_____.

19 위 글의 밑줄 친 ⓐthat idea가 가리키는 것을 본문에서 찾아 쓰시오.

➡ _____

20 아래 〈보기〉에서 위 글의 밑줄 친 ⓑto do와 to부정사의 용법이 같은 것의 개수를 고르시오.

> ┌ 보기 ┐
> ① He stopped to listen to music.
> ② Do you have any questions to ask?
> ③ He didn't want to do it.
> ④ She came home early to help her mother.
> ⑤ My dream is to be a famous pianist.

① 1개　② 2개　③ 3개　④ 4개　⑤ 5개

[19~21] 다음 글을 읽고 물음에 답하시오.

Q: I'm sure you were very excited when you found the books.

Dr. Park: Yes, I was, but more difficulties were waiting for me. I thought that the books should be returned to Korea, but

21 위 글의 밑줄 친 ⓒbecause of와 바꿔 쓸 수 없는 말을 고르시오.

① thanks to　② owing to
③ due to　④ because
⑤ on account of

Special

Creative Ideas in Stories

Words & Expressions

Key Words

- **batter** [bǽtər] 명 반죽
- **before** [bifɔ́ːr] 전 ~ 전에
- **button** [bʌ́tən] 명 버튼, 단추
- **counter** [káuntər] 명 계산대
- **creative** [kriéitiv] 형 창의적인
- **delicious** [dilíʃəs] 형 맛있는
- **diamond** [dáiəmənd] 명 다이아몬드
- **doughnut** [dóunət] 명 도넛
- **drop** [drɑp] 동 떨어지다
- **enough** [inʌ́f] 형 충분한
- **find** [faind] 동 찾다 (-found-found)
- **fresh** [freʃ] 형 신선한
- **fun** [fʌn] 형 재미있는, 즐거운
- **happen** [hǽpən] 동 발생하다, 일어나다
- **idea** [aidíːə] 명 아이디어
- **inside** [ìnsáid] 전 ~ 안에
- **leave** [liːv] 동 떠나다, ~에 두다 (-left-left)
- **lose** [luːz] 동 잃어버리다 (-lost-lost)
- **machine** [məʃíːn] 명 기계
- **mix** [miks] 동 섞다
- **oil** [ɔil] 명 기름

- **own** [oun] 동 소유하다
- **pile** [pail] 동 쌓아 올리다, 쌓다
- **prize** [praiz] 명 상금
- **P.S.** 추신 (= postscript)
- **push** [puʃ] 동 누르다
- **ready** [rédi] 형 준비된
- **recipe** [résəpi] 명 요리법
- **remember** [rimémbər] 동 기억하다
- **ring** [riŋ] 명 반지
- **sell** [sel] 동 팔다 (-sold-sold)
- **should** [ʃud] 조 ~해야 한다
- **shout** [ʃaut] 동 외치다, 소리치다
- **sign** [sain] 명 표지판
- **start** [stɑːrt] 동 (기계를) 작동시키다
- **taste** [teist] 동 ~한 맛이 나다
- **try** [trai] 동 시도하다, 먹어보다
- **visit** [vízit] 동 방문하다
- **watch** [wɑtʃ] 동 보다, (잠깐 동안) 봐 주다
- **work** [wəːrk] 동 효과가 있다, 작동하다
- **wrong** [rɔːŋ] 형 잘못된, 이상이 있는

Key Expressions

- **a lot of** 많은
- **a piece of paper** 종이 한 장
- **all of a sudden** 갑자기
- **be full of** ~으로 가득 차다
- **break up** ~을 부수다, 쪼개다
- **drop into** ~ 속으로 떨어지다
- **fall into** ~로 떨어지다
- **for a while** 잠시
- **get ~ back** ~을 되찾다
- **give ~ back** ~을 돌려주다
- **give a reward** 포상금을 지급하다
- **have to+동사원형** ~해야 한다
- **in front of** ~ 앞에
- **in the end** 결국, 마침내

- **just then** 바로 그때
- **keep+-ing** 계속해서 ~하다
- **look for** ~을 찾다
- **need to+동사원형** ~할 필요가 있다
- **one day** 어느 날
- **one of 복수명사** ~ 중 하나
- **pile A on B** A를 B에 쌓아 올리다
- **put A in B** A를 B에 넣다
- **right away** 즉시, 지금 당장
- **step out** ~에서 나오다, 내리다
- **take off** ~을 벗다
- **thank ~ for -ing** ~에게 -에 대해 감사하다
- **turn on** ~을 켜다, 작동시키다
- **with excitement** 흥분하여

Word Power

※ 서로 반대되는 뜻을 가진 어휘

□ **fun** (재미있는) ↔ **boring** (지루한)

□ **inside** (~ 안에) ↔ **outside** (~ 밖에)

□ **difficult** (어려운) ↔ **easy** (쉬운)

□ **leave** (떠나다) ↔ **arrive** (도착하다)

□ **push** (누르다) ↔ **pull** (당기다)

□ **wrong** (잘못된) ↔ **right** (옳은)

□ **sell** (팔다) ↔ **buy** (사다)

□ **remember** (기억하다) ↔ **forget** (잊다)

□ **take off** (벗다) ↔ **put on** (입다)

□ **turn on** (켜다) ↔ **turn off** (끄다)

※ 서로 비슷한 뜻을 가진 어휘

□ **a lot of** : **lots of** (많은)

□ **batter** : **dough** (반죽)

□ **creative** : **ingenious** (창의적인)

□ **delicious** : **tasty** (맛있는)

□ **shout** : **yell** (외치다)

□ **own** : **have** (소유하다)

□ **drop** : **fall** (떨어지다)

□ **happen** : **take place** (발생하다, 일어나다)

□ **mix** : **blend** (섞다)

□ **right away** : **right now** (즉시, 지금 당장)

□ **in the end** : **finally** (결국)

□ **be full of** : **be filled with** (~으로 가득 차다)

English Dictionary

□ **batter** 반죽
→ a mixture of flour, eggs, milk, etc. used in cooking and for making bread, cakes, etc.
요리를 하거나 빵이나 케이크를 만들기 위해 사용되는 밀가루, 달걀, 우유 등을 섞은 것

□ **compare** 비교하다
→ to think about how two or more things are different or the same
둘 또는 그 이상의 것이 어떻게 다르거나 같은지에 관해 생각하다

□ **counter** 계산대
→ the place where you pay in a shop, bank, restaurant, etc.
가게, 은행, 식당 등에서 돈을 지불하기 위한 장소

□ **doughnut** 도넛
→ a small round cake that usually has a hole in the middle
보통 중간에 구멍이 있는 작고 둥근 케이크

□ **excitement** 흥분
→ the feeling you have when you are excited
당신이 신날 때 갖는 느낌

□ **give a reward** 포상금을 주다
→ to give something to someone because he or she has done something good
좋은 일을 했기 때문에 누군가에게 무언가를 주다

□ **machine** 기계
→ a piece of equipment that you use to do a job
일을 할 때 사용하는 하나의 장비

□ **remember** 기억하다
→ to have an image in your mind of something that happened or was said in the past
과거에 일어났거나 말하여진 어떤 것의 이미지를 마음속에 갖다

□ **step out** ~에서 나오다
→ to go out for a short time
잠시 동안 밖으로 나가다

□ **work** 효과가 있다
→ to be effective or successful
효과적이거나 성공하다

The Doughnuts

machine 기계
batter 반죽
step out 내리다
diamond 다이아몬드

Homer's uncle, Bob, had a doughnut shop. Uncle Bob liked machines, so the shop was full of cooking machines. One day, Homer visited Uncle Bob's shop.
결과를 나타내는 접속사 be full of: ~으로 가득 차다 동명사(of의 목적어)

Homer: Hello, Uncle Bob!

Bob: Hi, Homer. Nice to see you. Look at this new doughnut machine. Isn't it great? Homer, I need to go back home for a while. Can you watch the shop for me and make some doughnuts?
need to+동사원형: ~할 필요가 있다   잠시 동안
watch와 make가 등위접속사 and로 연결

Homer: OK, I'll try but ....

Bob: It's easy to do. First, make the doughnut batter and put it in the machine. Then just start the machine. Here's the recipe.
부사적 용법(형용사 수식)   명령문으로 make와 put이 and로 연결   여기 있다

Homer: I can do that. Don't worry.

After Uncle Bob left, a big car stopped in front of the shop, and a lady stepped out.
~ 앞에

Lady: Can I have some doughnuts and a coffee?

Homer: I'm sorry, but the doughnuts aren't ready.

Lady: Are you making the doughnut batter now?
현재진행형 의문문

Homer: Yes, but this is my first time.

The lady took off her coat and her big diamond ring. She started to mix the batter.
take off: ~을 벗다   start+to부정사: ~하기 시작하다 = start+-ing

 확인문제

● 다음 문장이 본문의 내용과 일치하면 T, 일치하지 않으면 F를 쓰시오.

1 Bob's doughnut shop was filled with cooking machines. ☐

2 Bob allowed Homer to eat some doughnuts. ☐

3 Homer has made doughnuts before. ☐

Lady: I can help you. I can make delicious doughnuts.

Homer: Uh, OK. This is a lot of batter.

많은 ~(뒤에 셀 수 있는 명사와 셀 수 없는 명사 모두 올 수 있다)

Lady: Just wait and see. The doughnuts will taste great.

~의 맛이 나다, 맛이 ~하다(감각동사), 뒤에 형용사가 보어로 온다.

Homer turned on the doughnut machine. Rings of batter started

= started

dropping into the hot oil.

to drop

Lady: You try the first doughnut. Here.

명령문이므로 You를 생략할 수 있다.

Homer: Wow! It's really delicious!

Lady: I have to go now. This was so much fun! Good-bye!

have to+동사원형: ~해야 한다 (의무)

Homer: Thank you for helping me. Good-bye!

thank A for B: A에게 B에 대해 감사하다

Homer had enough doughnuts, so he pushed the stop button, but

'충분한'이라는 뜻의 형용사로 명사 앞에 위치. enough는 부사로도 쓰일 수 있다.

nothing happened. The doughnuts kept coming out of the machine.

keep+-ing: 계속해서 ~하다

Homer: Hmm... What's wrong? I think I should call Uncle Bob.

= What's the matter?

The shop was now full of doughnuts. Homer piled the doughnuts on

~으로 가득 찼다

the counter.

Homer: Uncle Bob! Please come back right away. Something's wrong

즉시   = There is something wrong

with the doughnut machine.

Bob: Oh, no! How can we sell all these doughnuts?

Just then the lady came back to the shop.

~으로 돌아왔따

Lady: I lost my diamond ring. I think I left it on the counter.

Homer: Oh, I remember. You took it off before you started to mix the

목적어가 인칭대명사일 때는 동사와 부사 사이에 위치. it = your diamond ring

batter.

turn on ~을 켜다
drop into ~ 속으로 떨어지다
out of ~에서, ~으로 부터
counter 계산대

확인문제

● 다음 문장이 본문의 내용과 일치하면 T, 일치하지 <u>않으면</u> F를 쓰시오.

1 When Homer turned on the doughnut machine, rings of batter started dropping into the hot oil. ☐

2 Homer pushed the stop button, but the doughnuts kept coming out of the machine. ☐

3 Homer piled the doughnuts on the floor. ☐

Everyone looked for the diamond ring, but they couldn't find it.
~을 찾았다   = the diamond ring

Homer: I can't find it.

Lady: I'll give a reward of one hundred dollars to the person who finds
give+사물+to+사람: ~에게 …을 주다
that ring!
주격 관계대명사절의 동사는 관계대명사 앞에 오는 명사 person에 수를 일치시킨다.

Homer: I know! The ring fell into the batter. I'm sure it's inside one of
fall-fell-fallen   one of+복수 명사: ~ 중의 하나
these doughnuts!

Lady: You're right!

Bob: Oh, no! Now we have to break up all of these doughnuts to find
쪼개다, 나누다   찾기 위해서(목적) = in order to find
the ring.

Homer: Don't worry, Uncle. I have an idea.

Homer took a piece of paper and made a sign.
종이 한 장
He then put it in the shop's window.

Fresh Doughnuts

2 for 5 cents

$100 prize for finding a ring inside a doughnut
동명사(for의 목적어)
P.S. You have to give the ring back.
타동사+목적어(명사)+부사

Then many people began to buy the doughnuts.
= began buying
All of a sudden, a man shouted with excitement.
흥분해서

Man: I found it! I found the ring!

Homer: See, my idea worked!
(어떤 계획이) 효과가 있다, 잘 작동하다
Lady: Here's one hundred dollars!

In the end, everybody was happy. The man went home with one
결국, 마침내
hundred dollars. The lady got her diamond ring back, and Uncle Bob
sold lots of doughnuts. And, what about Homer? He was happy that his
= a lot of   감정을 나타내는 형용사 뒤에 이어지는 that절은 그 감정의 원인을 나타낸다.
idea worked so well!

---

give a reward 보상금을 주다
give ~ back ~을 돌려주다
all of a sudden 갑자기
get ~ back ~을 돌려받다

📎 **확인문제**

● 다음 문장이 본문의 내용과 일치하면 T, 일치하지 않으면 F를 쓰시오.

1 They started to break up all the doughnuts to find the ring. ☐
2 A man found the ring inside a doughnut and received $100. ☐

● 우리말을 참고하여 빈칸에 알맞은 말을 쓰시오.

1   The _____

2   Homer's uncle, Bob, _____ a doughnut shop.

3   Uncle Bob liked machines, _____ the shop _____ _____ _____ cooking machines.

4   One day, Homer _____ Uncle Bob's shop.

5   Homer: Hello, _____ Bob!

6   Bob: Hi, Homer. Nice to see you. Look at this new doughnut machine. _____ _____ _____?

7   Bob: Homer, I need to go back home _____ _____ _____.

8   Can you watch the shop _____ _____ and make some doughnuts?

9   Homer: OK, I'll try but ....

10 Bob: It's easy to do. First, make the _____ _____ and put it in the machine.

11 Then just start the machine. Here's the _____.

12 Homer: I can do that. _____ _____.

13 After Uncle Bob left, a big car stopped in _____ of the shop, and a lady _____ _____.

14 Lady: _____ _____ _____ some doughnuts and a coffee?

15 Homer: I'm sorry, but the doughnuts _____ _____.

16 Lady: _____ _____ _____ the doughnut batter now?

17 Homer: Yes, but this is _____ _____ _____.

18 The lady _____ _____ her coat and her big diamond ring.

19 She started _____ _____ the batter.

20 Lady: _____ _____ _____ _____. I can make delicious doughnuts.

---

1   도넛

2   Homer의 삼촌인 Bob은 도넛 가게를 가지고 있었다.

3   Bob 삼촌은 기계를 좋아해서, 가게는 요리 기계들로 가득 차 있었다.

4   어느 날, Homer가 Bob 삼촌의 가게를 방문했다.

5   Homer: 안녕하세요, Bob 삼촌!

6   Bob: 안녕, Homer. 만나서 반갑구나. 이 새 도넛 기계 좀 봐. 멋지지 않니?

7   Bob: Homer, 내가 잠시 집에 가 봐야 해.

8   나 대신 가게를 봐 주고 도넛을 좀 만들어 줄 수 있겠니?

9   Homer: 네, 해 볼게요, 그런데 …

10 Bob: 하기 쉬워. 먼저, 도넛 반죽을 만들고 그것을 기계에 넣으렴.

11 그런 다음에 기계를 작동하기만 하면 돼. 여기 요리법이 있어.

12 Homer: 그건 할 수 있어요. 걱정하지 마세요.

13 Bob 삼촌이 떠난 후, 큰 차 한 대가 가게 앞에 섰고, 한 귀부인이 내렸다.

14 Lady: 도넛과 커피 한 잔 주겠니?

15 Homer: 그건 죄송하지만, 도넛이 준비가 안 됐어요.

16 Lady: 지금 도넛 반죽을 만들고 있는 거니?

17 Homer: 네, 하지만 처음 만드는 거예요.

18 그 귀부인은 외투를 벗고 커다란 다이아몬드 반지를 뺐다.

19 그녀는 반죽을 섞기 시작했다.

20 Lady: 내가 도와줄게. 나는 맛있는 도넛을 만들 수 있단다.

21 Homer: Uh, OK.

22 Homer: This is _____ _____ _____ batter.

23 Lady: Just _____ _____ _____ . The doughnuts will taste _____ .

24 Homer _____ _____ the doughnut machine.

25 Rings of batter started _____ _____ the hot oil.

26 Lady: You try the _____ doughnut. Here.

27 Homer: Wow! It's really _____ !

28 Lady: I have to go now. This was _____ _____ _____ ! Good-bye!

29 Homer: Thank you _____ _____ me. Good-bye!

30 Homer had _____ doughnuts, so he pushed the stop button, but _____ _____ .

31 The doughnuts _____ _____ out of the machine.

32 Homer: Hmm... What's wrong? I think I _____ _____ Uncle Bob.

33 The shop _____ now _____ _____ doughnuts. Homer _____ the doughnuts on the counter.

34 Homer: Uncle Bob! Please come back _____ _____ .

35 _____ _____ with the doughnut machine.

36 Bob: Oh, no! How can we sell _____ _____ doughnuts?

37 Just then the lady _____ _____ to the shop.

38 Lady: I lost my diamond ring. I think I _____ it on the counter.

39 Homer: Oh, I remember. You _____ _____ _____ before you started to mix the batter.

40 Everyone _____ _____ the diamond ring, but they couldn't find it.

21 Homer: 아, 좋아요.

22 Homer: 반죽이 많군요.

23 Lady: 좀 기다려 보렴. 도넛이 아주 맛있을 거야.

24 Homer는 도넛 기계를 작동했다.

25 링 모양의 반죽들이 뜨거운 기름 속으로 떨어지기 시작했다.

26 Lady: 첫 번째 도넛을 맛보렴. 여기 있어.

27 Homer: 와! 정말 맛있네요!

28 Lady: 난 이제 가 봐야 해. 정말 재미있었어! 잘 있으렴!

29 Homer: 도와주셔서 감사해요. 안녕히 가세요!

30 Homer는 도넛이 충분하게 있어서 정지 버튼을 눌렀지만, 아무 일도 일어나지 않았다.

31 도넛이 계속해서 기계에서 나오고 있었다.

32 Homer: 흐음 … 뭐가 잘못된 거지? Bob 삼촌에게 전화를 해야겠어.

33 가게는 이제 도넛으로 가득 찼다. Homer는 도넛들을 계산대 위로 쌓아 올렸다.

34 Homer: Bob 삼촌! 지금 당장 돌아와 주세요.

35 도넛 기계에 이상이 있어요.

36 Bob: 오, 이런! 이 도넛들을 모두 어떻게 팔지?

37 바로 그때 그 귀부인이 다시 가게로 돌아왔다.

38 Lady: 내 다이아몬드 반지를 잃어버렸어. 내 생각엔 계산대 위에 그것을 놓은 것 같은데.

39 Homer: 오, 기억나요. 반죽을 섞기 전에 그것을 뺐어요.

40 모두가 다이아몬드 반지를 찾았지만, 찾을 수 없었다.

41 Homer: I _____ _____ it.

42 Lady: I'll _____ _____ _____ of one hundred dollars to the person who finds that ring!

43 Homer: I know! The ring fell into the batter. _____ _____ it's inside one of these doughnuts!

44 Lady: You're _____!

45 Bob: Oh, no! Now we have to _____ _____ all of these doughnuts _____ _____ the ring.

46 Homer: _____ _____, Uncle. I have an idea.

47 Homer took a piece of paper and _____ _____ _____.

48 He then _____ _____ in the shop's window.

49 Fresh Doughnuts _____ _____ _____ _____

50 $100 prize _____ _____ a ring inside a doughnut

51 P.S. You have to _____ the ring _____.

52 Then many people began _____ _____ the doughnuts.

53 _____ _____ _____ _____, a man shouted with excitement.

54 Man: I _____ _____! I found the ring!

55 Homer: See, my idea _____!

56 Lady: _____ one hundred dollars!

57 _____ _____ _____, everybody was happy.

58 The man went home _____ one hundred dollars.

59 The lady _____ her diamond ring _____, and Uncle Bob sold _____ _____ doughnuts.

60 And, _____ _____ Homer?

61 He was happy that _____ _____ _____ so well!

---

41 Homer: 저는 못 찾겠어요.

42 Lady: 그 반지를 찾는 사람에게 100달러의 보상금을 드릴게요!

43 Homer: 알겠어요! 그 반지는 반죽 속으로 떨어졌어요. 반지는 이 도넛들 중 하나 안에 있다고 확신해요!

44 Lady: 네 말이 맞아!

45 Bob: 오, 안 돼! 이제 우리는 반지를 찾기 위해 이 도넛들을 모두 쪼개야 해요.

46 Homer: 걱정하지 마세요, 삼촌. 저에게 아이디어가 있어요.

47 Homer는 종이 한 장을 가져와 안내판을 만들었다.

48 그러고 나서 그것을 가게 창문에 걸었다.

49 신선한 도넛 2개에 5센트

50 도넛 안에 있는 반지를 찾으면 100달러의 상금을 드려요.

51 추신. 반지를 돌려주어야 합니다.

52 그러자, 많은 사람들이 도넛을 사기 시작했다.

53 갑자기, 한 남자가 흥분해서 소리쳤다.

54 Man: 찾았어요! 내가 반지를 찾았어요!

55 Homer: 보세요, 제 아이디어가 통했어요!

56 Lady: 여기 100달러예요!

57 결국 모두가 행복했다.

58 남자는 100달러를 갖고 집으로 갔다.

59 귀부인은 다이아몬드 반지를 다시 찾았고, Bob 삼촌은 도넛을 많이 팔았다.

60 그러면, Homer는 어떻게 됐을까?

61 그는 자신의 아이디어가 아주 잘 통해서 행복했다!

● 우리말을 참고하여 본문을 영작하시오.

1 도넛

➡ _____

2 Homer의 삼촌인 Bob은 도넛 가게를 가지고 있었다.

➡ _____

3 Bob 삼촌은 기계를 좋아해서, 가게는 요리 기계들로 가득 차 있었다.

➡ _____

4 어느 날, Homer가 Bob 삼촌의 가게를 방문했다.

➡ _____

5 Homer: 안녕하세요, Bob 삼촌!

➡ _____

6 Bob: 안녕, Homer. 만나서 반갑구나. 이 새 도넛 기계 좀 봐. 멋지지 않니?

➡ _____

7 Bob: Homer, 내가 잠시 집에 가 봐야 해.

➡ _____

8 나 대신 가게를 봐 주고 도넛을 좀 만들어 줄 수 있겠니?

➡ _____

9 Homer: 네, 해 볼게요, 그런데….

➡ _____

10 Bob: 하기 쉬워. 먼저, 도넛 반죽을 만들고 그것을 기계에 넣으렴.

➡ _____

11 그런 다음에 기계를 작동하기만 하면 돼. 여기 요리법이 있어.

➡ _____

12 Homer: 그건 할 수 있어요. 걱정하지 마세요.

➡ _____

13 Bob 삼촌이 떠난 후, 큰 차 한 대가 가게 앞에 섰고, 한 귀부인이 내렸다.

➡ _____

14 Lady: 도넛과 커피 한 잔 주겠니?

➡ _____

15 Homer: 죄송하지만, 도넛이 준비가 안 됐어요.

➡ _____

16 Lady: 지금 도넛 반죽을 만들고 있는 거니?

➡ _____

17 Homer: 네, 하지만 처음 만드는 거예요.

➡ _____

18 그 귀부인은 외투를 벗고 커다란 다이아몬드 반지를 뺐다.

➡ _____

19 그녀는 반죽을 섞기 시작했다.

➡ _____

20 Lady: 내가 도와줄게. 나는 맛있는 도넛을 만들 수 있단다.

➡ _____

21 Homer: 아, 좋아요.
➡ _____

22 Homer: 반죽이 많군요.
➡ _____

23 Lady: 좀 기다려 보렴. 도넛이 아주 맛있을 거야.
➡ _____

24 Homer는 도넛 기계를 작동했다.
➡ _____

25 링 모양의 반죽들이 뜨거운 기름 속으로 떨어지기 시작했다.
➡ _____

26 Lady: 첫 번째 도넛을 맛보렴. 여기 있어.
➡ _____

27 Homer: 와! 정말 맛있네요!
➡ _____

28 Lady: 난 이제 가 봐야 해. 정말 재미있었어! 잘 있으렴!
➡ _____

29 Homer: 도와주셔서 감사해요. 안녕히 가세요!
➡ _____

30 Homer는 도넛이 충분하게 있어서 정지 버튼을 눌렀지만, 아무 일도 일어나지 않았다.
➡ _____

31 도넛이 계속해서 기계에서 나오고 있었다.
➡ _____

32 Homer: 흐음 … 뭐가 잘못된 거지? Bob 삼촌에게 전화를 해야겠어.
➡ _____

33 가게는 이제 도넛으로 가득 찼다. Homer는 도넛들을 계산대 위로 쌓아 올렸다.
➡ _____

34 Homer: Bob 삼촌! 지금 당장 돌아와 주세요.
➡ _____

35 도넛 기계에 이상이 있어요.
➡ _____

36 Bob: 오, 이런! 이 도넛들을 모두 어떻게 팔지?
➡ _____

37 바로 그때 그 귀부인이 다시 가게로 돌아왔다.
➡ _____

38 Lady: 내 다이아몬드 반지를 잃어버렸어. 내 생각엔 계산대 위에 그것을 놓은 것 같은데.
➡ _____

39 Homer: 오, 기억나요. 반죽을 섞기 전에 그것을 뺐어요.
➡ _____

40 모두가 다이아몬드 반지를 찾았지만, 찾을 수 없었다.
➡ _____

41 Homer: 저는 못 찾겠어요.
➡ _____

42 Lady: 그 반지를 찾는 사람에게 100달러의 보상금을 드릴게요!
➡ _____

43 Homer: 알겠어요! 그 반지는 반죽 속으로 떨어졌어요. 반지는 이 도넛들 중 하나 안에 있다고 확신해요!
➡ _____

44 Lady: 네 말이 맞아!
➡ _____

45 Bob: 오, 안 돼! 이제 우리는 반지를 찾기 위해 이 도넛들을 모두 쪼개야 해요.
➡ _____

46 Homer: 걱정하지 마세요, 삼촌. 저에게 아이디어가 있어요.
➡ _____

47 Homer는 종이 한 장을 가져와 안내판을 만들었다.
➡ _____

48 그리고 나서 그것을 가게 창문에 걸었다.
➡ _____

49 신선한 도넛   2개에 5센트
➡ _____

50 도넛 안에 있는 반지를 찾으면 100달러의 상금을 드려요.
➡ _____

51 추신. 반지를 돌려주어야 합니다.
➡ _____

52 그러자, 많은 사람들이 도넛을 사기 시작했다.
➡ _____

53 갑자기, 한 남자가 흥분해서 소리쳤다.
➡ _____

54 Man: 찾았어요! 내가 반지를 찾았어요!
➡ _____

55 Homer: 보세요, 제 아이디어가 통했어요!
➡ _____

56 Lady: 여기 100달러예요!
➡ _____

57 결국 모두가 행복했다.
➡ _____

58 남자는 100달러를 갖고 집으로 갔다.
➡ _____

59 귀부인은 다이아몬드 반지를 다시 찾았고, Bob 삼촌은 도넛을 많이 팔았다.
➡ _____

60 그러면, Homer는 어떻게 됐을까?
➡ _____

61 그는 자신의 아이디어가 아주 잘 통해서 행복했다!
➡ _____

서술형 실전문제

01 다음 문장에 공통으로 들어갈 말을 쓰시오.

> (1) Can I _____ some doughnuts and a coffee?
>
> (2) I _____ to go now. This was so much fun! Good-bye!

02 다음 빈칸에 들어갈 말을 〈보기〉에서 찾아 쓰시오. (필요하면 변형하여 쓰시오.)

┌─ 보기 ┐
drop into reward batter step out
└────────┘

(1) I'll give a _____ of one hundred dollars to the person who finds that ring!

(2) Rings of batter started _____ _____ the hot oil.

(3) After Uncle Bob left, a big car stopped in front of the shop, and a lady _____ _____.

03 다음 영영풀이에 해당하는 단어를 〈보기〉에서 찾아 첫 번째 칸에 쓰고, 두 번째 칸에는 우리말 뜻을 쓰시오.

┌─ 보기 ┐
compare remember batter
excitement machine work
└────────┘

(1) _____ : to have an image in your mind of something that happened or was said in the past: _____

(2) _____ : to think about how two or more things are different or the same: _____

(3) _____ : the feeling you have when you are excited: _____

(4) _____ : to be effective or successful: _____

04 다음 우리말 해석과 같은 뜻이 되도록 주어진 철자로 시작하여 빈칸을 채우시오.

(1) Homer의 삼촌인 Bob은 도넛 가게를 갖고 있었다.
➡ Homer's uncle, Bob, o_____ a doughnut shop.

(2) 내가 잠시 집으로 되돌아가야 해.
➡ I need to go back home f_____ _____.

(3) 그 귀부인은 외투를 벗고 커다란 다이아몬드 반지를 뺐다.
➡ The lady t_____ _____ her coat and her big diamond ring.

05 다음 문장에서 어법상 어색한 부분을 바르게 고쳐 다시 쓰시오.

(1) Bob liked books, because his room was full of books.
➡ _____

(2) That is easy to make doughnuts.
➡ _____

(3) Homer thinks that the doughnuts smell greatly.
➡ _____

(4) After Bob made doughnuts with the doughnut machine, he turned off it.
➡ _____
_____

(5) We ordered three piece of pizzas and two can of colas at the restaurant.
➡ _____
_____

06 다음 두 문장을 관계대명사를 이용하여 한 문장으로 연결하여 쓰시오.

(1) • Have you met the girl?
  • She is talking to Judy.

  ➡ _____

  _____

(2) • Yuna is good at figure skating.
  • Figure skating is hard to learn.

  ➡ _____

  _____

(3) • The hotel was clean and beautiful.
  • I stayed at the hotel.

  ➡ _____

  _____

  _____

[07~09] 다음 글을 읽고, 물음에 답하시오.

Homer's uncle, Bob, had a doughnut shop. Uncle Bob liked machines, so the shop was full of cooking machines. One day, Homer visited Uncle Bob's shop.

Homer: Hello, Uncle Bob!

Bob: Hi, Homer. Nice to see you. Look at this new doughnut machine. Isn't it great?

Bob: Homer, I need to go back home for a while. Can you watch the shop for me and make some doughnuts?

Homer: OK, I'll try but ....

Bob: It's easy to do. First, make the doughnut batter and put it in the machine. Then just start the machine. Here's the recipe.

Homer: I can do that. Don't worry.

After Uncle Bob left, a big car stopped in front of the shop, and a lady stepped out.

07 Why was Bob's doughnut shop filled with cooking machines? Answer in English. (4 words)

  ➡ _____

08 위 글에서 다음 영영풀이에 해당하는 단어를 찾아 쓰시오.

a mixture of flour, eggs, and milk that is used in cooking

  ➡ _____

09 위 글에서 Bob 삼촌이 말하는 도넛 만드는 법을 우리말로 쓰시오.

(1) _____
(2) _____
(3) _____

[10~12] 다음 글을 읽고, 물음에 답하시오.

Just then the lady came back to the shop.

Lady: I lost my diamond ring. I think I left it on the counter.

Homer: Oh, I remember. ⓐ반죽을 섞기 전에 그것을 뺐어요.

Everyone looked for the diamond ring, but they couldn't find it.

Homer: I can't find it.

Lady: ⓑI'll give a reward of one hundred dollars to the person who finds that ring!

Homer: I know! The ring fell into the batter. I'm sure it's inside one of these doughnuts!

Lady: You're right!

Bob: Oh, no! Now we have to break up all of these doughnuts ⓒto find the ring.

10 위 글의 밑줄 친 ⓐ의 우리말에 맞게 한 단어를 보충하여, 주어진 어휘를 알맞게 배열하시오.

started / it / you / to mix / before / took / the batter / you

  ➡ _____

11 위 글의 밑줄 친 문장 ⓑ를 4형식 문장으로 고치시오.

➡ _____

_____

12 위 글의 밑줄 친 ⓒ를 다음과 같이 바꿔 쓸 때 빈칸에 들어갈 알맞은 말을 쓰시오.

(1) _____ _____ _____ the ring

(2) _____ _____ _____ _____ the ring

(3) _____ _____ we can find the ring

(4) _____ _____ we _____ find the ring

[13~16] 다음 글을 읽고, 물음에 답하시오.

Homer: Don't worry, Uncle. I have an idea.

Homer took a piece of paper and made a sign.

He then put it in the shop's window.

Fresh Doughnuts

2 for 5 cents

$100 prize for finding a ring inside a doughnut

P.S. You have to give the ring back.

Then many people began to buy the doughnuts.

All of a sudden, a man shouted with excitement.

Man: I found it! I found the ring!

Homer: See, my idea worked!

Lady: Here's one hundred dollars!

In the end, everybody was happy. The man went home with one hundred dollars. The lady got her diamond ring back, and Uncle Bob sold lots of doughnuts. And, what about Homer? He was happy that his idea <u>worked</u> so well!

13 If a person buys 10 doughnuts, what's the price of them?

➡ _____

14 다음 빈칸에 들어갈 알맞은 단어를 본문에서 찾아 넣어 위 글의 요지를 완성하시오.

> The main idea of this text is how creative ideas can _____ in solving problems.

➡ _____

15 위 글의 등장인물들 각자에게 어떤 일이 일어났는지 결말을 우리말로 쓰시오.

• Man: _____

• Lady: _____

• Uncle Bob: _____

• Homer: _____

16 위 글의 밑줄 친 worked와 같은 의미로 쓰인 것을 고르시오.

① He worked for a bank.

② She worked a farm.

③ The plan worked well.

④ This machine is worked by wind power.

⑤ They often worked very long hours.

단원별 예상문제

01 다음 단어에 대한 영어 설명이 <u>어색한</u> 것은?

① doughnut: a small round cake that usually has a hole in the middle

② give a reward: to give something to someone because he or she has done something good

③ counter: the place where you pay in a shop, bank, restaurant, etc.

④ batter: a mixture of flour, eggs, milk, etc. used in cooking and for making bread, cakes, etc.

⑤ step out: to fall or to allow something to fall

02 다음 짝지어진 단어의 관계가 같도록 빈칸에 알맞은 말을 쓰시오.

mix : blend = fall : _____

03 다음 영영풀이에 해당하는 단어를 고르시오.

a set of instructions telling you how to prepare and cook food

① recipe   ② batter   ③ machine
④ counter   ⑤ cooker

04 다음 그림에 맞게 대화의 빈칸에 들어갈 말을 쓰시오.

Lady: Are you making the doughnut _____ now?
Boy: Yes, but this is my first time.

05 다음 문장의 밑줄 친 단어와 같은 말을 네 단어로 쓰시오.

- All at once it became dark.
- I suddenly remembered I had left something at home.

➡ _____

06 다음 빈칸에 들어갈 말이 알맞게 짝지어진 것은?

- Homer turned on the doughnut machine. Rings of batter started dropping _____ the hot oil.
- The shop was now full _____ doughnuts.
- Now we have to break _____ all of these doughnuts to find the ring.

① on – with – down   ② into – of – up
③ by – of – up   ④ into – with – down
⑤ by – of – down

07 다음 중 짝지어진 단어의 관계가 <u>다른</u> 것은?

① easy : difficult   ② sell : buy
③ push : pull   ④ shout : yell
⑤ fun : boring

08 다음 문장의 빈칸에 공통으로 들어갈 말을 쓰시오.

> • Homer, I need to go _____ home for a while.
> • Uncle Bob! Please come _____ right away. Something's wrong with the doughnut machine.
> • You have to give the ring _____.
> • The lady got her diamond ring _____, and Uncle Bob sold lots of doughnuts.

09 다음 문장에서 어법상 <u>어색한</u> 부분을 바르게 고쳐 다시 쓰시오.

(1) Homer is the person which is very creative.

➡ _____

(2) Bob had to fix the machine making doughnuts.

➡ _____

(3) Homer found the lost ring with easy.

➡ _____

(4) Sean was happy what his idea was finally accepted.

➡ _____

10 다음 빈칸에 알맞은 말을 <u>모두</u> 고르시오.

> The food _____ really delicious.

① bought　② brought　③ asked
④ tasted　⑤ smelled

11 다음 중 〈보기〉의 밑줄 친 부분과 용법이 같은 것을 고르시오.

┤ 보기 ├
We eat <u>to live</u>, not live <u>to eat</u>.

① It is very important for him <u>to eat</u> delicious food.
② We decided <u>to eat</u> pizza.
③ They had nothing <u>to eat</u>.
④ We went to the restaurant <u>to eat</u> lunch.
⑤ What I like is <u>to eat</u> delicious food.

12 우리말을 괄호 안에 주어진 어휘를 이용하여 영작하시오.

(1) Grace는 스커트를 하나 사서 그것을 입었다. (buy, and, put)

➡ _____

(2) Charlie Brown은 운이 없는 소녀이다. (bad luck, a boy, have, who)

➡ _____

(3) 그 금속은 촉감이 매끄럽고 차가웠다. (metal, smooth, cold, feel)

➡ _____

(4) 그녀는 그녀의 손가락을 튼튼하게 하기 위하여 피아노를 치기 시작했다. (make, start, playing, strong, fingers)

➡ _____
_____

출제율 90%

13 다음 중 어법상 옳지 <u>않은</u> 것은?

① The rock looks like a big battle ship.

② A teacher is a person whom teaches students at school.

③ Will you throw them away, please?

④ Her face turned red with excitement.

⑤ The hens are hungry, so I must feed them now.

[14~16] 다음 글을 읽고 물음에 답하시오.

Homer's uncle, Bob, had a doughnut shop. ⓐUnderline Bob liked machines, so the shop was full of cooking machines. One day, Homer visited Uncle Bob's shop.

Homer: Hello, Uncle Bob!

Bob: Hi, Homer. Nice to see you. Look at this new doughnut machine. Isn't it great?

Bob: Homer, I need to go back home for a while. Can you watch the shop for me and make some doughnuts?

Homer: OK, I'll try but ....

Bob: It's easy to do. First, make the doughnut batter and put ⓑit in the machine. Then just start the machine. Here's the recipe.

Homer: I can do that. Don't worry.

After Uncle Bob left, a big car stopped in front of the shop, and a lady stepped out.

출제율 95%

14 위 글의 밑줄 친 ⓐ를 다음과 같이 바꿔 쓸 때 빈칸에 들어갈 알맞은 단어를 고르시오.

_____ Uncle Bob liked machines, the shop was full of cooking machines.

① That　　② If　　③ As

④ While　　⑤ Though

출제율 95%

15 위 글의 밑줄 친 ⓑit이 가리키는 것을 본문에서 찾아 쓰시오.

➡ _____

출제율 100%

16 위 글의 내용과 일치하도록 다음 빈칸 (A)와 (B)에 들어갈 알맞은 말을 쓰시오.

Uncle Bob wanted Homer to (A) _____ _____ _____ for him and (B)_____ _____ _____.

[17~19] 다음 글을 읽고, 물음에 답하시오.

Lady: Can I have some doughnuts and a coffee?

Homer: I'm sorry, but the doughnuts aren't ready.

Lady: Are you making the doughnut batter now?

Homer: Yes, but this is my first time.

The lady (A)[put on / took off] her coat and her big diamond ring.

She started to mix the batter.

Lady: I can help you. I can make delicious doughnuts.

Homer: Uh, OK.

Homer: This is a lot of batter.

Lady: Just wait and see. The doughnuts will taste (B)[great / greatly].

Homer (C)[turned on / turned off] the doughnut machine. Rings of batter started dropping into the hot oil.

Lady: You try the first doughnut. Here.

Homer: Wow! It's really delicious!

출제율 85%

17 위 글의 괄호 (A)~(C)에서 문맥이나 어법상 알맞은 낱말을 골라 쓰시오.

(A) _____　(B) _____　(C) _____

18 출제율 90%

위 글에서 알 수 있는 'Lady'의 성격으로 가장 알맞은 것을 고르시오.

① curious   ② polite
③ patient   ④ kind
⑤ creative

19 출제율 95%

위 글의 내용과 일치하지 않는 것은?

① The lady asked Homer if she could have some doughnuts and a coffee.
② Homer said that the doughnuts weren't ready.
③ Homer was making the doughnut batter for the first time.
④ Homer made a lot of batter.
⑤ The lady gave Homer the first doughnut.

[20~22] 다음 글을 읽고 물음에 답하시오.

Lady: I have to go now. This was so much fun! Good-bye!
Homer: Thank you for helping me. Good-bye!
　Homer had enough doughnuts, so he pushed the stop button, but nothing happened. (①)
Homer: Hmm... What's wrong? (②) I think I should call Uncle Bob. (③)
　The shop was now ⓐ<u>full of</u> doughnuts. (④) Homer piled the doughnuts on the counter. (⑤)
Homer: Uncle Bob! Please come back right away. ⓑ<u>Something's wrong with the doughnut machine.</u>
Bob: Oh, no! How can we sell all these doughnuts?

20 출제율 100%

위 글의 흐름으로 보아, 주어진 문장이 들어가기에 가장 적절한 곳은?

> The doughnuts kept coming out of the machine.

①   ②   ③   ④   ⑤

21 출제율 90%

위 글의 밑줄 친 ⓐfull of와 바꿔 쓸 수 있는 두 단어를 쓰시오.

➡ _____

22 출제율 95%

위 글의 밑줄 친 ⓑ가 가리키는 내용을 본문에서 찾아 쓰시오.

➡ _____
_____

[23~26] 다음 글을 읽고 물음에 답하시오.

　Just then the lady came back to the shop.
Lady: I lost my diamond ring. I think I ___ⓐ___ it on the counter.
Homer: Oh, I remember. You took it off before you started to mix the batter.
　Everyone looked for the diamond ring, but they couldn't find it.
Homer: I can't find it.
Lady: I'll give a reward of one hundred dollars to the person who finds that ring!
Homer: I know! The ring fell into the batter. I'm sure it's inside one of these doughnuts!
Lady: You're right!
Bob: Oh, no! Now we have to break up all of these doughnuts ⓑ<u>to find</u> the ring.

출제율 90%

23 위 글의 빈칸 ⓐ에 들어갈 알맞은 말을 고르시오.

① lay   ② held   ③ gave

④ left   ⑤ found

출제율 95%

24 아래 〈보기〉에서 위 글의 밑줄 친 ⓑto find와 to부정사의 용법이 같은 것의 개수를 고르시오.

> ① They went there to find the ring.
> ② It was not easy to find the ring.
> ③ Can you think of the way to find the ring?
> ④ I wanted to find the ring.
> ⑤ I wonder who will be the person to find the ring.

① 1개   ② 2개   ③ 3개   ④ 4개   ⑤ 5개

출제율 100%

25 위 글의 마지막 부분에서 알 수 있는 'Uncle Bob'의 심경으로 가장 알맞은 것을 고르시오.

① embarrassed   ② excited

③ ashamed   ④ bored

⑤ relieved

출제율 95%

26 위 글의 내용과 일치하지 않는 것은? (2개)

① The lady came back to the shop because she lost her diamond ring.

② Homer remembers that she took off her ring before she started to mix the batter.

③ Homer thinks that the lady lost the ring on the street.

④ The person who finds that ring will receive a reward from Homer.

⑤ Homer says that the ring fell into the batter.

[27~29] 다음 글을 읽고, 물음에 답하시오.

Homer: Don't worry, Uncle. I have an idea.
Homer took a piece of paper and made a sign. He then put it in the shop's window.

Fresh Doughnuts
2 for 5 cents
$100 prize for finding a ring inside a doughnut
P.S. You have to give the ring back.

Then many people began to buy the doughnuts. ⓐAll of a sudden, a man shouted with excitement.
Man: I found it! I found the ring!
Homer: See, my idea worked!
Lady: ⓑHere're one hundred dollars!
In the end, everybody was happy. The man went home with one hundred dollars. The lady got her diamond ring back, and Uncle Bob sold lots of doughnuts. And, what about Homer? He was happy that his idea worked so well!

출제율 90%

27 위 글의 제목으로 알맞은 것을 고르시오.

① Homer Made a Sign!

② Put the Sign in the Shop's Window

③ $100 Prize for Finding a Ring

④ Uncle Bob Sold Lots of Doughnuts

⑤ Creative Idea Worked Well!

출제율 95%

28 위 글의 밑줄 친 ⓐAll of a sudden과 바꿔 쓸 수 있는 말을 모두 고르시오.

① At one time   ② Suddenly

③ Actually   ④ All at once

⑤ Immediately

출제율 85%

29 위 글의 밑줄 친 문장 ⓑ에서 어법상 틀린 부분을 찾아 고치시오.

_____ ➡ _____

INSIGHT
on the textbook

교과서 파헤치기

※ 다음 영어를 우리말로 쓰시오.

01 arrive _____

02 adventure _____

03 taste _____

04 amazing _____

05 difficult _____

06 float _____

07 shout _____

08 balloon _____

09 container _____

10 different _____

11 curious _____

12 thirsty _____

13 everywhere _____

14 space station _____

15 exploration _____

16 finally _____

17 since _____

18 foreign _____

19 excited _____

20 lie _____

21 swallow _____

22 shake _____

23 towards _____

24 spaceship _____

25 fix _____

26 wet _____

27 laugh _____

28 save _____

29 recently _____

30 space suit _____

31 form _____

32 secret _____

33 soft _____

34 thrilling _____

35 don't have to+동사원형 _____

36 each other _____

37 be covered with _____

38 pull down _____

39 lie down _____

40 for example _____

41 be curious about ~ _____

42 run up to ~ _____

43 not ~ anymore _____

※ 다음 우리말을 영어로 쓰시오.

01	모험	
02	풍선	
03	어려운	
04	떠가다	
05	신난, 흥분한	
06	다른	
07	탐험, 탐사	
08	부드러운	
09	놀라운	
10	마침내	
11	~한 이래로	
12	고치다	
13	외국의	
14	우주선	
15	비밀, 기밀	
16	모든 곳에	
17	바람	
18	외치다	
19	흔들다	
20	궁금한, 호기심이 많은	
21	~쪽으로, ~을 향하여	

22	우주복	
23	목마른	
24	그릇, 용기	
25	삼키다	
26	언덕	
27	눕다	
28	아주 신나는	
29	웃다	
30	젖은	
31	풀, 잔디	
32	최근에	
33	구하다	
34	맛	
35	~에 관해 궁금해 하다	
36	~하려고 시도하다	
37	놀라서	
38	더 이상 ~ 않다	
39	~으로 뒤덮이다	
40	~에 타다	
41	예를 들어	
42	(둘 사이의) 서로	
43	굴러 내려가다	

※ 다음 영영풀이에 알맞은 단어를 <보기>에서 골라 쓴 후, 우리말 뜻을 쓰시오.

1 _____ : extremely surprising: _____

2 _____ : to stay on the surface of a liquid and not sink: _____

3 _____ : a vehicle used for travel in space: _____

4 _____ : to make something into a particular shape: _____

5 _____ : to reach a place, especially at the end of a journey: _____

6 _____ : to keep someone or something safe from death, harm, loss, etc.:
_____

7 _____ : interested in learning about people or things around you: _____

8 _____ : covered with or containing liquid, especially water: _____

9 _____ : the activity of searching and finding out about something: _____

10 _____ : belonging or connected to a country that is not your own: _____

11 _____ : in the direction of, or closer to someone or something: _____

12 _____ : a place or vehicle in space where people can stay: _____

13 _____ : an unusual, exciting, and possibly dangerous activity, such as a trip:
_____

14 _____ : to cause food, drink, pills, etc. to move from your mouth into your
stomach by using the muscles of your throat: _____

15 _____ : to arrive on the ground or other surface after moving down through the
air: _____

16 _____ : a piece of information that is only known by one person or a few people
and should not be told to others: _____

보기			
land	foreign	amazing	spaceship
form	arrive	towards	secret
adventure	float	wet	save
swallow	space station	curious	exploration

※ 다음 우리말과 일치하도록 빈칸에 알맞은 말을 쓰시오.

Listen and Talk A-1

B: Did you _____ _____ the first spaceship _____ _____ _____ _____?

G: No, I didn't. I'm _____ _____ it.

B: This is a poster of the _____.

G: Really? I _____ _____ _____ it.

Listen and Talk A-2

G: _____ you _____ _____ the new book about Mars?

B: No, I didn't. _____ _____ _____ _____ _____ Mars.

G: Look. It's _____ _____. It's _____ Mars and its moons.

B: Great. I think I'll _____ the book.

Listen and Talk A-3

G: _____ _____ _____ _____ the space marathon?

B: No, _____ _____.

G: It's a marathon on a _____ _____. _____ _____ this video.

B: OK. _____ _____ _____ _____ it.

Listen and Talk A-4

G: Did you hear _____ the new _____ _____?

B: Yes, I did. It's _____ _____ _____ ice cream.

G: Yes, and _____ _____ _____. It _____ _____.

B: I'm really _____ _____ _____ _____.

Listen and Talk B

1. A: Look at this. Did you hear _____ the new musical?

   B: Yes, I did. I _____ it has great songs.

   A: Oh, I'm really _____ _____ it.

2. A: _____ _____ this. Did you _____ _____ the new musical?

   B: _____, I _____.

   A: I heard _____ _____ _____ _____.

   B: Oh, I'm _____ _____ it.

Listen and Talk C

B: Subin, did you _____ _____ the new movie, *Life on the Moon*?

G: No, I _____.

B: I _____ it's really _____.

G: I'm really _____ _____ the movie. What's it _____?

B: It's _____ a man _____ is _____ _____ _____ on the moon.

G: That _____ _____.

B: Look. The movie _____ _____ at the Space Theater here.

G: _____ _____ is the movie?

B: It _____ _____ 2:30.

G: _____ _____ _____ first _____ _____ see the movie.

B: OK. I'm _____. _____ _____!

B: 수빈아, "달에서의 생활"이라는 새 영화에 대해서 들어 봤니?
G: 아니.
B: 굉장히 좋다고 들었거든.
G: 그 영화가 정말 궁금하네. 뭐에 관한 거야?
B: 달에서 살기 위해 노력하는 한 남자에 관한 영화래.
G: 그거 재미있겠다.
B: 봐. 그 영화가 여기 우주 극장에서 상영되고 있어.
G: 영화가 몇 시에 상영되는데?
B: 2시 30분에 시작해.
G: 우선 점심부터 먹고 영화를 보자.
B: 좋아. 나 배고파. 가자!

Review 1

G: Tony, _____ _____ _____ _____ the movie, *My Hero*?

B: _____, I _____.

G: Well, I _____ it's really good.

B: I'm really _____ _____ the movie. What's it _____?

G: It's _____ a father _____ _____ _____ _____.

G: Tony, 영화 My Hero에 대해 들어 봤니?
B: 아니, 못 들어 봤어.
G: 음, 정말 좋다고 들었어.
B: 그 영화에 대해 정말 궁금하다. 무엇에 대한 것이니?
G: 그것은 아들을 구하는 아빠에 관한 거야.

Review 2

G: _____ you _____ _____ the new book, *Living in a Foreign Country*?

B: No, I didn't.

G: Look. It's _____ here. It's _____ _____ in New York.

B: Great. I'm _____ _____ _____ this book.

G: _____, _____.

G: 새 책인 "Living in a Foreign Country"에 대해 들어 봤니?
B: 아니, 못 들어 봤어.
G: 봐. 바로 여기 있어. 그것은 뉴욕에서의 삶에 관한 거야.
B: 멋지다. 이 책이 정말 궁금해.
G: 나도 그래.

대화문 Test

※ 다음 우리말에 맞도록 대화를 영어로 쓰시오.

Listen and Talk A-1

B: _____

G: _____

B: _____

G: _____

B: 너는 우주에 간 첫 번째 우주선에 대해 들어 봤니?
G: 아니, 못 들어 봤어. 궁금하다.
B: 이것이 그 우주선 포스터야.
G: 정말? 그것을 사고 싶다.

Listen and Talk A-2

G: _____

B: _____

G: _____

B: _____

G: 너는 화성에 관한 새로운 책에 관해 들어 봤니?
B: 아니, 못 들어 봤어. 나는 화성에 관해 정말 궁금해.
G: 봐. 바로 여기 있어. 그것은 화성과 그것의 위성들에 관한 내용이야.
B: 멋지다. 이 책을 사야겠어.

Listen and Talk A-3

G: _____

B: _____

G: _____

B: _____

G: 너는 우주 마라톤에 대해 들어 봤니?
B: 아니, 못 들어 봤어.
G: 그것은 우주 정거장에서 하는 마라톤이야. 이 비디오를 봐.
B: 알겠어. 정말 궁금하다.

Listen and Talk A-4

G: _____

B: _____

G: _____

B: _____

G: 너는 새로운 우주 음식에 대해 들어 봤니?
B: 응, 들어 봤어. 그건 일종의 아이스크림이야.
G: 응, 여기 있어. 맛있어 보인다.
B: 그 맛이 참 궁금하다.

Listen and Talk B

1. A: _____

   B: _____

   A: _____

2. A: _____

   B: _____

   A: _____

   B: _____

1. A: 이것 봐. 새 뮤지컬에 대해 들어 봤니?
   B: 응, 들어 봤어. 좋은 노래들이 나온다고 들었어.
   A: 오, 정말 궁금하다.

2. A: 이것 봐. 새 뮤지컬에 대해 들어 봤니?
   B: 아니, 못 들어 봤어.
   A: 좋은 노래들이 나온다고 들었어.
   B: 오, 정말 궁금하다.

Listen and Talk C

B: _____

G: _____

B: _____

G: _____

B: _____

G: _____

B: _____

G: _____

B: _____

G: _____

B: _____

B: 수빈아, "달에서의 생활"이라는 새 영화에 대해서 들어 봤니?

G: 아니.

B: 굉장히 좋다고 들었거든.

G: 그 영화가 정말 궁금하네. 뭐에 관한 거야?

B: 달에서 살기 위해 노력하는 한 남자에 관한 영화래.

G: 그거 재미있겠다.

B: 봐. 그 영화가 여기 우주 극장에서 상영되고 있어.

G: 영화가 몇 시에 상영되는데?

B: 2시 30분에 시작해.

G: 우선 점심부터 먹고 영화를 보자.

B: 좋아. 나 배고파. 가자!

Review 1

G: _____

B: _____

G: _____

B: _____

G: _____

G: Tony, 영화 My Hero에 대해 들어 봤니?

B: 아니, 못 들어 봤어.

G: 음, 정말 좋다고 들었어.

B: 그 영화에 대해 정말 궁금하다. 무엇에 대한 것이니?

G: 그것은 아들을 구하는 아빠에 관한 거야.

Review 2

G: _____

B: _____

G: _____

B: _____

G: _____

G: 새 책인 "Living in a Foreign Country"에 대해 들어 봤니?

B: 아니, 못 들어 봤어.

G: 봐. 바로 여기 있어. 그것은 뉴욕에서의 삶에 관한 거야.

B: 멋지다. 이 책이 정말 궁금해.

G: 나도 그래.

※ 다음 우리말과 일치하도록 빈칸에 알맞은 것을 골라 쓰시오.

1 The _____ New _____
A. Thing   B. Best

2 Rada lived on a _____ world, _____ _____ in space.
A. out   B. little   C. far

3 She _____ _____ her father, mother, and brother Jonny.
A. with   B. there   C. lived

4 Rada's father and _____ people _____ _____ spaceships.
A. on   B. other   C. worked

5 _____ Rada and Jonny were children, and they _____ _____ in space.
A. were   B. only   C. born

6 _____ day, Dad told Rada and Jonny, "We're _____ to Earth tomorrow."
A. going   B. one   C. back

7 Rada and Jonny looked at Dad _____ _____ and _____ _____ him.
A. towards   B. in   C. floated   D. surprise

8 Rada asked Dad, "_____ _____ _____ on Earth?"
A. it   B. what's   C. like

9 "_____ is _____ there.
A. different   B. everything

10 _____ _____ , the sky is blue," _____ Dad.
A. answered   B. example   C. for

11 "I've _____ _____ a blue sky," _____ Jonny.
A. seen   B. never   C. said

12 "The sky _____ _____ _____ here," said Rada.
A. always   B. is   C. black

13 "You _____ _____ to wear your big heavy space _____ because _____ is air everywhere.
A. have   B. there   C. don't   D. suits

14 It's also _____ to jump there _____ Earth _____ you _____ ," said Dad.
A. pulls   B. hard   C. down   D. because

15 "_____ _____ ?" asked Rada.
A. else   B. what

16 "There are hills, and they are _____ _____ soft green _____ .
A. with   B. grass   C. covered

---

1 최고의 새로운 것

2 Rada는 먼 우주의 작은 세계에 살고 있었다.

3 그녀는 아빠, 엄마 그리고 남동생 Jonny와 함께 그곳에서 살고 있었다.

4 Rada의 아빠와 다른 사람들은 우주선에서 일했다.

5 Rada와 Jonny만이 아이들이었고, 그들은 우주에서 태어났다.

6 어느 날, 아빠가 Rada와 Jonny에게, "우리는 내일 지구로 돌아갈 거야."라고 말했다.

7 Rada와 Jonny는 깜짝 놀라 아빠를 바라보았고, 그에게 둥둥 떠서 갔다.

8 Rada가 아빠에게, "지구는 어떤 곳인가요?"라고 물었다.

9 "그곳에선 모든 것이 다르단다.

10 예를 들어, 하늘은 파란색이지." 라고 아빠가 대답했다.

11 "전 한 번도 파란 하늘을 본 적이 없어요."라고 Jonny가 말했다.

12 "여기는 하늘이 항상 검은색이잖아요."라고 Rada가 말했다.

13 "그곳에는 모든 곳에 공기가 있기 때문에 크고 무거운 우주복을 입을 필요가 없단다.

14 또한 지구가 너희들을 끌어당기기 때문에 거기에서는 점프하는 것도 어렵단다." 아빠가 말했다.

15 "그 밖에 또 뭐가 있어요?" Rada가 물었다.

16 "언덕들이 있는데 그것들은 부드러운 초록색의 잔디로 뒤덮여 있단다.

17 You can _____ _____ the hills," _____ Mom.

A. down   B. roll   C. answered

18 "Dad, _____ you _____ _____ _____ a hill?" asked Rada.

A. ever   B. down   C. have   D. rolled

19 "Yes, it's really _____!" _____ Dad.

A. answered   B. amazing

20 Jonny was _____, so he _____ a milk container and _____ it.

A. shook   B. thirsty   C. opened

21 The milk _____ in the _____ and _____ balls.

A. formed   B. floated   C. air

22 Jonny _____ the _____.

A. balls   B. swallowed

23 "Jonny, _____ you drink milk that _____ on Earth, you'll _____ _____," said Mom.

A. way   B. wet   C. get   D. if

24 _____ that night, Rada and Jonny _____ a _____ time about Earth.

A. long   B. talked   C. later

25 It was _____ to think about _____ the new _____ they were _____ to see and do.

A. things   B. exciting   C. all   D. going

26 There was _____ _____ _____ Rada and Jonny really wanted to do.

A. new   B. thing   C. one

27 They _____ about it _____ and didn't tell Mom and Dad _____ it.

A. night   B. thought   C. all   D. about

28 It was _____ _____.

A. secret   B. their

29 The _____ day, Rada's family _____ _____ a spaceship.

A. got   B. next   C. on

30 "It's _____ to _____ a long _____," said Mom.

A. trip   B. going   C. be

31 "That's _____. I'm _____ _____!" said Rada.

A. so   B. alright   C. excited

32 The spaceship _____ _____.

A. landed   B. finally

---

17 언덕을 굴러 내려갈 수도 있어." 엄마가 대답했다.

18 "아빠, 언덕을 굴러 내려가 본 적 있어요?" Rada가 물었다.

19 "그럼, 정말 놀라워!" 아빠가 대답했다.

20 Jonny는 목이 말라서 우유 용기를 열어 그것을 흔들었다.

21 우유가 공기 중으로 떠서 방울을 형성했다.

22 Jonny는 그 우유 방울을 삼켰다.

23 "Jonny, 만약 네가 지구에서 그런 식으로 우유를 마신다면, 다 젖을 거야." 엄마가 말했다.

24 그날 밤 늦게, Rada와 Jonny는 지구에 대해서 오랜 시간 이야기했다.

25 그들이 보고, 하게 될 모든 새로운 것들을 생각하는 것은 흥미로웠다.

26 Rada와 Jonny가 정말로 하고 싶었던 한 가지 새로운 것이 있었다.

27 그들은 밤새 그것에 대해서 생각했고 엄마와 아빠에게는 그것을 말하지 않았다.

28 그것은 그들의 비밀이었다.

29 다음날, Rada의 가족은 우주선에 올랐다.

30 "긴 여행이 될 거야." 엄마가 말했다.

31 "괜찮아요. 정말 신나요!" Rada가 말했다.

32 우주선이 마침내 착륙했다.

33 "Dad, it's _____ _____ _____ on Earth," said Rada.

A. walk   B. to   C. difficult

34 "I know. Earth is _____ _____ _____," said Dad.

A. down   B. you   C. pulling

35 Rada and Jonny _____ _____ _____.

A. float   B. couldn't   C. anymore

36 That was the _____ _____ _____.

A. new   B. first   C. thing

37 "_____ that _____?" asked Rada.

A. sound   B. what's

38 "A _____ is _____," said Mom.

A. singing   B. bird

39 "I've _____ _____ a bird _____," said Rada.

A. heard   B. sing   C. never

40 "And I've _____ _____ the _____," said Jonny.

A. felt   B. wind   C. never

41 _____ were _____ _____ things.

A. new   B. these   C. all

42 Rada and Jonny _____ _____ _____ _____ hill.

A. ran   B. nearest   C. up   D. the

43 At the _____, they looked at _____ _____ and _____.

A. other   B. top   C. laughed   D. each

44 Then they _____ _____ on the _____ green grass and _____ down the hill.

A. rolled   B. down   C. lay   D. soft

45 That was _____ _____!

A. secret   B. their

46 "This is the _____ _____ thing of all!" _____ Rada and Jonny.

A. shouted   B. new   C. best

47 And they _____ _____ _____ the _____ of the hill again.

A. top   B. up   C. ran   D. to

---

33 "아빠, 지구에서는 걷는 것이 어려워요." Rada가 말했다.

34 "그래. 지구가 너를 끌어당기고 있거든." 아빠가 말했다.

35 Rada와 Jonny는 더 이상 떠다닐 수 없었다.

36 그것이 첫 번째 새로운 것이었다.

37 "저건 무슨 소리죠?"라고 Rada가 물었다.

38 "새가 노래하는 거야." 엄마가 말했다.

39 "새가 노래하는 것을 들어 본 적이 없어요."라고 Rada가 말했다.

40 "그리고 저는 바람을 느껴 본 적도 없어요."라고 Jonny가 말했다.

41 이러한 것들이 모두 새로운 것들이었다.

42 Rada와 Jonny는 가장 가까운 언덕으로 뛰어 올라갔다.

43 꼭대기에서, 그들은 서로를 쳐다보고 웃었다.

44 그러고 나서 그들은 부드러운 초록 잔디에 누워서 언덕 아래로 굴러 내려갔다.

45 그것이 그들의 비밀이었다!

46 "이것이 모든 것들 중에서 최고의 새로운 것이에요!" Rada와 Jonny는 외쳤다.

47 그리고 그들은 언덕 꼭대기로 다시 뛰어 올라갔다.

※ 다음 우리말과 일치하도록 빈칸에 알맞은 말을 쓰시오.

1 The _____ New _____

2 Rada lived on a little world, _____ _____ _____ _____.

3 She _____ _____ _____ her father, mother, and _____ Jonny.

4 Rada's father and _____ people _____ _____ spaceships.

5 _____ Rada and Jonny were children, and they _____ _____ _____ _____.

6 _____ _____, Dad told Rada and Jonny, "We're _____ _____ _____ Earth tomorrow."

7 Rada and Jonny looked at Dad _____ _____ and _____ _____ him.

8 Rada asked Dad, "_____ _____ _____ on Earth?"

9 "_____ _____ _____ there.

10 _____ _____ _____, the sky is blue," answered Dad.

11 "_____ _____ _____ a blue sky," said Jonny.

12 "The sky _____ _____ _____ here," said Rada.

13 "You _____ _____ _____ wear your big heavy space suits _____ _____ _____ _____ everywhere.

14 It's also hard to _____ there because Earth _____ _____ _____," said Dad.

15 "_____ _____?" asked Rada.

16 "There are hills, and they _____ _____ _____ soft green grass.

17 You can _____ _____ the hills," answered Mom.

18 "Dad, _____ _____ _____ _____ _____ _____ a hill?" asked Rada.

19 "Yes, it's _____ _____!" answered Dad.

20 Jonny was _____, _____ he _____ a milk container and _____ it.

21 The milk _____ in the air and _____ balls.

22 Jonny _____ the balls.

23 "Jonny, _____ you drink milk _____ _____ on Earth, you'll _____ _____," said Mom.

1 최고의 새로운 것

2 Rada는 먼 우주의 작은 세계에 살고 있었다.

3 그녀는 아빠, 엄마 그리고 남동생 Jonny와 함께 그곳에서 살고 있었다.

4 Rada의 아빠와 다른 사람들은 우주선에서 일했다.

5 Rada와 Jonny만이 아이들이었고, 그들은 우주에서 태어났다.

6 어느 날, 아빠가 Rada와 Jonny에게, "우리는 내일 지구로 돌아갈 거야."라고 말했다.

7 Rada와 Jonny는 깜짝 놀라 아빠를 바라보았고, 그에게 둥둥 떠서 갔다.

8 Rada가 아빠에게, "지구는 어떤 곳인가요?"라고 물었다.

9 "그곳에선 모든 것이 다르단다.

10 예를 들어, 하늘은 파란색이지."라고 아빠가 대답했다.

11 "전 한 번도 파란 하늘을 본 적이 없어요."라고 Jonny가 말했다.

12 "여기는 하늘이 항상 검은색이잖아요."라고 Rada가 말했다.

13 "그곳에는 모든 곳에 공기가 있기 때문에 크고 무거운 우주복을 입을 필요가 없단다.

14 또한 지구가 너희들을 끌어당기기 때문에 거기에서는 점프하는 것도 어렵단다." 아빠가 말했다.

15 "그 밖에 또 뭐가 있어요?" Rada가 물었다.

16 "언덕들이 있는데 그것들은 부드러운 초록색의 잔디로 뒤덮여 있단다.

17 언덕을 굴러 내려갈 수도 있어." 엄마가 대답했다.

18 "아빠, 언덕을 굴러 내려가 본 적 있어요?" Rada가 물었다.

19 "그럼, 정말 놀라워!" 아빠가 대답했다.

20 Jonny는 목이 말라서 우유 용기를 열어 그것을 흔들었다.

21 우유가 공기 중으로 떠서 방울을 형성했다.

22 Jonny는 그 우유 방울을 삼켰다.

23 "Jonny, 만약 네가 지구에서 그런 식으로 우유를 마신다면, 다 젖을 거야." 엄마가 말했다.

24 _____ _____ _____, Rada and Jonny talked _____ _____ _____ about Earth.

25 It was _____ to _____ about _____ _____ _____ they were _____ _____ see and do.

26 There was _____ _____ _____ Rada and Jonny really _____ _____ _____.

27 They thought about it _____ _____ and didn't tell Mom and Dad about it.

28 It was _____ _____.

29 The next day, Rada's family _____ _____ a spaceship.

30 "_____ _____ _____ a long trip," said Mom.

31 "That's _____. I'm _____ _____!" said Rada.

32 The spaceship _____ _____.

33 "Dad, it's difficult _____ _____ on Earth," said Rada.

34 "I know. Earth is _____ _____ _____," said Dad.

35 Rada and Jonny _____ _____ _____.

36 That was _____ _____ _____ _____.

37 "_____ that _____?" asked Rada.

38 "A bird _____ _____," said Mom.

39 "_____ _____ _____ a bird _____," said Rada.

40 "And _____ _____ _____ the wind," said Jonny.

41 _____ were _____ _____ _____.

42 Rada and Jonny _____ _____ _____ _____ hill.

43 At the top, they looked at _____ and _____.

44 Then they _____ on the soft green grass and _____ the hill.

45 That was _____ _____!

46 "This is the _____ _____ _____ of all!" shouted Rada and Jonny.

47 And they ran _____ _____ _____ of the hill again.

---

24 그날 밤 늦게, Rada와 Jonny는 지구에 대해서 오랜 시간 이야기했다.

25 그들이 보고, 하게 될 모든 새로운 것들을 생각하는 것은 흥미로웠다.

26 Rada와 Jonny가 정말로 하고 싶었던 한 가지 새로운 것이 있었다.

27 그들은 밤새 그것에 대해서 생각했고 엄마와 아빠에게는 그것을 말하지 않았다.

28 그것은 그들의 비밀이었다.

29 다음날, Rada의 가족은 우주선에 올랐다.

30 "긴 여행이 될 거야." 엄마가 말했다.

31 "괜찮아요. 정말 신나요!" Rada가 말했다.

32 우주선이 마침내 착륙했다.

33 "아빠, 지구에서는 걷는 것이 어려워요." Rada가 말했다.

34 "그래. 지구가 너를 끌어당기고 있거든." 아빠가 말했다.

35 Rada와 Jonny는 더 이상 떠다닐 수 없었다.

36 그것이 첫 번째 새로운 것이었다.

37 "저건 무슨 소리죠?"라고 Rada가 물었다.

38 "새가 노래하는 거야." 엄마가 말했다.

39 "새가 노래하는 것을 들어 본 적이 없어요."라고 Rada가 말했다.

40 "그리고 저는 바람을 느껴 본 적도 없어요."라고 Jonny가 말했다.

41 이러한 것들이 모두 새로운 것들이었다.

42 Rada와 Jonny는 가장 가까운 언덕으로 뛰어 올라갔다.

43 꼭대기에서, 그들은 서로를 쳐다보고 웃었다.

44 그리고 나서 그들은 부드러운 초록 잔디에 누워서 언덕 아래로 굴러 내려갔다.

45 그것이 그들의 비밀이었다!

46 "이것이 모든 것들 중에서 최고의 새로운 것이에요!" Rada와 Jonny는 외쳤다.

47 그리고 그들은 언덕 꼭대기로 다시 뛰어 올라갔다.

※ 다음 문장을 우리말로 쓰시오.

1 The Best New Thing
➡ _____

2 Rada lived on a little world, far out in space.
➡ _____

3 She lived there with her father, mother, and brother Jonny.
➡ _____

4 Rada's father and other people worked on spaceships.
➡ _____

5 Only Rada and Jonny were children, and they were born in space.
➡ _____

6 One day, Dad told Rada and Jonny, "We're going back to Earth tomorrow."
➡ _____

7 Rada and Jonny looked at Dad in surprise and floated towards him.
➡ _____

8 Rada asked Dad, "What's it like on Earth?"
➡ _____

9 "Everything is different there.
➡ _____

10 For example, the sky is blue," answered Dad.
➡ _____

11 "I've never seen a blue sky," said Jonny.
➡ _____

12 "The sky is always black here," said Rada.
➡ _____

13 "You don't have to wear your big heavy space suits because there is air everywhere.
➡ _____

14 It's also hard to jump there because Earth pulls you down," said Dad.
➡ _____

15 "What else?" asked Rada.
➡ _____

16 "There are hills, and they are covered with soft green grass.
➡ _____

17 You can roll down the hills," answered Mom.
➡ _____

18 "Dad, have you ever rolled down a hill?" asked Rada.
➡ _____

19 "Yes, it's really amazing!" answered Dad.
➡ _____

20 Jonny was thirsty, so he opened a milk container and shook it.
➡ _____

21 The milk floated in the air and formed balls.
➡ _____

22 Jonny swallowed the balls.
➡ _____

23 "Jonny, if you drink milk that way on Earth, you'll get wet," said Mom.
➡ _____

24 Later that night, Rada and Jonny talked a long time about Earth.
➡ _____

25 It was exciting to think about all the new things they were going to see and do.
➡ _____

26 There was one new thing Rada and Jonny really wanted to do.
➡ _____

27 They thought about it all night and didn't tell Mom and Dad about it.
➡ _____

28 It was their secret.
➡ _____

29 The next day, Rada's family got on a spaceship.
➡ _____

30 "It's going to be a long trip," said Mom.
➡ _____

31 That's alright. I'm so excited!" said Rada.
➡ _____

32 The spaceship finally landed.
➡ _____

33 "Dad, it's difficult to walk on Earth," said Rada.
➡ _____

34 "I know. Earth is pulling you down," said Dad.
➡ _____

35 Rada and Jonny couldn't float anymore.
➡ _____

36 That was the first new thing.
➡ _____

37 "What's that sound?" asked Rada.
➡ _____

38 "A bird is singing," said Mom.
➡ _____

39 "I've never heard a bird sing," said Rada.
➡ _____

40 "And I've never felt the wind," said Jonny.
➡ _____

41 These were all new things.
➡ _____

42 Rada and Jonny ran up the nearest hill.
➡ _____

43 At the top, they looked at each other and laughed.
➡ _____

44 Then they lay down on the soft green grass and rolled down the hill.
➡ _____

45 That was their secret!
➡ _____

46 "This is the best new thing of all!" shouted Rada and Jonny.
➡ _____

47 And they ran up to the top of the hill again.
➡ _____

※ 다음 괄호 안의 단어들을 우리말에 맞도록 바르게 배열하시오.

1 (Best / Thing / New / The)
➡ _____

2 (lived / Rada / a / on / world, / little / out / far / space. / in)
➡ _____

3 (there / lived / she / with / father, / her / and / mother, / Jonny. / brother)
➡ _____

4 (father / Rada's / and / people / other / on / spaceships. / worked)
➡ _____

5 (Rada / only / and / were / Jonny / children, / and / were / they / space. / in / born)
➡ _____

6 (day, / one / told / Dad / Rada / Jonny, / and / "we're / back / going / to / tomorrow." / Earth)
➡ _____

7 (Jonny / and / Rada / at / looked / Dad / surprise / in / and / him. / towards / floated)
➡ _____

8 (asked / Rada / Dad, / it / "what's / on / Earth?" / like)
➡ _____

9 (is / "everything / there. / different)
➡ _____

10 (example, / for / sky / the / blue," / is / Dad. / answered)
➡ _____

11 (never / "I've / seen / a / sky," / blue / Jonny. / said)
➡ _____

12 (sky / "the / always / is / here," / black / Rada. / said)
➡ _____

13 (don't / "you / to / wear / have / big / your / heavy / suits / space / because / is / there / everywhere. / air)
➡ _____
_____

14 (also / it's / to / hard / jump / there / Earth / because / pulls / down," / you / Dad. / said)
➡ _____

15 (else?" / "what / Rada. / asked)
➡ _____

16 (are / "there / hills, / and / are / they / with / covered / soft / grass. / green)
➡ _____

1 최고의 새로운 것

2 Rada는 먼 우주의 작은 세계에 살고 있었다.

3 그녀는 아빠, 엄마 그리고 남동생 Jonny와 함께 그곳에서 살고 있었다.

4 Rada의 아빠와 다른 사람들은 우주선에서 일했다.

5 Rada와 Jonny만이 아이들이었고, 그들은 우주에서 태어났다.

6 어느 날, 아빠가 Rada와 Jonny에게, "우리는 내일 지구로 돌아갈 거야."라고 말했다.

7 Rada와 Jonny는 깜짝 놀라 아빠를 바라보았고, 그에게 둥둥 떠서 갔다.

8 Rada가 아빠에게, "지구는 어떤 곳인가요?"라고 물었다.

9 "그곳에선 모든 것이 다르단다.

10 예를 들어, 하늘은 파란색이지."라고 아빠가 대답했다.

11 "전 한 번도 파란 하늘을 본 적이 없어요."라고 Jonny가 말했다.

12 "여기는 하늘이 항상 검은색이잖아요."라고 Rada가 말했다.

13 "그곳에는 모든 곳에 공기가 있기 때문에 크고 무거운 우주복을 입을 필요가 없단다.

14 또한 지구가 너희들을 끌어당기기 때문에 거기에서는 점프하는 것도 어렵단다." 아빠가 말했다.

15 "그 밖에 또 뭐가 있어요?" Rada가 물었다.

16 "언덕들이 있는데 그것들은 부드러운 초록색의 잔디로 뒤덮여 있단다.

17 (you / roll / can / down / hills," / the / Mom. / answered)

➡ _____

18 (have / "Dad / ever / you / down / rolled / hill?" / a / Rada. / asked)

➡ _____

19 ("yes, / really / it's / amazing!" Dad. / answered)

➡ _____

20 (was / Jonny / thirsty, / he / so / opened / a / container / milk / and / it. / shook)

➡ _____

21 (milk / the / in / floated / the / air / and / balls. / formed)

➡ _____

22 (swallowed / Jonny / balls. / the)

➡ _____

23 ("Jonny, / you / if / milk / drink / way / that / Earth, / on / get / you'll / wet," / Mom. / said)

➡ _____

24 (that / later / night, / Jonny / and / Rada / talked / long / a / Earth. / about / time)

➡ _____

25 (was / it / exciting / think / to / all / about / new / the / things / were / they / going / see / do. / and / to)

➡ _____

26 (was / there / new / one / Rada / thing / and / really / Jonny / do. / to / wanted)

➡ _____

27 (thought / they / it / about / night / all / and / didn't / Mom / tell / and / it. / about / Dad)

➡ _____

28 (was / it / secret. / their)

➡ _____

29 (next / the / day, / family / Rada's / on / got / spaceship. / a)

➡ _____

30 (going / "it's / be / to / long / a / trip," Mom. / said)

➡ _____

31 (alright. / "that's // so / I'm / excited!" Rada. / said)

➡ _____

32 (spaceship / the / landed. / finally)

➡ _____

17 언덕을 굴러 내려갈 수도 있어." 엄마가 대답했다.

18 "아빠, 언덕을 굴러 내려가 본 적 있어요?" Rada가 물었다.

19 "그럼, 정말 놀라워!" 아빠가 대답했다.

20 Jonny는 목이 말라서 우유 용기를 열어 그것을 흔들었다.

21 우유가 공기 중으로 떠서 방울을 형성했다.

22 Jonny는 그 우유 방울을 삼켰다.

23 "Jonny, 만약 네가 지구에서 그런 식으로 우유를 마신다면, 다 젖을 거야." 엄마가 말했다.

24 그날 밤 늦게, Rada와 Jonny는 지구에 대해서 오랜 시간 이야기했다.

25 그들이 보고, 하게 될 모든 새로운 것들을 생각하는 것은 흥미로웠다.

26 Rada와 Jonny가 정말로 하고 싶었던 한 가지 새로운 것이 있었다.

27 그들은 밤새 그것에 대해서 생각했고 엄마와 아빠에게는 그것을 말하지 않았다.

28 그것은 그들의 비밀이었다.

29 다음날, Rada의 가족은 우주선에 올랐다.

30 "긴 여행이 될 거야." 엄마가 말했다.

31 "괜찮아요. 정말 신나요!" Rada가 말했다.

32 우주선이 마침내 착륙했다.

33 ("Dad, / difficult / it's / walk / to / Eaeth," / on / Rada. / said)

➡ _____

34 (know. / "I / is / Earth / you / pulling / down," / Dad. / said)

➡ _____

35 (Jonny / and / Rada / couldn't / anymore. / float)

➡ _____

36 (was / that / first / the / thing. / new)

➡ _____

37 ("what's / sound?" / that / Rada. / asked)

➡ _____

38 (bird / "a / singing," / is / Mom. / said)

➡ _____

39 (never / "I've / heard / bird / a / sing," / Rada. / said)

➡ _____

40 ("and / never / I've / felt / wind," / the / Jonny. / said)

➡ _____

41 (were / these / new / things. / all)

➡ _____

42 (Jonny / and / Rada / up / ran / nearest / the / hill.)

➡ _____

43 (the / at / top, / looked / they / each / at / other / laughed. / and)

➡ _____

44 (they / then / down / lay / the / on / green / soft / grass / and / down / rolled / hill. / the)

➡ _____

45 (was / that / secret! / their)

➡ _____

46 (is / "this / best / the / thing / new / all!" / of / Rada / shouted / Jonny. / and)

➡ _____

47 (and / ran / they / up / the / to / top / of / hill / again. / the)

➡ _____

33 "아빠, 지구에서는 걷는 것이 어려워요." Rada가 말했다.

34 "그래. 지구가 너를 끌어당기고 있거든." 아빠가 말했다.

35 Rada와 Jonny는 더 이상 떠다닐 수 없었다.

36 그것이 첫 번째 새로운 것이었다.

37 "저건 무슨 소리죠?"라고 Rada가 물었다.

38 "새가 노래하는 거야." 엄마가 말했다.

39 "새가 노래하는 것을 들어 본 적이 없어요."라고 Rada가 말했다.

40 "그리고 저는 바람을 느껴 본 적도 없어요."라고 Jonny가 말했다.

41 이러한 것들이 모두 새로운 것들이었다.

42 Rada와 Jonny는 가장 가까운 언덕으로 뛰어 올라갔다.

43 꼭대기에서, 그들은 서로를 쳐다보고 웃었다.

44 그리고 나서 그들은 부드러운 초록 잔디에 누워서 언덕 아래로 굴러 내려갔다.

45 그것이 그들의 비밀이었다!

46 "이것이 모든 것들 중에서 최고의 새로운 것이에요!" Rada와 Jonny는 외쳤다.

47 그리고 그들은 언덕 꼭대기로 다시 뛰어 올라갔다.

18 Lesson 7. Life in Space

※ 다음 우리말을 영어로 쓰시오.

1 최고의 새로운 것
➡ _____

2 Rada는 먼 우주의 작은 세계에 살고 있었다.
➡ _____

3 그녀는 아빠, 엄마 그리고 남동생 Jonny와 함께 그곳에서 살고 있었다.
➡ _____

4 Rada의 아빠와 다른 사람들은 우주선에서 일했다.
➡ _____

5 Rada와 Jonny만이 아이들이었고, 그들은 우주에서 태어났다.
➡ _____

6 어느 날, 아빠가 Rada와 Jonny에게, "우리는 내일 지구로 돌아갈 거야."라고 말했다.
➡ _____

7 Rada와 Jonny는 깜짝 놀라 아빠를 바라보았고, 그에게 둥둥 떠서 갔다.
➡ _____

8 Rada가 아빠에게, "지구는 어떤 곳인가요?"라고 물었다.
➡ _____

9 "그곳에선 모든 것이 다르단다.
➡ _____

10 예를 들어, 하늘은 파란색이지."라고 아빠가 대답했다.
➡ _____

11 "전 한 번도 파란 하늘을 본 적이 없어요."라고 Jonny가 말했다.
➡ _____

12 "여기는 하늘이 항상 검은색이잖아요."라고 Rada가 말했다.
➡ _____

13 "그곳에는 모든 곳에 공기가 있기 때문에 크고 무거운 우주복을 입을 필요가 없단다.
➡ _____

14 또한 지구가 너희들을 끌어당기기 때문에 거기에서는 점프하는 것도 어렵단다." 아빠가 말했다.
➡ _____

15 "그 밖에 또 뭐가 있어요?" Rada가 물었다.
➡ _____

16 "언덕들이 있는데 그것들은 부드러운 초록색의 잔디로 뒤덮여 있단다.
➡ _____

17 언덕을 굴러 내려갈 수도 있어." 엄마가 대답했다.
➡ _____

18 "아빠, 언덕을 굴러 내려가 본 적 있어요?" Rada가 물었다.
➡ _____

19 "그럼, 정말 놀라워!" 아빠가 대답했다.
➡ _____

20 Jonny는 목이 말라서 우유 용기를 열어 그것을 흔들었다.
➡ _____

21 우유가 공기 중으로 떠서 방울을 형성했다.
➡ _____

22 Jonny는 그 우유 방울을 삼켰다.
➡ _____

23 "Jonny, 만약 네가 지구에서 그런 식으로 우유를 마신다면, 다 젖을 거야." 엄마가 말했다.
➡ _____

24 그날 밤 늦게, Rada와 Jonny는 지구에 대해서 오랜 시간 이야기했다.
➡ _____

25 그들이 보고, 하게 될 모든 새로운 것들을 생각하는 것은 흥미로웠다.
➡ _____

26 Rada와 Jonny가 정말로 하고 싶었던 한 가지 새로운 것이 있었다.
➡ _____

27 그들은 밤새 그것에 대해서 생각했고 엄마와 아빠에게는 그것을 말하지 않았다.
➡ _____

28 그것은 그들의 비밀이었다.
➡ _____

29 다음날, Rada의 가족은 우주선에 올랐다.
➡ _____

30 "긴 여행이 될 거야." 엄마가 말했다.
➡ _____

31 "괜찮아요. 정말 신나요!" Rada가 말했다.
➡ _____

32 우주선이 마침내 착륙했다.
➡ _____

33 "아빠, 지구에서는 걷는 것이 어려워요." Rada가 말했다.
➡ _____

34 "그래. 지구가 너를 끌어당기고 있거든." 아빠가 말했다.
➡ _____

35 Rada와 Jonny는 더 이상 떠다닐 수 없었다.
➡ _____

36 그것이 첫 번째 새로운 것이었다.
➡ _____

37 "저건 무슨 소리죠?"라고 Rada가 물었다.
➡ _____

38 "새가 노래하는 거야." 엄마가 말했다.
➡ _____

39 "새가 노래하는 것을 들어 본 적이 없어요."라고 Rada가 말했다.
➡ _____

40 "그리고 저는 바람을 느껴 본 적도 없어요."라고 Jonny가 말했다.
➡ _____

41 이러한 것들이 모두 새로운 것들이었다.
➡ _____

42 Rada와 Jonny는 가장 가까운 언덕으로 뛰어 올라갔다.
➡ _____

43 꼭대기에서, 그들은 서로를 쳐다보고 웃었다.
➡ _____

44 그러고 나서 그들은 부드러운 초록 잔디에 누워서 언덕 아래로 굴러 내려갔다.
➡ _____

45 그것이 그들의 비밀이었다!
➡ _____

46 "이것이 모든 것들 중에서 최고의 새로운 것이에요!" Rada와 Jonny는 외쳤다.
➡ _____

47 그리고 그들은 언덕 꼭대기로 다시 뛰어 올라갔다.
➡ _____

※ 다음 우리말과 일치하도록 빈칸에 알맞은 말을 쓰시오.

One Minute Speech

1. Did you _____ _____ the new book, *Dave's Adventures*?

2. This book _____ _____ Dave and his _____ in the _____.

3. The _____ _____ are Dave and a big bear. The story is fun.

4. _____ you _____ _____ the book?

5. Then you _____ _____ it!

1. 새 책인 Dave의 모험에 관해 들어 봤니?
2. 이 책은 Dave와 숲에서의 그의 모험에 관한 거야.
3. 주인공은 Dave와 큰 곰이야. 이야기가 재미있어.
4. 그 책에 관해 궁금하니?
5. 그러면 그것을 꼭 읽어 봐야 해!

Read and Complete

1. Rada's family lived in space. One day, they _____ _____ _____ _____ to Earth.

2. Rada's family talked about life on Earth. They talked about the blue sky and hills which _____ _____ _____ green grass.

3. The next day, Rada's family _____ _____ a spaceship. It was _____ _____ _____ to Earth.

4. When they _____ _____ Earth, Rada and Jonny _____ _____ the nearest hill and _____ _____ it. That was _____ _____ _____ to them.

1. Rada의 가족은 우주에서 살고 있었다. 어느 날, 그들은 지구로 돌아가기로 결정했다.
2. Rada의 가족은 지구의 생활에 대해 이야기했다. 그들은 파란 하늘과 초록색 잔디로 뒤덮인 언덕에 대해 이야기했다.
3. 다음날, Rada의 가족은 우주선에 올랐다. 그것은 지구로의 긴 여행이었다.
4. 그들이 지구에 도착했을 때, Rada와 Jonny는 가장 가까운 언덕으로 뛰어 올라가 아래로 굴러 내려갔다. 그것은 그들에게 최고의 새로운 것이었다.

Around the World

1. Russia _____ the first dog _____ _____. It was small, and _____ _____ was Laika.

2. Yuri Gagarin _____ _____ space _____ _____ _____ _____.

3. The USA _____ the _____ _____ _____ _____ the moon. His name was Neil Armstrong.

4. Russia _____ the first space station. It _____ _____ the Earth _____ 3,000 times.

1. 러시아는 우주에 최초의 개를 보냈다. 그것은 작았고, 이름은 Laika였다.
2. Yuri Gagarin이 최초로 우주에 갔다.
3. 미국은 달에 최초의 인간을 보냈다. 그의 이름은 Neil Armstrong이었다.
4. 러시아가 최초의 우주정거장을 건설하였다. 그것은 거의 3천 번 지구 주변을 돌았다.

※ 다음 우리말을 영어로 쓰시오.

One Minute Speech

1. 새 책인 Dave의 모험에 관해 들어 봤니?
➡ _____

2. 이 책은 Dave와 숲에서의 그의 모험에 관한 거야.
➡ _____

3. 주인공은 Dave와 큰 곰이야. 이야기가 재미있어.
➡ _____

4. 그 책에 관해 궁금하니?
➡ _____

5. 그러면 그것을 꼭 읽어 봐야 해!
➡ _____

Read and Complete

1. Rada의 가족은 우주에서 살고 있었다. 어느 날, 그들은 지구로 돌아가기로 결정했다.
➡ _____

2. Rada의 가족은 지구의 생활에 대해 이야기했다. 그들은 파란 하늘과 초록색 잔디로 뒤덮인 언덕에 대해 이야기했다.
➡ _____
_____

3. 다음날, Rada의 가족은 우주선에 올랐다. 그것은 지구로의 긴 여행이었다.
➡ _____

4. 그들이 지구에 도착했을 때, Rada와 Jonny는 가장 가까운 언덕으로 뛰어 올라가 아래로 굴러 내려갔다. 그것은 그들에게 최고의 새로운 것이었다.
➡ _____
_____

Around the World

1. 러시아는 우주에 최초의 개를 보냈다. 그것은 작았고, 이름은 Laika였다.
➡ _____

2. Yuri Gagarin이 최초로 우주에 갔다.
➡ _____

3. 미국은 달에 최초의 인간을 보냈다. 그의 이름은 Neil Armstrong이었다.
➡ _____

4. 러시아가 최초의 우주정거장을 건설하였다. 그것은 거의 3천 번 지구 주변을 돌았다.
➡ _____

※ 다음 영어를 우리말로 쓰시오.

01 college

02 grass

03 display

04 exhibition

05 fan dance

06 continue

07 abroad

08 treasure

09 army

10 behind

11 research

12 wedding

13 storm

14 researcher

15 allow

16 traditional

17 museum

18 fitting room

19 government

20 result

21 historian

22 printing

23 instrument

24 succeed

25 value

26 royal

27 finally

28 pride

29 prove

30 delicious

31 steal

32 publish

33 difficulty

34 whole

35 because of+명사

36 give up

37 be full of

38 would like to+동사원형

39 as soon as+주어+동사

40 try on

41 right away

42 thanks to

43 spend+시간+ -ing

※ 다음 우리말을 영어로 쓰시오.

01	해외에서, 해외로	_____
02	자부심, 긍지	_____
03	정부	_____
04	대학	_____
05	맛있는	_____
06	성공하다	_____
07	허락하다, 허용하다	_____
08	반환	_____
09	입증하다, 증명하다	_____
10	왕실의	_____
11	박람회, 전시회	_____
12	어려움	_____
13	전시	_____
14	역사학자	_____
15	보물	_____
16	계속하다	_____
17	악기	_____
18	폭풍	_____
19	마침내, 결국	_____
20	연구가	_____
21	탈의실	_____
22	결과, 결실	_____
23	해고하다	_____
24	금속	_____
25	전통적인	_____
26	도둑질하다, 훔치다	_____
27	군대	_____
28	소리, 소음	_____
29	100만, 수많은	_____
30	결혼식	_____
31	출판하다, 발행하다	_____
32	연구, 조사	_____
33	도둑	_____
34	가치	_____
35	~ 덕분에	_____
36	~하자마자	_____
37	바로, 즉시	_____
38	~을 입어 보다	_____
39	포기하다	_____
40	~하면서 시간을 보내다	_____
41	~ 때문에	_____
42	~로 가득 차 있다	_____
43	~을 찾다	_____

※ 다음 영영풀이에 알맞은 단어를 <보기>에서 골라 쓴 후, 우리말 뜻을 쓰시오.

1 _____ : to use time doing something: _____

2 _____ : in or to a foreign country: _____

3 _____ : to show that something is true: _____

4 _____ : a feeling of satisfaction and pleasure in what you have done: _____

5 _____ : to say that someone can do something: _____

6 _____ : the work of finding out facts about something: _____

7 _____ : something that happens because of something else: _____

8 _____ : to do something that you tried or aimed to do: _____

9 _____ : relating to or belonging to a king or queen: _____

10 _____ : to take something that belongs to someone else: _____

11 _____ : to try to find someone or something by looking very carefully: _____

12 _____ : a group of valuable things, especially gold, silver, or jewels: _____

13 _____ : to print a book, magazine, or newspaper for people to buy: _____

14 _____ : the group of people who are responsible for controlling a country or state: _____

15 _____ : a bright light on a camera that flashes as you take a photograph in order to provide enough light: _____

16 _____ : a room in a clothes shop where you can put on clothes before you buy them: _____

보기

flash	abroad	allow	succeed
prove	fitting room	government	treasure
royal	pride	result	search
spend	steal	publish	research

※ 다음 우리말과 일치하도록 빈칸에 알맞은 말을 쓰시오.

Listen and Talk A-1

B: _____ me. What's this? _____ _____ _____ any food _____ this.

W: Oh, it's Tteok, a Korean _____.

B: _____ _____ _____ _____ _____ some?

W: Sure. _____ _____. It's really _____.

Listen and Talk A-2

G: Excuse me. Is it OK _____ _____ _____ _____?

M: You _____, on the grass?

G: Yes. Is it _____ _____?

M: I'm sorry, but _____ on the grass _____ _____ _____.

G: OK, I _____.

Listen and Talk A-3

B: Excuse me. What's this? It _____ _____.

W: Oh, that's a haegeum, a _____ Korean _____ _____.

B: _____ _____ _____ _____ _____ it?

W: _____ _____, but it's only _____ _____. _____ it is not _____.

B: I see.

Listen and Talk A-4

G: _____ me. _____ _____ _____ _____ _____ pictures here?

M: Yes, it's _____ _____.

G: _____ _____ _____ a flash? Can I use it, _____?

M: I'm _____ _____. _____ a flash is _____ _____ here.

G: Oh, I see. Thank you.

Listen and Talk B

A: _____ _____ _____ _____ _____ _____ _____?

B: I'm _____ _____. _____ is _____ _____ here.

A: Oh, I see.

B: 실례합니다. 이것이 무엇인가요? 저는 이런 음식을 본 적이 없어요.
W: 오, 그것은 한국의 후식인 떡이에요.
B: 먹어 봐도 될까요?
W: 물론이죠. 그렇게 하세요. 정말 맛있답니다.

G: 실례합니다. 저기에 앉아도 되나요?
M: 잔디 위를 말하는 건가요?
G: 네. 괜찮은가요?
M: 미안하지만, 잔디 위에 앉는 것은 허락되지 않습니다.
G: 알겠습니다, 이해합니다.

B: 실례합니다. 이것은 무엇인가요? 흥미롭게 생겼네요.
W: 오, 그것은 한국의 전통 악기인 해금이에요.
B: 연주를 해 봐도 될까요?
W: 미안하지만, 전시용입니다. 연주를 하는 것은 허락되지 않습니다.
B: 알겠습니다.

G: 실례합니다. 여기서 사진을 찍어도 되나요?
M: 네, 괜찮습니다.
G: 플래시를 사용하는 것은 어떤가요? 사용해도 되나요?
M: 안 될 것 같아요. 플래시를 사용하는 것은 여기서 허용되지 않습니다.
G: 오, 알겠어요. 감사합니다.

A: 여기 앉아도 될까요?
B: 안 될 것 같아요. 여기에 앉는 것은 허용되지 않습니다.
A: 오, 알겠습니다.

Talk and Play

A: _____ place do you want _____ _____ first in the museum?

B: _____ _____ _____ guess?

A: OK. _____ _____ _____ _____ _____ food there?

B: Yes. _____ _____ is _____.

A: _____ _____ _____ _____ _____ pictures?

B: No. Taking pictures _____ _____ _____.

A: I _____ _____. You're _____ _____ _____ to the Video Room.

B: You're right.

Listen and Talk C

G: Excuse me, but _____ _____ _____ to try on this hanbok?

M: Sure. The _____ _____ is _____ _____.

G: Thanks. Wait a _____. That's also very pretty.

M: Oh, the little hat _____ _____?

G: Yes. What is it?

M: It's a jokduri, a _____ Korean hat _____ _____. It's usually _____ on a _____ day.

G: Really? _____ _____ _____ _____ _____ _____ _____, too?

M: I'm sorry, but it's only _____ _____. Trying it _____ is _____ _____.

G: Oh. Then, I'll just _____ _____ this hanbok.

Review 1

G: _____ _____. What's this? It _____ _____.

B: Oh, that's a janggu, a _____ Korean _____ _____.

G: _____ _____ _____ _____ play it?

B: I'm sorry, but it's only _____ _____. Playing it is not _____.

G: I see.

Review 2

G: Excuse me, but _____ _____ _____ to take pictures here?

M: Yes. Go _____.

G: _____ _____ _____ a flash, _____?

M: Yes. That's _____ OK.

G: I'm sorry, _____ I have _____ _____ question. Can I eat food here?

M: I'm sorry, but that's _____ _____.

A: 박물관에서 어떤 장소를 먼저 가고 싶니?

B: 알아맞혀 볼래?

A: 좋아. 거기에서 음식을 먹어도 되니?

B: 응. 음식을 먹는 것은 허용돼.

A: 사진을 찍어도 되니?

B: 아니. 사진을 찍는 것은 허용되지 않아.

A: 알겠다. 너는 Video Room에 갈 생각이구나.

B: 맞아.

G: 실례지만, 이 한복을 입어 봐도 될까요?

M: 물론이죠. 탈의실은 저쪽입니다.

G: 고마워요. 잠깐만요. 저것도 매우 예쁘네요.

M: 오, 저기 있는 작은 모자요?

G: 네. 그건 뭔가요?

M: 그것은 여자들이 쓰는 한국 전통 모자인 족두리예요. 주로 결혼식 날 쓰죠.

G: 정말요? 그것도 써 봐도 될까요?

M: 죄송하지만, 그것은 전시만 하는 거예요. 써 보시는 건 안 돼요.

G: 오. 그럼, 그냥 이 한복만 입어 볼게요.

G: 실례합니다. 이것은 무엇인가요? 흥미로워 보이네요.

B: 오, 저것은 한국의 전통 악기인 장구예요.

G: 연주해 봐도 되나요?

B: 미안하지만, 전시용이에요. 연주하는 것은 허용되지 않아요.

G: 알겠어요.

G: 실례합니다만, 여기서 사진을 찍어도 되나요?

M: 네. 그렇게 하세요.

G: 플래시를 사용해도 되나요?

M: 네. 그것도 괜찮습니다.

G: 죄송하지만, 질문이 하나 더 있어요. 여기서 음식을 먹어도 되나요?

M: 미안하지만, 그것은 허용되지 않습니다.

※ 다음 우리말에 맞도록 대화를 영어로 쓰시오.

Listen and Talk A-1

B: _____

W: _____

B: _____

W: _____

B: 실례합니다. 이것이 무엇인가요? 저는 이런 음식을 본 적이 없어요.
W: 오, 그것은 한국의 후식인 떡이에요.
B: 먹어 봐도 될까요?
W: 물론이죠. 그렇게 하세요. 정말 맛있답니다.

Listen and Talk A-2

G: _____

M: _____

G: _____

M: _____

G: _____

G: 실례합니다. 저기에 앉아도 되나요?
M: 잔디 위를 말하는 건가요?
G: 네. 괜찮은가요?
M: 미안하지만, 잔디 위에 앉는 것은 허락되지 않습니다.
G: 알겠습니다, 이해합니다.

Listen and Talk A-3

B: _____

W: _____

B: _____

W: _____

B: _____

B: 실례합니다. 이것은 무엇인가요? 흥미롭게 생겼네요.
W: 오, 그것은 한국의 전통 악기인 해금이에요.
B: 연주를 해 봐도 될까요?
W: 미안하지만, 전시용입니다. 연주를 하는 것은 허락되지 않습니다.
B: 알겠습니다.

Listen and Talk A-4

G: _____

M: _____

G: _____

M: _____

G: _____

G: 실례합니다. 여기서 사진을 찍어도 되나요?
M: 네, 괜찮습니다.
G: 플래시를 사용하는 것은 어떤가요? 사용해도 되나요?
M: 안 될 것 같아요. 플래시를 사용하는 것은 여기서 허용되지 않습니다.
G: 오, 알겠어요. 감사합니다.

Listen and Talk B

A: _____

B: _____

A: _____

A: 여기 앉아도 될까요?
B: 안 될 것 같아요. 여기에 앉는 것은 허용되지 않습니다.
A: 오, 알겠습니다.

Talk and Play

A: _____

B: _____

A: _____

B: _____

A: _____

B: _____

A: _____

B: _____

A: 박물관에서 어떤 장소를 먼저 가고 싶니?
B: 알아맞혀 볼래?
A: 좋아. 거기에서 음식을 먹어도 되니?
B: 응. 음식을 먹는 것은 허용돼.
A: 사진을 찍어도 되니?
B: 아니. 사진을 찍는 것은 허용되지 않아.
A: 알겠다. 너는 Video Room에 갈 생각이구나.
B: 맞아.

Listen and Talk C

G: _____

M: _____

G: _____

M: _____

G: _____

M: _____

G: _____

M: _____

G: _____

G: 실례지만, 이 한복을 입어 봐도 될까요?
M: 물론이죠. 탈의실은 저쪽입니다.
G: 고마워요. 잠깐만요. 저것도 매우 예쁘네요.
M: 오, 저기 있는 작은 모자요?
G: 네. 그건 뭔가요?
M: 그것은 여자들이 쓰는 한국 전통 모자인 족두리예요. 주로 결혼식 날 쓰죠.
G: 정말요? 그것도 써 봐도 될까요?
M: 죄송하지만, 그것은 전시만 하는 거예요. 써 보시는 건 안 돼요.
G: 오. 그럼, 그냥 이 한복만 입어 볼게요.

Review 1

G: _____

B: _____

G: _____

B: _____

G: _____

G: 실례합니다. 이것은 무엇인가요? 흥미로워 보이네요.
B: 오, 저것은 한국의 전통 악기인 장구예요.
G: 연주해 봐도 되나요?
B: 미안하지만, 전시용이에요. 연주하는 것은 허용되지 않아요.
G: 알겠어요.

Review 2

G: _____

M: _____

G: _____

M: _____

G: _____

M: _____

G: 실례합니다만, 여기서 사진을 찍어도 되나요?
M: 네. 그렇게 하세요.
G: 플래시를 사용해도 되나요?
M: 네. 그것도 괜찮습니다.
G: 죄송하지만, 질문이 하나 더 있어요. 여기서 음식을 먹어도 되나요?
M: 미안하지만, 그것은 허용되지 않습니다.

※ 다음 우리말과 일치하도록 빈칸에 알맞은 것을 골라 쓰시오.

1 An _____ _____ Dr. Park Byeong-seon
A. with   B. Interview

2 _____ May 27, 2011, 297 books of *Uigwe*, a _____ of royal books the French army _____ in 1866, came _____ to Korea.
A. back   B. on   C. collection   D. took

3 The person _____ this _____ is Dr. Park Byeong-seon, a historian who spent her whole life _____ for Korean national treasures _____.
A. return   B. abroad   C. behind   D. searching

4 Q: Can you tell me _____ you _____ _____ in *Uigwe*?
A. interested   B. how   C. became

5 Dr. Park: I _____ _____ in _____.
A. college   B. history   C. studied

6 I went to France _____ _____ my _____ in 1955.
A. continue   B. studies   C. to

7 _____ you know, the French _____ took many of our national _____ in 1866.
A. treasures   B. as   C. army

8 I wanted to _____ them _____ I was _____ there.
A. while   B. find   C. studying

9 *Uigwe* was _____ _____ _____.
A. them   B. one   C. of

10 Q: You _____ 297 _____ of *Uigwe* in the National Library of France, _____ Paris.
A. books   B. found   C. in

11 Please _____ me _____ you _____ them.
A. how   B. tell   C. found

12 Dr. Park: _____ _____ as I became a researcher at the National Library in 1967, I began to _____ _____ *Uigwe*.
A. for   B. soon   C. look   D. as

13 _____ 10 years, in 1977, I _____ _____ the books.
A. finally   B. after   C. found

14 I think I _____ _____ more _____ 30 _____ books.
A. million   B. than   C. at   D. looked

15 Q: I'm _____ you were very _____ when you _____ the books.
A. excited   B. found   C. sure

16 Dr. Park: Yes, I was, but _____ _____ were _____ _____ me.
A. for   B. difficulties   C. more   D. waiting

17 I _____ that the books _____ be _____ to Korea, _____ my bosses at the library didn't like that idea.
A. returned   B. thought   C. should   D. but

1 박병선 박사와의 인터뷰

2 2011년 5월 27일에 프랑스군이 1866년에 가져갔던 왕실 서적인 "의궤" 297권이 한국으로 돌아왔다.

3 이 반환 뒤에 있는 인물이 해외에 있는 한국의 문화재를 찾기 위해 전 생애를 바친 역사학자 박병선 박사이다.

4 Q: "의궤"에 어떻게 관심을 갖게 되셨는지 말씀해 주시겠어요?

5 Dr. Park: 저는 대학에서 역사를 공부했어요.

6 저는 1955년에 학업을 계속하기 위해 프랑스에 갔습니다.

7 아시다시피, 프랑스군은 1866년에 우리 문화재를 많이 가져갔어요.

8 저는 그곳에서 공부하는 동안 그것들을 찾고 싶었어요.

9 "의궤"는 그것들 중의 하나였어요.

10 Q: 당신은 파리에 있는 프랑스 국립도서관에서 297권의 "의궤"를 발견하셨어요.

11 그것들을 어떻게 발견하셨는지 말씀해 주세요.

12 Dr. Park: 1967년에 국립도서관의 연구원이 되자마자, 저는 "의궤"를 찾기 시작했어요.

13 10년 후인 1977년에 마침내 그 책들을 발견했죠.

14 제 생각에 3천만 권 이상의 책을 본 것 같아요.

15 Q: 그 책들을 발견했을 때 무척 흥분하셨겠어요.

16 Dr. Park: 네, 하지만 더 큰 어려움이 저를 기다리고 있었어요.

17 저는 그 책들이 한국에 반환되어야 한다고 생각했지만, 도서관의 제 상사들은 그 생각을 좋아하지 않았어요.

18 They _____ _____ that I was a Korean spy and _____ me.

    A. fired   B. thought   C. even

19 After that, I had to go to the library _____ a visitor, _____ it was not easy to _____ research _____ *Uigwe*.

    A. as   B. on   C. so   D. do

20 _____, I didn't _____ _____.

    A. give   B. however   C. up

21 For _____ than ten years, I went to the library _____ day _____ finish my _____.

    A. every   B. research   C. to   D. more

22 I _____ to _____ people the _____ of *Uigwe*.

    A. show   B. wanted   C. value

23 Q: The _____ of your _____ were _____ _____ a book in Korea in 1990.

    A. as   B. results   C. published   D. research

24 Many Koreans became _____ _____ *Uigwe* _____ _____ your book.

    A. because   B. interested   C. of   D. in

25 Dr. Park: Yes. In 1992, the Korean government _____ the French government _____ its _____ and, _____, the 297 books are here now.

    A. for   B. finally   C. asked   D. return

26 Q: Before I _____ this interview, I'd _____ to ask you about *Jikji*, a book that _____ the history of _____.

    A. printing   B. changed   C. like   D. finish

27 Dr. Park: I _____ it _____ my first _____ at the library.

    A. year   B. in   C. found

28 I knew _____ _____ that it was very _____.

    A. special   B. away   C. right

29 I worked _____ to _____ its _____ and finally _____.

    A. succeeded   B. value   C. prove   D. hard

30 At a book _____ in Paris in 1972, *Jikji* was _____ _____ the oldest book in the world that was printed with movable _____ type.

    A. displayed   B. metal   C. exhibition   D. as

31 Q: Dr. Park, _____ _____ your hard work, *Jikji* and *Uigwe* were found, and all Koreans _____ you _____ that.

    A. thank   B. to   C. for   D. thanks

32 Dr. Park: I hope people will become more _____ in our national _____ _____ and work for their _____.

    A. treasures   B. return   C. interested   D. abroad

---

18 그들은 심지어 제가 한국의 스파이라고 생각했고 저를 해고했죠.

19 그 후에, 저는 방문객으로 도서관에 가야만 했고, 그래서 "의궤"를 연구하는 것이 쉽지 않았어요.

20 하지만 저는 포기하지 않았죠.

21 10년 넘게, 연구를 끝마치기 위해 매일 도서관에 갔어요.

22 저는 사람들에게 "의궤"의 가치를 보여 주고 싶었어요.

23 Q: 당신의 연구 결과가 1990년 한국에서 책으로 출판되었죠.

24 많은 한국인들이 당신의 책 때문에 "의궤"에 관심을 갖게 되었어요.

25 Dr. Park: 네. 1992년에 한국 정부는 프랑스 정부에 그것의 반환을 요청했고, 마침내 297권의 책이 지금 여기 있게 된 거죠.

26 Q: 인터뷰를 마치기 전에, 인쇄의 역사를 바꾼 책인 "직지"에 대해 여쭙고 싶어요.

27 Dr. Park: 저는 도서관에서 근무한 첫해에 그것을 발견했어요.

28 그것이 아주 특별하다는 것을 바로 알았어요.

29 저는 그것의 가치를 증명하기 위해 열심히 연구했고 마침내 성공했죠.

30 1972년에 파리 도서 박람회에서 "직지"는 금속 활자로 인쇄된 세계에서 가장 오래된 책으로 전시되었죠.

31 Q: 박 박사님, 당신의 노고 덕분에 "직지"와 "의궤"가 발견되었고, 모든 한국인들이 그 점을 당신에게 감사하고 있어요.

32 Dr. Park: 저는 사람들이 해외에 있는 우리의 문화재에 더 많은 관심을 갖고 그것의 반환을 위해 애써 주시기를 바랍니다.

※ 다음 우리말과 일치하도록 빈칸에 알맞은 말을 쓰시오.

1 An _____ _____ Dr. Park Byeong-seon

2 _____ May 27, 2011, 297 books of *Uigwe*, _____ _____ _____ _____ _____ the French army took in 1866, _____ _____ _____ Korea.

3 The person _____ _____ _____ is Dr. Park Byeong-seon, a historian who _____ her _____ _____ _____ _____ Korean national treasures _____.

4 Q: Can you tell me _____ you _____ _____ _____ *Uigwe*?

5 Dr. Park: I _____ _____ _____ _____ .

6 I went to France _____ _____ my studies in 1955.

7 _____ _____ _____ , the French army took many of our _____ _____ in 1866.

8 I wanted to find them _____ I _____ _____ there.

9 *Uigwe* was _____ _____ _____ .

10 Q: You found _____ _____ in the _____ _____ of France, in Paris.

11 Please _____ _____ _____ you _____ them.

12 Dr. Park: _____ _____ _____ I became a _____ at the National Library in 1967, I began to _____ _____ *Uigwe*.

13 _____ 10 years, in 1977, I _____ _____ the books.

14 I think I _____ _____ more than _____ _____ books.

15 Q: _____ _____ you were very _____ when you found the books.

16 Dr. Park: Yes, I was, but _____ _____ were _____ me.

17 I thought that the books _____ _____ _____ _____ Korea, but my bosses at the library didn't like _____ _____ .

---

1 박병선 박사와의 인터뷰

2 2011년 5월 27일에 프랑스군이 1866년에 가져갔던 왕실 서적인 "의궤" 297권이 한국으로 돌아왔다.

3 이 반환 뒤에 있는 인물이 해외에 있는 한국의 문화재를 찾기 위해 전 생애를 바친 역사학자 박병선 박사이다.

4 Q: "의궤"에 어떻게 관심을 갖게 되셨는지 말씀해 주시겠어요?

5 Dr. Park: 저는 대학에서 역사를 공부했어요.

6 저는 1955년에 학업을 계속하기 위해 프랑스에 갔습니다.

7 아시다시피, 프랑스군은 1866년에 우리 문화재를 많이 가져갔어요.

8 저는 그곳에서 공부하는 동안 그것들을 찾고 싶었어요.

9 "의궤"는 그것들 중의 하나였어요.

10 Q: 당신은 파리에 있는 프랑스 국립도서관에서 297권의 "의궤"를 발견하셨어요.

11 그것들을 어떻게 발견하셨는지 말씀해 주세요.

12 Dr. Park: 1967년에 국립도서관의 연구원이 되자마자, 저는 "의궤"를 찾기 시작했어요.

13 10년 후인 1977년에 마침내 그 책들을 발견했죠.

14 제 생각에 3천만 권 이상의 책을 본 것 같아요.

15 Q: 그 책들을 발견했을 때 무척 흥분하셨겠어요.

16 Dr. Park: 네, 하지만 더 큰 어려움이 저를 기다리고 있었어요.

17 저는 그 책들이 한국에 반환되어야 한다고 생각했지만, 도서관의 제 상사들은 그 생각을 좋아하지 않았어요.

18 They _____ _____ that I was a Korean spy and _____ me.

19 After that, I had to go to the library _____ _____ _____, _____ it was not easy _____ _____ _____ _____ *Uigwe*.

20 _____, I didn't give up.

21 _____ _____ _____ ten years, I went to the library every day _____ _____ _____ _____ _____.

22 I wanted to show people _____ _____ _____ _____.

23 Q: The results of your research _____ _____ _____ a book in Korea in 1990.

24 Many Koreans _____ _____ _____ *Uigwe* _____ _____ your book.

25 Dr. Park: Yes. In 1992, the Korean government _____ the French government _____ _____ _____ and, finally, the 297 books _____ _____ _____.

26 Q: Before I finish this interview, _____ _____ _____ you about *Jikji*, a book that _____ the history of _____.

27 Dr. Park: I found it _____ _____ _____ _____ at the library.

28 I knew _____ _____ that it was _____ _____.

29 I worked hard _____ _____ _____ _____ and finally _____.

30 At a book exhibition in Paris in 1972, *Jikji* _____ _____ _____ the _____ _____ in the world that was printed with _____ _____ _____.

31 Q: Dr. Park, _____ _____ your hard work, *Jikji* and *Uigwe* were found, and all Koreans _____ you _____ that.

32 Dr. Park: I hope people will become more interested in _____ _____ _____ _____ and work for their _____.

18 그들은 심지어 제가 한국의 스파이라고 생각했고 저를 해고했죠.

19 그 후에, 저는 방문객으로 도서관에 가야만 했고, 그래서 "의궤"를 연구하는 것이 쉽지 않았어요.

20 하지만 저는 포기하지 않았죠.

21 10년 넘게, 연구를 끝마치기 위해 매일 도서관에 갔어요.

22 저는 사람들에게 "의궤"의 가치를 보여 주고 싶었어요.

23 Q: 당신의 연구 결과가 1990년 한국에서 책으로 출판되었죠.

24 많은 한국인들이 당신의 책 때문에 "의궤"에 관심을 갖게 되었어요.

25 Dr. Park: 네. 1992년에 한국 정부는 프랑스 정부에 그것의 반환을 요청했고, 마침내 297권의 책이 지금 여기 있게 된 거죠.

26 Q: 인터뷰를 마치기 전에, 인쇄의 역사를 바꾼 책인 "직지"에 대해 여쭙고 싶어요.

27 Dr. Park: 저는 도서관에서 근무한 첫해에 그것을 발견했어요.

28 그것이 아주 특별하다는 것을 바로 알았어요.

29 저는 그것의 가치를 증명하기 위해 열심히 연구했고 마침내 성공했죠.

30 1972년에 파리 도서 박람회에서 "직지"는 금속 활자로 인쇄된 세계에서 가장 오래된 책으로 전시되었죠.

31 Q: 박 박사님, 당신의 노고 덕분에 "직지"와 "의궤"가 발견되었고, 모든 한국인들이 그 점을 당신에게 감사하고 있어요.

32 Dr. Park: 저는 사람들이 해외에 있는 우리의 문화재에 더 많은 관심을 갖고 그것의 반환을 위해 애써 주시기를 바랍니다.

※ 다음 문장을 우리말로 쓰시오.

1 An Interview with Dr. Park Byeong-seon
➡ _____

2 On May 27, 2011, 297 books of *Uigwe*, a collection of royal books the French army took in 1866, came back to Korea.
➡ _____

3 The person behind this return is Dr. Park Byeong-seon, a historian who spent her whole life searching for Korean national treasures abroad.
➡ _____

4 Q: Can you tell me how you became interested in *Uigwe*?
➡ _____

5 Dr. Park: I studied history in college.
➡ _____

6 I went to France to continue my studies in 1955.
➡ _____

7 As you know, the French army took many of our national treasures in 1866.
➡ _____

8 I wanted to find them while I was studying there.
➡ _____

9 *Uigwe* was one of them.
➡ _____

10 Q: You found 297 books of *Uigwe* in the National Library of France, in Paris.
➡ _____

11 Please tell me how you found them.
➡ _____

12 Dr. Park: As soon as I became a researcher at the National Library in 1967, I began to look for *Uigwe*.
➡ _____

13 After 10 years, in 1977, I finally found the books.
➡ _____

14 I think I looked at more than 30 million books.
➡ _____

15 Q: I'm sure you were very excited when you found the books.
➡ _____

16 Dr. Park: Yes, I was, but more difficulties were waiting for me.
➡ _____

17 I thought that the books should be returned to Korea, but my bosses at the library didn't like that idea.
➡ _____

18 They even thought that I was a Korean spy and fired me.

➡ _____

19 After that, I had to go to the library as a visitor, so it was not easy to do research on *Uigwe*.

➡ _____

20 However, I didn't give up.

➡ _____

21 For more than ten years, I went to the library every day to finish my research.

➡ _____

22 I wanted to show people the value of *Uigwe*.

➡ _____

23 Q: The results of your research were published as a book in Korea in 1990.

➡ _____

24 Many Koreans became interested in *Uigwe* because of your book.

➡ _____

25 Dr. Park: Yes. In 1992, the Korean government asked the French government for its return and, finally, the 297 books are here now.

➡ _____

_____

26 Q: Before I finish this interview, I'd like to ask you about *Jikji*, a book that changed the history of printing.

➡ _____

27 Dr. Park: I found it in my first year at the library.

➡ _____

28 I knew right away that it was very special.

➡ _____

29 I worked hard to prove its value and finally succeeded.

➡ _____

30 At a book exhibition in Paris in 1972, *Jikji* was displayed as the oldest book in the world that was printed with movable metal type.

➡ _____

31 Q: Dr. Park, thanks to your hard work, *Jikji* and *Uigwe* were found, and all Koreans thank you for that.

➡ _____

32 Dr. Park: I hope people will become more interested in our national treasures abroad and work for their return.

➡ _____

_____

※ 다음 괄호 안의 단어들을 우리말에 맞도록 바르게 배열하시오.

1 (Interview / An / Dr. / with / Byeong-seon / Park)
➡ _____

2 (May / on / 2011, / 27, / books / 297 *Uigwe* / of / collection / a / royal / of / books / French / the / army / in / took / 1866, / back / came / Korea. / to)
➡ _____

3 (person / the / behind / return / this / Dr. / is / Park / a / Byeong-seon / historian / spent / who / whole / her / searching / life / for / national / Korean / abroad. / treasures)
➡ _____

4 (Q: / you / can / me / tell / you / how / interested / became / *Uigwe*? / in)
➡ _____

5 (Dr. Park: / I / history / studied / college. / in)
➡ _____

6 (went / I / France / to / continue / to / studies / 1955. / in / my)
➡ _____

7 (you / as / know, / French / the / took / army / of / many / our / treasures / 1866. / in / national)
➡ _____

8 (wanted / I / find / to / them / I / while / was / there. / studying)
➡ _____

9 (was / *Uigwe* / of / them. / one)
➡ _____

10 (Q: / found / you / books / 297 / *Uigwe* / of / the / in / Library / of / National / Paris. / in / France)
➡ _____

11 (tell / please / how / me / found / them. / you)
➡ _____

12 (Dr. Park: / soon / as / I / as / became / researcher / a / at / Library / the / National / 1976, / in / began / I / look / to / *Uigwe*. / for)
➡ _____

13 (10 / after / years, / 1977, / in / finally / I / books. / the / found)
➡ _____

14 (I / looked / I / think / more / at / 30 / than / books. / million)
➡ _____

15 (Q: / sure / I'm / were / you / excited / very / you / when / books. / the / found)
➡ _____

16 (Dr. Park: / I / yes, / was, / more / but / were / difficulties / waiting / me. / for)
➡ _____

17 (thought / I / that / books / the / be / should / to / returned / Korea, / my / but / bosses / at / library / didn't / the / idea. / that / like)
➡ _____

1 박병선 박사와의 인터뷰

2 2011년 5월 27일에 프랑스군이 1866년에 가져갔던 왕실 서적인 "의궤" 297권이 한국으로 돌아왔다.

3 이 반환 뒤에 있는 인물이 해외에 있는 한국의 문화재를 찾기 위해 전 생애를 바친 역사학자 박병선 박사이다.

4 Q: "의궤"에 어떻게 관심을 갖게 되셨는지 말씀해 주시겠어요?

5 Dr. Park: 저는 대학에서 역사를 공부했어요.

6 저는 1955년에 학업을 계속하기 위해 프랑스에 갔습니다.

7 아시다시피, 프랑스군은 1866년에 우리 문화재를 많이 가져갔어요.

8 저는 그곳에서 공부하는 동안 그것들을 찾고 싶었어요.

9 "의궤"는 그것들 중의 하나였어요.

10 Q: 당신은 파리에 있는 프랑스 국립도서관에서 297권의 "의궤"를 발견하셨어요.

11 그것들을 어떻게 발견하셨는지 말씀해 주세요.

12 Dr. Park: 1967년에 국립도서관의 연구원이 되자마자, 저는 "의궤"를 찾기 시작했어요.

13 10년 후인 1977년에 마침내 그 책들을 발견했죠.

14 제 생각에 3천만 권 이상의 책을 본 것 같아요.

15 Q: 그 책들을 발견했을 때 무척 흥분하셨겠어요.

16 Dr. Park: 네, 하지만 더 큰 어려움이 저를 기다리고 있었어요.

17 저는 그 책들이 한국에 반환되어야 한다고 생각했지만, 도서관의 제 상사들은 그 생각을 좋아하지 않았어요.

18 (even / they / thought / I / that / a / was / Korean / and / spy / me. / fired)
➡ _____

19 (that, / after / had / I / go / to / to / library / the / a / as / visitor, / it / so / was / easy / not / do / to / *Uigwe.* / on / research)
➡ _____

20 (I / however, / didn't / up. / give)
➡ _____

21 (more / for / ten / than / years, / went / I / to / library / the / day / every / to / my / research. / finish)
➡ _____

22 (wanted / I / to / people / show / value / the *Uigwe.* / of)
➡ _____

23 (Q: / results / the / your / of / were / research / as / published / a / in / book / in / 1990. / Korea)
➡ _____

24 (Koreans / many / interested / became / in / because / *Uigwe* / of / book. / your)
➡ _____

25 (Dr. Park: / yes. // 1992, / in / Korean / the / government / asked / French / the / government / its / for / and, / return / finally, / 297 / the / are / now. / here / books)
➡ _____

26 (Q: / I / before / this / finish / interview, / like / I'd / ask / to / about / you *Jikji,* / book / a / changed / that / history / the / painting. / of)
➡ _____

27 (Dr. Park: / found / I / it / my / in / year / first / at / library. / the)
➡ _____

28 (knew / I / away / right / that / was / it / special. / very)
➡ _____

29 (worked / I / to / hard / its / prove / value / succeeded. / finally / and)
➡ _____

30 (a / at / exhibition / book / Paris / in / 1972, / in / was *Jikji* / as / displayed / the / book / oldest / the / in / world / was / that / with / printed / metal / movable / type.)
➡ _____

31 (Q: / Park, / Dr. / to / thanks / your / work, / hard *Uigwe* / and *Jikji* / found, / were / and / Koreans / all / you / that. / for / thank)
➡ _____

32 (Dr. Park: / hope / I / will / people / become / interested / more / national / our / in / abroad / treasures / and / for / return. / their / work)
➡ _____

18 그들은 심지어 제가 한국의 스파이라고 생각했고 저를 해고했죠.
19 그 후에, 저는 방문객으로 도서관에 가야만 했고, 그래서 "의궤"를 연구하는 것이 쉽지 않았어요.
20 하지만 저는 포기하지 않았죠.
21 10년 넘게, 연구를 끝마치기 위해 매일 도서관에 갔어요.
22 저는 사람들에게 "의궤"의 가치를 보여 주고 싶었어요.
23 Q: 당신의 연구 결과가 1990년 한국에서 책으로 출판되었죠.
24 많은 한국인들이 당신의 책 때문에 "의궤"에 관심을 갖게 되었어요.
25 Dr. Park: 네. 1992년에 한국 정부는 프랑스 정부에 그것의 반환을 요청했고, 마침내 297권의 책이 지금 여기 있게 된 거죠.
26 Q: 인터뷰를 마치기 전에, 인쇄의 역사를 바꾼 책인 "직지"에 대해 여쭙고 싶어요.
27 Dr. Park: 저는 도서관에서 근무한 첫해에 그것을 발견했어요.
28 그것이 아주 특별하다는 것을 바로 알았어요.
29 저는 그것의 가치를 증명하기 위해 열심히 연구했고 마침내 성공했죠.
30 1972년에 파리 도서 박람회에서 "직지"는 금속 활자로 인쇄된 세계에서 가장 오래된 책으로 전시되었죠.
31 Q: 박 박사님, 당신의 노고 덕분에 "직지"와 "의궤"가 발견되었고, 모든 한국인들이 그 점을 당신에게 감사하고 있어요.
32 Dr. Park: 저는 사람들이 해외에 있는 우리의 문화재에 더 많은 관심을 갖고 그것의 반환을 위해 애써 주시기를 바랍니다.

※ 다음 우리말을 영어로 쓰시오.

1 박병선 박사와의 인터뷰

➡ _____

2 2011년 5월 27일에 프랑스군이 1866년에 가져갔던 왕실 서적인 "의궤" 297권이 한국으로 돌아왔다.

➡ _____

3 이 반환 뒤에 있는 인물이 해외에 있는 한국의 문화재를 찾기 위해 전 생애를 바친 역사학자 박병선 박사이다.

➡ _____

4 Q: "의궤"에 어떻게 관심을 갖게 되셨는지 말씀해 주시겠어요?

➡ _____

5 Dr. Park: 저는 대학에서 역사를 공부했어요.

➡ _____

6 저는 1955년에 학업을 계속하기 위해 프랑스에 갔습니다.

➡ _____

7 아시다시피, 프랑스군은 1866년에 우리 문화재를 많이 가져갔어요.

➡ _____

8 저는 그곳에서 공부하는 동안 그것들을 찾고 싶었어요.

➡ _____

9 "의궤"는 그것들 중의 하나였어요.

➡ _____

10 Q: 당신은 파리에 있는 프랑스 국립도서관에서 297권의 "의궤"를 발견하셨어요.

➡ _____

11 그것들을 어떻게 발견하셨는지 말씀해 주세요.

➡ _____

12 Dr. Park: 1967년에 국립도서관의 연구원이 되자마자, 저는 "의궤"를 찾기 시작했어요.

➡ _____

13 10년 후인 1977년에 마침내 그 책들을 발견했죠.

➡ _____

14 제 생각에 3천만 권 이상의 책을 본 것 같아요.

➡ _____

15 Q: 그 책들을 발견했을 때 무척 흥분하셨겠어요.

➡ _____

16 Dr. Park: 네, 하지만 더 큰 어려움이 저를 기다리고 있었어요.

➡ _____

17 저는 그 책들이 한국에 반환되어야 한다고 생각했지만, 도서관의 제 상사들은 그 생각을 좋아하지 않았어요.

➡ _____

18 그들은 심지어 제가 한국의 스파이라고 생각했고 저를 해고했죠.

➡ _____

19 그 후에, 저는 방문객으로 도서관에 가야만 했고, 그래서 "의궤"를 연구하는 것이 쉽지 않았어요.

➡ _____

20 하지만 저는 포기하지 않았죠.

➡ _____

21 10년 넘게, 연구를 끝마치기 위해 매일 도서관에 갔어요.

➡ _____

22 저는 사람들에게 "의궤"의 가치를 보여 주고 싶었어요.

➡ _____

23 Q: 당신의 연구 결과가 1990년 한국에서 책으로 출판되었죠.

➡ _____

24 많은 한국인들이 당신의 책 때문에 "의궤"에 관심을 갖게 되었어요.

➡ _____

25 Dr. Park: 네. 1992년에 한국 정부는 프랑스 정부에 그것의 반환을 요청했고, 마침내 297권의 책이 지금 여기 있게 된 거죠.

➡ _____

➡ _____

26 Q: 인터뷰를 마치기 전에, 인쇄의 역사를 바꾼 책인 "직지"에 대해 여쭙고 싶어요.

➡ _____

➡ _____

27 Dr. Park: 저는 도서관에서 근무한 첫해에 그것을 발견했어요.

➡ _____

28 그것이 아주 특별하다는 것을 바로 알았어요.

➡ _____

29 저는 그것의 가치를 증명하기 위해 열심히 연구했고 마침내 성공했죠.

➡ _____

30 1972년에 파리 도서 박람회에서 "직지"는 금속 활자로 인쇄된 세계에서 가장 오래된 책으로 전시되었죠.

➡ _____

➡ _____

31 Q: 박 박사님, 당신의 노고 덕분에 "직지"와 "의궤"가 발견되었고, 모든 한국인들이 그 점을 당신에게 감사하고 있어요.

➡ _____

➡ _____

32 Dr. Park: 저는 사람들이 해외에 있는 우리의 문화재에 더 많은 관심을 갖고 그것의 반환을 위해 애써 주시기를 바랍니다.

➡ _____

➡ _____

※ 다음 우리말과 일치하도록 빈칸에 알맞은 말을 쓰시오.

After You Read C Think and Talk

1. A: _____ do you _____ _____ Dr. Park?

2. B: I _____ she had a strong _____. She had many _____, but she didn't _____ _____.

3. C: I think she had a _____ _____ for her work.

4. _____ a historian, she was very _____ about _____ Korean national treasures _____.

Think and Write Step 2

1. An _____ _____ Kim Yubin

2. The _____ is the interview I had with Kim Yubin, a _____ _____ _____.

3. Q: Can you tell me _____ _____ _____ _____ _____ _____?

4. A: I _____ _____ in Seoul _____ March 11, 1980.

5. Q: I'd _____ _____ know _____ _____ _____ _____ _____ _____.

6. A: _____ _____ in life is _____ _____ a better world.

7. Q: Can you tell me _____ _____ _____ about your job?

8. A: I _____ _____ people.

9. I think _____ Kim Yubin is a great _____ _____.

Team Project Create

1. *Jikji*, _____ _____ _____ _____ No. 1132

2. *Jikji* _____ _____ at Heungdeoksa in 1377.

3. It is now in the _____ _____ of France, in Paris.

4. It is the _____ _____ _____ that was printed with movable _____ _____.

1. A: 박 박사에 대해 어떻게 생각하니?
2. B: 그녀는 강한 의지를 가졌다고 생각해. 그녀는 많은 어려움을 겪었지만 포기하지 않았어.
3. C: 그녀는 자신의 일에 대해 강한 열정을 가졌다고 생각해.
4. 역사학자로서, 그녀는 해외에 있는 한국의 문화재를 찾는 것에 대해 매우 열정적이었어.

1. 김유빈 씨와의 인터뷰
2. 다음은 제가 지역 경찰관 김유빈 씨와 한 인터뷰입니다.
3. Q: 당신은 언제, 어디서 태어나셨는지 말씀해 주시겠어요?
4. A: 저는 1980년 3월 11일에 서울에서 태어났어요.
5. Q: 당신의 인생의 목표가 무엇인지 알고 싶어요.
6. A: 저의 인생의 목표는 더 나은 세상을 만드는 것입니다.
7. Q: 당신의 직업에 관해 당신이 좋아하는 것이 무엇인지 말씀해 주시겠어요?
8. A: 저는 사람들을 돕는 것이 좋아요.
9. 저는 김유빈 씨가 대단한 경찰관이라고 생각합니다.

1. 직지, 한국의 국보 1132번
2. 직지는 1377년 흥덕사에서 인쇄되었다.
3. 현재는 파리의 프랑스 국립도서관에 있다.
4. 직지는 금속활자로 인쇄된 세계에서 가장 오래된 책이다.

※ 다음 우리말을 영어로 쓰시오.

After You Read C Think and Talk

1. A: 박 박사에 대해 어떻게 생각하니?
   ➡ _____

2. B: 그녀는 강한 의지를 가졌다고 생각해. 그녀는 많은 어려움을 겪었지만 포기하지 않았어.
   ➡ _____

3. C: 그녀는 자신의 일에 대해 강한 열정을 가졌다고 생각해.
   ➡ _____

4. 역사학자로서, 그녀는 해외에 있는 한국의 문화재를 찾는 것에 대해 매우 열정적이었어.
   ➡ _____

Think and Write Step 2

1. 김유빈 씨와의 인터뷰
   ➡ _____

2. 다음은 제가 지역 경찰관 김유빈 씨와 한 인터뷰입니다.
   ➡ _____

3. Q: 당신은 언제, 어디서 태어나셨는지 말씀해 주시겠어요?
   ➡ _____

4. A: 저는 1980년 3월 11일에 서울에서 태어났어요.
   ➡ _____

5. Q: 당신의 인생의 목표가 무엇인지 알고 싶어요.
   ➡ _____

6. A: 저의 인생의 목표는 더 나은 세상을 만드는 것입니다.
   ➡ _____

7. Q: 당신의 직업에 관해 당신이 좋아하는 것이 무엇인지 말씀해 주시겠어요?
   ➡ _____

8 A: 저는 사람들을 돕는 것이 좋아요.
   ➡ _____

9. 저는 김유빈 씨가 대단한 경찰관이라고 생각합니다.
   ➡ _____

Team Project Create

1. 직지, 한국의 국보 1132번
   ➡ _____

2. 직지는 1377년 흥덕사에서 인쇄되었다.
   ➡ _____

3. 현재는 파리의 프랑스 국립도서관에 있다.
   ➡ _____

4. 직지는 금속활자로 인쇄된 세계에서 가장 오래된 책이다.
   ➡ _____

※ 다음 영어를 우리말로 쓰시오.

01	button	
02	fun	
03	creative	
04	delicious	
05	enough	
06	taste	
07	work	
08	pile	
09	batter	
10	own	
11	counter	
12	recipe	
13	mix	
14	drop	
15	fresh	
16	sell	
17	inside	
18	push	
19	happen	
20	prize	
21	sign	
22	machine	
23	shout	
24	P.S.(=postscript)	
25	ready	
26	try	
27	lose	
28	wrong	
29	leave	
30	remember	
31	break up	
32	all of a sudden	
33	with excitement	
34	for a while	
35	in the end	
36	be full of	
37	drop into	
38	pile A on B	
39	give ~ back	
40	right away	
41	step out	
42	give a reward	
43	keep+-ing	

※ 다음 우리말을 영어로 쓰시오.

01 도넛 _____

02 반죽 _____

03 쌓아 올리다, 쌓다 _____

04 창의적인 _____

05 표지판 _____

06 상금 _____

07 ~한 맛이 나다 _____

08 떨어지다 _____

09 잃어버리다 _____

10 외치다, 소리치다 _____

11 계산대 _____

12 발생하다, 일어나다 _____

13 ~ 전에 _____

14 시도하다, 먹어보다 _____

15 반지 _____

16 잘못된, 이상이 있는 _____

17 떠나다, ~에 두다 _____

18 섞다 _____

19 팔다 _____

20 요리법 _____

21 기계 _____

22 누르다 _____

23 효과가 있다, 작동하다 _____

24 준비된 _____

25 ~ 안에 _____

26 소유하다 _____

27 맛있는 _____

28 충분한 _____

29 신선한 _____

30 기억하다 _____

31 ~ 앞에 _____

32 잠시 _____

33 결국, 마침내 _____

34 ~으로 가득 차다 _____

35 ~에서 나오다, 내리다 _____

36 ~을 벗다 _____

37 ~을 부수다, 쪼개다 _____

38 갑자기 _____

39 어느 날 _____

40 종이 한 장 _____

41 ~로 떨어지다 _____

42 ~을 되찾다 _____

43 즉시, 지금 당장 _____

※ 다음 영영풀이에 알맞은 단어를 <보기>에서 골라 쓴 후, 우리말 뜻을 쓰시오.

1 _____ : to go out for a short time: _____

2 _____ : to be effective or successful: _____

3 _____ : a piece of jewelry that is worn usually on a finger: _____

4 _____ : the feeling you have when you are excited: _____

5 _____ : a set of instructions for making food: _____

6 _____ : to say something in a loud voice: _____

7 _____ : to give something to somebody in exchange for money: _____

8 _____ : to think about how two or more things are different or the same:
_____

9 _____ : a small round cake that usually has a hole in the middle: _____

10 _____ : a piece of equipment that you use to do a job: _____

11 _____ : the place where you pay in a shop, bank, restaurant, etc.: _____

12 _____ : to give something to someone because he or she has done something
good: _____

13 _____ : a mixture of flour, eggs, milk, etc. used in cooking and for making bread,
cakes, etc.: _____

14 _____ : an award that is given to a person who wins a competition, race, etc. or
who does very good work: _____

15 _____ : a piece of paper, wood, or metal that has writing or a picture on it that
gives you information, instructions, a warning, etc.: _____

16 _____ : to have an image in your mind of a something that happened or was said
in the past: _____

 보기

sign	remember	excitement	doughnut
shout	ring	counter	give a reward
batter	prize	compare	machine
work	sell	step out	recipe

※ 다음 우리말과 일치하도록 빈칸에 알맞은 것을 골라 쓰시오.

1 _____ _____
A. Doughnuts   B. The

2 Homer's _____, Bob, _____ a doughnut _____.
A. had   B. uncle   C. shop

3 Uncle Bob liked machines, _____ the shop was _____
_____ _____ machines.
A. full   B. so   C. cooking   D. of

4 _____ day, Homer _____ Uncle Bob's _____.
A. shop   B. one   C. visited

5 Homer: Hello, _____ _____!
A. Bob   B. Uncle

6 Bob: Hi, Homer. _____ to see you. Look _____ this
new doughnut machine. _____ it great?
A. at   B. isn't   C. nice

7 Bob: Homer, I need to go _____ home _____ a _____.
A. while   B. back   C. for

8 Can you _____ the shop _____ me and _____ some
doughnuts?
A. for   B. make   C. watch

9 Homer: OK, I'll _____ _____ ....
A. try   B. but

10 Bob: It's _____ to do. First, _____ the doughnut _____
and _____ it in the machine.
A. put   B. make   C. easy   D. batter

11 Then _____ start the _____. Here's the _____.
A. recipe   B. machine   C. just

12 Homer: I can _____ that. _____ _____.
A. do   B. worry   C. don't

13 After Uncle Bob left, a big car _____ in _____ of the shop,
and a lady _____ _____.
A. front   B. out   C. stopped   D. stepped

14 Lady: _____ I _____ _____ doughnuts and a coffee?
A. some   B. have   C. can

15 Homer: I'm sorry, _____ the doughnuts _____ _____.
A. ready   B. but   C. aren't

16 Lady: Are you _____ the doughnut _____ now?
A. batter   B. making

17 Homer: Yes, but this is _____ _____ _____.
A. first   B. my   C. time

18 The lady _____ her coat and _____ big diamond
_____.
A. off   B. ring   C. took   D. her

19 She _____ _____ _____ the batter.
A. mix   B. to   C. started

20 Lady: I _____ _____ you. I can make _____ doughnuts.
A. delicious   B. help   C. can

1 도넛

2 Homer의 삼촌인 Bob은 도넛 가게를 가지고 있었다.

3 Bob 삼촌은 기계를 좋아해서, 가게는 요리 기계들로 가득 차 있었다.

4 어느 날, Homer가 Bob 삼촌의 가게를 방문했다.

5 Homer: 안녕하세요, Bob 삼촌!

6 Bob: 안녕, Homer. 만나서 반갑구나. 이 새 도넛 기계 좀 봐. 멋지지 않니?

7 Bob: Homer, 내가 잠시 집에 가 봐야 해.

8 나 대신 가게를 봐 주고 도넛을 좀 만들어 줄 수 있겠니?

9 Homer: 네, 해 볼게요, 그런데 …

10 Bob: 하기 쉬워. 먼저, 도넛 반죽을 만들고 그것을 기계에 넣으렴.

11 그런 다음에 기계를 작동하기만 하면 돼. 여기 요리법이 있어.

12 Homer: 그건 할 수 있어요. 걱정하지 마세요.

13 Bob 삼촌이 떠난 후, 큰 차 한 대가 가게 앞에 섰고, 한 귀부인이 내렸다.

14 Lady: 도넛과 커피 한 잔 주겠니?

15 Homer: 그건 죄송하지만, 도넛이 준비가 안 됐어요.

16 Lady: 지금 도넛 반죽을 만들고 있는 거니?

17 Homer: 네, 하지만 처음 만드는 거예요.

18 그 귀부인은 외투를 벗고 커다란 다이아몬드 반지를 뺐다.

19 그녀는 반죽을 섞기 시작했다.

20 Lady: 내가 도와줄게. 나는 맛있는 도넛을 만들 수 있단다.

21 Homer: _____ , _____ .

    A. OK   B. uh

22 Homer: This is _____ _____ _____ batter.

    A. of   B. lot   C. a

23 Lady: Just _____ and see. The doughnuts will _____ _____ .

    A. great   B. wait   C. taste

24 Homer _____ _____ the doughnut _____ .

    A. machine   B. on   C. turned

25 _____ of batter started _____ _____ the hot oil.

    A. dropping   B. rings   C. into

26 Lady: You _____ the _____ doughnut. Here.

    A. first   B. try

27 Homer: Wow! It's _____ _____ !

    A. delicious   B. really

28 Lady: I _____ _____ go now. This was _____ _____ fun! Good-bye!

    A. so   B. have   C. much   D. to

29 Homer: _____ you _____ _____ me. Good-bye!

    A. for   B. thank   C. helping

30 Homer had _____ doughnuts, so he _____ the stop button, but _____ _____ .

    A. happened   B. enough   C. pushed   D. nothing

31 The doughnuts _____ _____ _____ of the machine.

    A. out   B. coming   C. kept

32 Homer: Hmm... What's _____ ? I think I _____ _____ Uncle Bob.

    A. call   B. wrong   C. should

33 The shop was now _____ _____ doughnuts. Homer _____ the doughnuts on the counter.

    A. piled   B. full   C. of

34 Homer: Uncle Bob! Please come _____ _____ _____ .

    A. away   B. back   C. right

35 _____ _____ _____ the doughnut machine.

    A. wrong   B. with   C. something's

36 Bob: Oh, no! _____ can we sell _____ _____ doughnuts?

    A. these   B. all   C. how

37 _____ then the lady _____ to the shop.

    A. back   B. just   C. came

38 Lady: I _____ my diamond _____ . I think I _____ it on the _____ .

    A. left   B. lost   C. counter   D. ring

39 Homer: Oh, I remember. You _____ it _____ before you started to _____ the batter.

    A. off   B. mix   C. took

40 Everyone _____ _____ the diamond ring, but they _____ find it.

    A. couldn't   B. for   C. looked

---

21 Homer: 아, 좋아요.

22 Homer: 반죽이 많군요.

23 Lady: 좀 기다려 보렴. 도넛이 아주 맛있을 거야.

24 Homer는 도넛 기계를 작동했다.

25 링 모양의 반죽들이 뜨거운 기름 속으로 떨어지기 시작했다.

26 Lady: 첫 번째 도넛을 맛보렴. 여기 있어.

27 Homer: 와! 정말 맛있네요!

28 Lady: 난 이제 가 봐야 해. 정말 재미있었어! 잘 있으렴!

29 Homer: 도와주셔서 감사해요. 안녕히 가세요!

30 Homer는 도넛이 충분하게 있어서 정지 버튼을 눌렀지만, 아무 일도 일어나지 않았다.

31 도넛이 계속해서 기계에서 나오고 있었다.

32 Homer: 흠음 ⋯ 뭐가 잘못된 거지? Bob 삼촌에게 전화를 해야겠어.

33 가게는 이제 도넛으로 가득 찼다. Homer는 도넛들을 계산대 위로 쌓아 올렸다.

34 Homer: Bob 삼촌! 지금 당장 돌아와 주세요.

35 도넛 기계에 이상이 있어요.

36 Bob: 오, 이런! 이 도넛들을 모두 어떻게 팔지?

37 바로 그때 그 귀부인이 다시 가게로 돌아왔다.

38 Lady: 내 다이아몬드 반지를 잃어버렸어. 내 생각엔 계산대 위에 그것을 놓은 것 같은데.

39 Homer: 오, 기억나요. 반죽을 섞기 전에 그것을 뺐어요.

40 모두가 다이아몬드 반지를 찾았지만, 찾을 수 없었다.

41 Homer: I _____ _____ it.
A. find   B. can't

42 Lady: I'll _____ a _____ of one hundred dollars to the person _____ _____ that ring!
A. reward   B. finds   C. give   D. who

43 Homer: I know! The ring _____ _____ the batter. I'm sure it's _____ one of these doughnuts!
A. inside   B. fell   C. into

44 Lady: _____ _____!
A. right   B. you're

45 Bob: Oh, no! Now we have to _____ _____ all of these doughnuts _____ _____ the ring.
A. up   B. to   C. break   D. find

46 Homer: _____ _____, Uncle. I _____ an idea.
A. have   B. worry   C. don't

47 Homer _____ a _____ of paper and _____ a _____.
A. made   B. took   C. sign   D. piece

48 He then _____ it _____ the _____ window.
A. in   B. put   C. shop's

49 Fresh Doughnuts   2 _____ 5 _____
A. cents   B. for

50 $100 prize _____ _____ a ring _____ a doughnut
A. finding   B. inside   C. for

51 P.S. You _____ to _____ the ring _____.
A. back   B. have   C. give

52 Then _____ people began _____ _____ the doughnuts.
A. buy   B. many   C. to

53 _____ of a _____, a man shouted _____ _____.
A. with   B. sudden   C. excitement   D. all

54 Man: I _____ it! I found the _____!
A. ring   B. found

55 Homer: See, my _____ _____!
A. idea   B. worked

56 Lady: _____ one _____ dollars!
A. hundred   B. here's

57 _____ the _____, everybody _____ happy.
A. end   B. was   C. in

58 The man _____ home _____ one _____ dollars.
A. went   B. hundred   C. with

59 The lady _____ her diamond ring _____, and Uncle Bob _____ _____ of doughnuts.
A. back   B. sold   C. lots   D. got

60 And, _____ _____ Homer?
A. about   B. what

61 He was happy _____ his idea _____ so _____!
A. worked   B. well   C. that

---

41 Homer: 저는 못 찾겠어요.

42 Lady: 그 반지를 찾는 사람에게 100달러의 보상금을 드릴게요!

43 Homer: 알겠어요! 그 반지는 반죽 속으로 떨어졌어요. 반지는 이 도넛들 중 하나 안에 있다고 확신해요!

44 Lady: 네 말이 맞아!

45 Bob: 오, 안 돼! 이제 우리는 반지를 찾기 위해 이 도넛들을 모두 쪼개야 해요.

46 Homer: 걱정하지 마세요, 삼촌. 저에게 아이디어가 있어요.

47 Homer는 종이 한 장을 가져와 안내판을 만들었다.

48 그러고 나서 그것을 가게 창문에 걸었다.

49 신선한 도넛   2개에 5센트

50 도넛 안에 있는 반지를 찾으면 100달러의 상금을 드려요.

51 추신. 반지를 돌려주어야 합니다.

52 그러자, 많은 사람들이 도넛을 사기 시작했다.

53 갑자기, 한 남자가 흥분해서 소리쳤다.

54 Man: 찾았어요! 내가 반지를 찾았어요!

55 Homer: 보세요, 제 아이디어가 통했어요!

56 Lady: 여기 100달러예요!

57 결국 모두가 행복했다.

58 남자는 100달러를 갖고 집으로 갔다.

59 귀부인은 다이아몬드 반지를 다시 찾았고, Bob 삼촌은 도넛을 많이 팔았다.

60 그러면, Homer는 어떻게 됐을까?

61 그는 자신의 아이디어가 아주 잘 통해서 행복했다!

※ 다음 우리말과 일치하도록 빈칸에 알맞은 말을 쓰시오.

1 The _____

2 Homer's _____, Bob, _____ a doughnut shop.

3 Uncle Bob liked machines, _____ the shop _____ _____ _____ _____ _____.

4 _____ _____, Homer _____ Uncle Bob's shop.

5 Homer: Hello, _____ Bob!

6 Bob: Hi, Homer. Nice to see you. _____ _____ this new doughnut machine. _____ _____ _____?

7 Bob: Homer, I need to go back home _____ _____ _____.

8 Can you watch the shop _____ _____ and make some doughnuts?

9 Homer: OK, I'll _____ but ....

10 Bob: It's _____ _____ _____. First, make the _____ _____ and _____ it _____ the machine.

11 Then just start the _____. Here's the _____.

12 Homer: I _____ that. _____ _____.

13 After Uncle Bob left, a big car stopped _____ _____ _____ the shop, and a lady _____ _____.

14 Lady: _____ _____ _____ some doughnuts and a coffee?

15 Homer: I'm sorry, but the doughnuts _____ _____.

16 Lady: _____ _____ _____ the doughnut _____ now?

17 Homer: Yes, but this is _____ _____ _____.

18 The lady _____ _____ her coat and her big diamond _____.

19 She _____ _____ _____ the batter.

20 Lady: _____ _____ _____. I can _____ _____ doughnuts.

1 도넛

2 Homer의 삼촌인 Bob은 도넛 가게를 가지고 있었다.

3 Bob 삼촌은 기계를 좋아해서, 가게는 요리 기계들로 가득 차 있었다.

4 어느 날, Homer가 Bob 삼촌의 가게를 방문했다.

5 Homer: 안녕하세요, Bob 삼촌!

6 Bob: 안녕, Homer. 만나서 반갑구나. 이 새 도넛 기계 좀 봐. 멋지지 않니?

7 Bob: Homer, 내가 잠시 집에 가 봐야 해.

8 나 대신 가게를 봐 주고 도넛을 좀 만들어 줄 수 있겠니?

9 Homer: 네, 해 볼게요, 그런데 …

10 Bob: 하기 쉬워. 먼저, 도넛 반죽을 만들고 그것을 기계에 넣으렴.

11 그런 다음에 기계를 작동하기만 하면 돼. 여기 요리법이 있어.

12 Homer: 그건 할 수 있어요. 걱정하지 마세요.

13 Bob 삼촌이 떠난 후, 큰 차 한 대가 가게 앞에 섰고, 한 귀부인이 내렸다.

14 Lady: 도넛과 커피 한 잔 주겠니?

15 Homer: 그건 죄송하지만, 도넛이 준비가 안 됐어요.

16 Lady: 지금 도넛 반죽을 만들고 있는 거니?

17 Homer: 네, 하지만 처음 만드는 거예요.

18 그 귀부인은 외투를 벗고 커다란 다이아몬드 반지를 뺐다.

19 그녀는 반죽을 섞기 시작했다.

20 Lady: 내가 도와줄게. 나는 맛있는 도넛을 만들 수 있단다.

21 Homer: Uh, _____.

22 Homer: This is _____ _____ _____ batter.

23 Lady: Just _____ _____ _____. The doughnuts _____ _____ _____.

24 Homer _____ _____ the doughnut machine.

25 Rings of batter started _____ _____ the _____ _____.

26 Lady: You _____ the _____ doughnut. Here.

27 Homer: Wow! It's really _____!

28 Lady: I _____ _____ _____ now. This was _____ _____ _____! Good-bye!

29 Homer: Thank you _____ _____ me. Good-bye!

30 Homer had _____ doughnuts, so he pushed the stop button, but _____ _____.

31 The doughnuts _____ _____ _____ _____ the machine.

32 Homer: Hmm... What's _____? I think I _____ _____ Uncle Bob.

33 The shop _____ now _____ _____ doughnuts. Homer _____ the doughnuts _____ _____ _____.

34 Homer: Uncle Bob! Please come _____ _____ _____.

35 _____ _____ _____ the doughnut machine.

36 Bob: Oh, no! How can we sell _____ _____ doughnuts?

37 Just then the lady _____ _____ _____ the shop.

38 Lady: I _____ my diamond ring. I think I _____ it on the counter.

39 Homer: Oh, I remember. You _____ _____ _____ before you started to _____ _____ _____.

40 Everyone _____ _____ the diamond ring, but they _____ _____ it.

21 Homer: 아, 좋아요.

22 Homer: 반죽이 많군요.

23 Lady: 좀 기다려 보렴. 도넛이 아주 맛있을 거야.

24 Homer는 도넛 기계를 작동했다.

25 링 모양의 반죽들이 뜨거운 기름 속으로 떨어지기 시작했다.

26 Lady: 첫 번째 도넛을 맛보렴. 여기 있어.

27 Homer: 와! 정말 맛있네요!

28 Lady: 난 이제 가 봐야 해. 정말 재미있었어! 잘 있으렴!

29 Homer: 도와주셔서 감사해요. 안녕히 가세요!

30 Homer는 도넛이 충분하게 있어서 정지 버튼을 눌렀지만. 아무 일도 일어나지 않았다.

31 도넛이 계속해서 기계에서 나오고 있었다.

32 Homer: 흐음 … 뭐가 잘못된 거지? Bob 삼촌에게 전화를 해야겠어.

33 가게는 이제 도넛으로 가득 찼다. Homer는 도넛들을 계산대 위로 쌓아 올렸다.

34 Homer: Bob 삼촌! 지금 당장 돌아와 주세요.

35 도넛 기계에 이상이 있어요.

36 Bob: 오, 이런! 이 도넛들을 모두 어떻게 팔지?

37 바로 그때 그 귀부인이 다시 가게로 돌아왔다.

38 Lady: 내 다이아몬드 반지를 잃어버렸어. 내 생각엔 계산대 위에 그것을 놓은 것 같은데.

39 Homer: 오, 기억나요. 반죽을 섞기 전에 그것을 뺐어요.

40 모두가 다이아몬드 반지를 찾았지만, 찾을 수 없었다.

41 Homer: I _____ _____ it.

42 Lady: I'll _____ _____ _____ of one hundred dollars to the person _____ _____ that ring!

43 Homer: I know! The ring _____ _____ the batter. _____ _____ it's _____ one of these doughnuts!

44 Lady: You're _____!

45 Bob: Oh, no! Now we _____ _____ _____ _____ all of these doughnuts _____ _____ the ring.

46 Homer: _____ _____, Uncle. I have an idea.

47 Homer took a _____ of paper and _____ _____ _____.

48 He then _____ _____ in the shop's window.

49 Fresh Doughnuts _____ _____ _____ _____

50 $100 prize _____ _____ a ring _____ a doughnut

51 P.S. You _____ _____ _____ the ring _____.

52 Then many people began _____ _____ the doughnuts.

53 _____ _____ _____, a man shouted with excitement.

54 Man: I _____ _____! I found the ring!

55 Homer: See, my idea _____!

56 Lady: _____ one _____ dollars!

57 _____ _____ _____, everybody _____ happy.

58 The man went home _____ one hundred dollars.

59 The lady _____ her diamond ring _____, and Uncle Bob sold _____ _____ doughnuts.

60 And, _____ _____ Homer?

61 He was happy that _____ _____ _____ so well!

41 Homer: 저는 못 찾겠어요.

42 Lady: 그 반지를 찾는 사람에게 100달러의 보상금을 드릴게요!

43 Homer: 알겠어요! 그 반지는 반죽 속으로 떨어졌어요. 반지는 이 도넛들 중 하나 안에 있다고 확신해요!

44 Lady: 네 말이 맞아!

45 Bob: 오, 안 돼! 이제 우리는 반지를 찾기 위해 이 도넛들을 모두 쪼개야 해요.

46 Homer: 걱정하지 마세요, 삼촌. 저에게 아이디어가 있어요.

47 Homer는 종이 한 장을 가져와 안내판을 만들었다.

48 그리고 나서 그것을 가게 창문에 걸었다.

49 신선한 도넛 2개에 5센트

50 도넛 안에 있는 반지를 찾으면 100달러의 상금을 드려요.

51 추신. 반지를 돌려주어야 합니다.

52 그러자, 많은 사람들이 도넛을 사기 시작했다.

53 갑자기, 한 남자가 흥분해서 소리쳤다.

54 Man: 찾았어요! 내가 반지를 찾았어요!

55 Homer: 보세요, 제 아이디어가 통했어요!

56 Lady: 여기 100달러예요!

57 결국 모두가 행복했다.

58 남자는 100달러를 갖고 집으로 갔다.

59 귀부인은 다이아몬드 반지를 다시 찾았고, Bob 삼촌은 도넛을 많이 팔았다.

60 그러면, Homer는 어떻게 됐을까?

61 그는 자신의 아이디어가 아주 잘 통해서 행복했다!

※ 다음 문장을 우리말로 쓰시오.

1 ▶ The Doughnuts
➡ _____

2 ▶ Homer's uncle, Bob, had a doughnut shop.
➡ _____

3 ▶ Uncle Bob liked machines, so the shop was full of cooking machines.
➡ _____

4 ▶ One day, Homer visited Uncle Bob's shop.
➡ _____

5 ▶ Homer: Hello, Uncle Bob!
➡ _____

6 ▶ Bob: Hi, Homer. Nice to see you. Look at this new doughnut machine. Isn't it great?
➡ _____

7 ▶ Bob: Homer, I need to go back home for a while.
➡ _____

8 ▶ Can you watch the shop for me and make some doughnuts?
➡ _____

9 ▶ Homer: OK, I'll try but ....
➡ _____

10 ▶ Bob: It's easy to do. First, make the doughnut batter and put it in the machine.
➡ _____

11 ▶ Then just start the machine. Here's the recipe.
➡ _____

12 ▶ Homer: I can do that. Don't worry.
➡ _____

13 ▶ After Uncle Bob left, a big car stopped in front of the shop, and a lady stepped out.
➡ _____

14 ▶ Lady: Can I have some doughnuts and a coffee?
➡ _____

15 ▶ Homer: I'm sorry, but the doughnuts aren't ready.
➡ _____

16 ▶ Lady: Are you making the doughnut batter now?
➡ _____

17 ▶ Homer: Yes, but this is my first time.
➡ _____

18 ▶ The lady took off her coat and her big diamond ring.
➡ _____

19 ▶ She started to mix the batter.
➡ _____

20 ▶ Lady: I can help you. I can make delicious doughnuts.
➡ _____

21 Homer: Uh, OK.
➡ _____

22 Homer: This is a lot of batter.
➡ _____

23 Lady: Just wait and see. The doughnuts will taste great.
➡ _____

24 Homer turned on the doughnut machine.
➡ _____

25 Rings of batter started dropping into the hot oil.
➡ _____

26 Lady: You try the first doughnut. Here.
➡ _____

27 Homer: Wow! It's really delicious!
➡ _____

28 Lady: I have to go now. This was so much fun! Good-bye!
➡ _____

29 Homer: Thank you for helping me. Good-bye!
➡ _____

30 Homer had enough doughnuts, so he pushed the stop button, but nothing happened.
➡ _____

31 The doughnuts kept coming out of the machine.
➡ _____

32 Homer: Hmm... What's wrong? I think I should call Uncle Bob.
➡ _____

33 The shop was now full of doughnuts. Homer piled the doughnuts on the counter.
➡ _____

34 Homer: Uncle Bob! Please come back right away.
➡ _____

35 Something's wrong with the doughnut machine.
➡ _____

36 Bob: Oh, no! How can we sell all these doughnuts?
➡ _____

37 Just then the lady came back to the shop.
➡ _____

38 Lady: I lost my diamond ring. I think I left it on the counter.
➡ _____

39 Homer: Oh, I remember. You took it off before you started to mix the batter.
➡ _____

40 Everyone looked for the diamond ring, but they couldn't find it.
➡ _____

41 Homer: I can't find it.
➡ _____

42 Lady: I'll give a reward of one hundred dollars to the person who finds that ring!
➡ _____

43 Homer: I know! The ring fell into the batter. I'm sure it's inside one of these doughnuts!
➡ _____

44 Lady: You're right!
➡ _____

45 Bob: Oh, no! Now we have to break up all of these doughnuts to find the ring.
➡ _____

46 Homer: Don't worry, Uncle. I have an idea.
➡ _____

47 Homer took a piece of paper and made a sign.
➡ _____

48 He then put it in the shop's window.
➡ _____

49 Fresh Doughnuts   2 for 5 cents
➡ _____

50 $100 prize for finding a ring inside a doughnut
➡ _____

51 P.S. You have to give the ring back.
➡ _____

52 Then many people began to buy the doughnuts.
➡ _____

53 All of a sudden, a man shouted with excitement.
➡ _____

54 Man: I found it! I found the ring!
➡ _____

55 Homer: See, my idea worked!
➡ _____

56 Lady: Here's one hundred dollars!
➡ _____

57 In the end, everybody was happy.
➡ _____

58 The man went home with one hundred dollars.
➡ _____

59 The lady got her diamond ring back, and Uncle Bob sold lots of doughnuts.
➡ _____

60 And, what about Homer?
➡ _____

61 He was happy that his idea worked so well!
➡ _____

※ 다음 괄호 안의 단어들을 우리말에 맞도록 바르게 배열하시오.

1 (Doughnuts / The)
➡ _____

2 (uncle, / Homer's / Bob, / a / had / shop. / doughnut)
➡ _____

3 (Bob / Uncle / machines, / liked / so / shop / the / was / of / full / machines. / cooking)
➡ _____

4 (day, / one / visited / Homer / Uncle / shop. / Bob's)
➡ _____

5 (Homer: / Bob! / Uncle / Hello,)
➡ _____

6 (Bob: / Homer. / hi, // to / nice / you. / see // at / look / new / this / machine / doughnut // isn't / great? / it)
➡ _____

7 (Bob: / Homer, / need / I / go / to / back / for / while. / home / a)
➡ _____

8 (you / can / watch / shop / the / me / for / and / make / doughnuts? / some)
➡ _____

9 (Homer: / OK, / try / but / I'll / ....)
➡ _____

10 (Bob: / easy / it's / do. / to // first, / the / make / batter / doughnut / and / it / put / the / machine. / in)
➡ _____

11 (then / start / just / machine. / the // recipe. / the / here's)
➡ _____

12 (Homer: / can / I / that. / do // worry. / don't)
➡ _____

13 (Uncle / left, / after / Bob / big / a / car / stopped / front / of / in / shop, / the / and / lady / a / out. / stepped)
➡ _____

14 (Lady: / I / can / have / doughnuts / some / and / coffee? / a)
➡ _____

15 (Homer: / sorry, / I'm / but / doughnuts / the / ready. / aren't)
➡ _____

16 (Lady: / you / are / making / doughnut / the / now? / batter)
➡ _____

17 (Homer: / yes, / this / but / is / my / first)
➡ _____

18 (lady / the / off / took / coat / her / and / her / diamond / ring. / big)
➡ _____

19 (started / she / mix / to / batter. / the)
➡ _____

20 (Lady: / can / I / you. / help // can / I / make / doughnuts. / delicious)
➡ _____

1 도넛

2 Homer의 삼촌인 Bob은 도넛 가게를 가지고 있었다.

3 Bob 삼촌은 기계를 좋아해서, 가게는 요리 기계들로 가득 차 있었다.

4 어느 날, Homer가 Bob 삼촌의 가게를 방문했다.

5 Homer: 안녕하세요, Bob 삼촌!

6 Bob: 안녕, Homer. 만나서 반갑구나. 이 새 도넛 기계 좀 봐. 멋지지 않니?

7 Bob: Homer, 내가 잠시 집에 가 봐야 해.

8 나 대신 가게를 봐 주고 도넛을 좀 만들어 줄 수 있겠니?

9 Homer: 네, 해 볼게요, 그런데 …

10 Bob: 하기 쉬워. 먼저, 도넛 반죽을 만들고 그것을 기계에 넣으렴.

11 그런 다음에 기계를 작동하기만 하면 돼. 여기 요리법이 있어.

12 Homer: 그건 할 수 있어요. 걱정하지 마세요.

13 Bob 삼촌이 떠난 후, 큰 차 한 대가 가게 앞에 섰고, 한 귀부인이 내렸다.

14 Lady: 도넛과 커피 한 잔 주겠니?

15 Homer: 그건 죄송하지만, 도넛이 준비가 안 됐어요.

16 Lady: 지금 도넛 반죽을 만들고 있는 거니?

17 Homer: 네, 하지만 처음 만드는 거예요.

18 그 귀부인은 외투를 벗고 커다란 다이아몬드 반지를 뺐다.

19 그녀는 반죽을 섞기 시작했다.

20 Lady: 내가 도와줄게. 나는 맛있는 도넛을 만들 수 있단다.

21 (Homer: / OK. / uh,)
➡ _____

22 (Homer: / is / this / a / batter. / of / lot)
➡ _____

23 (Lady: / wait / just / see. / and // doughnuts / the / great. / taste / will)
➡ _____

24 (turned / Homer / the / on / machine. / doughnut)
➡ _____

25 (batter / of / rings / started / into / dropping / the / oil. / hot)
➡ _____

26 (Lady: / try / you / first / doughnut. / the // here.)
➡ _____

27 (Homer: / wow! // really / it's / delicious!)
➡ _____

28 (Lady: / have / I / go / to / now. // was / this / much / so / fun! // good-bye!)
➡ _____

29 (Homer: / you / thank / helping / for / me. // good-bye!)
➡ _____

30 (Homer / enough / had / doughnuts, / so / pushed / he / stop / the / button, / but / happened. / nothing)
➡ _____

31 (doughnuts / the / coming / kept / of / out / machine. / the)
➡ _____

32 (Homer: / hmm... // wrong? / what's // think / I / should / I / Bob. / call / Uncle)
➡ _____

33 (shop / the / was / full / now / doughnuts. / of // Homer / the / piled / doughnuts / the / counter. / on)
➡ _____

34 (Homer: / Bob! / Uncle // come / please / right / back / away.)
➡ _____

35 (wrong / something's / with / the / machine. / doughnut)
➡ _____

36 (Bob: / no! / oh, // can / how / sell / we / all / doughnuts? / these)
➡ _____

37 (then / just / lady / the / back / came / shop. / the / to)
➡ _____

38 (Lady: / lost / I / ring. / diamond / my // I / left / I / think / it / counter. / the / on)
➡ _____

39 (Homer: / oh, / remember. / I // took / you / off / it / before / started / you / mix / batter. / the / to)
➡ _____

40 (looked / everyone / the / for / ring, / diamond / but / they / find / it. / couldn't)
➡ _____

21 Homer: 아, 좋아요.

22 Homer: 반죽이 많군요.

23 Lady: 좀 기다려 보렴. 도넛이 아주 맛있을 거야.

24 Homer는 도넛 기계를 작동했다.

25 링 모양의 반죽들이 뜨거운 기름 속으로 떨어지기 시작했다.

26 Lady: 첫 번째 도넛을 맛보렴. 여기 있어.

27 Homer: 와! 정말 맛있네요!

28 Lady: 난 이제 가 봐야 해. 정말 재미있었어! 잘 있으렴!

29 Homer: 도와주셔서 감사해요. 안녕히 가세요!

30 Homer는 도넛이 충분하게 있어서 정지 버튼을 눌렀지만, 아무 일도 일어나지 않았다.

31 도넛이 계속해서 기계에서 나오고 있었다.

32 Homer: 흐음 … 뭐가 잘못된 거지? Bob 삼촌에게 전화를 해야겠어.

33 가게는 이제 도넛으로 가득 찼다. Homer는 도넛들을 계산대 위로 쌓아 올렸다.

34 Homer: Bob 삼촌! 지금 당장 돌아와 주세요.

35 도넛 기계에 이상이 있어요.

36 Bob: 오, 이런! 이 도넛들을 모두 어떻게 팔지?

37 바로 그때 그 귀부인이 다시 가게로 돌아왔다.

38 Lady: 내 다이아몬드 반지를 잃어버렸어. 내 생각엔 계산대 위에 그것을 놓은 것 같은데.

39 Homer: 오, 기억나요. 반죽을 섞기 전에 그것을 뺐어요.

40 모두가 다이아몬드 반지를 찾았지만, 찾을 수 없었다.

41 (Homer: / I / find / it. / can't)
➡ _____

42 (Lady: / give / I'll / reward / a / one / of / dollars / hundred / the / to / person / finds / who / ring! / that)
➡ _____

43 (Homer: / know! / I // ring / the / into / fell / batter. / the // I'm / it's / sure / one / inside / of / doughnuts! / these)
➡ _____
_____

44 (Lady: / right! / you're)
➡ _____

45 (Bob: / no! / oh, // we / now / to / have / break / all / up / these / of / to / doughnuts / ring. / the / find)
➡ _____

46 (Homer: / worry, / don't / Uncle. // have / I / idea. / an)
➡ _____

47 (took / Homer / piece / a / paper / of / and / sign. / a / made)
➡ _____

48 (then / he / it / put / in / shop's / the / window.)
➡ _____

49 (Doughnuts / Fresh // for / 2 / cents / 5)
➡ _____

50 (prize / $100 / finding / for / ring / a / inside / doughnut / a)
➡ _____

51 (P.S. / have / you / give / to / back. / ring / the)
➡ _____

52 (many / then / began / people / buy / to / doughnuts / the)
➡ _____

53 (of / all / sudden, / a / man / a / with / shouted / excitement.)
➡ _____

54 (Man: / found / I / it! // the / I / ring! / found)
➡ _____

55 (Homer: / my / see, / worked! / idea)
➡ _____

56 (Lady: / one / here's / dallars! / hundred)
➡ _____

57 (the / in / end, / was / happy. / everybody)
➡ _____

58 (man / the / home / went / with / hundred / dollars. / one)
➡ _____

59 (lady / the / her / got / ring / diamond / back, / and / Bob / Uncle / lots / sold / doughnuts. / of)
➡ _____

60 (and, / Homer? / about / what)
➡ _____

61 (was / he / happy / that / idea / his / well! / so / worked)
➡ _____

41 Homer: 저는 못 찾겠어요.

42 Lady: 그 반지를 찾는 사람에게 100달러의 보상금을 드릴게요!

43 Homer: 알겠어요! 그 반지는 반죽 속으로 떨어졌어요. 반지는 이 도넛들 중 하나 안에 있다고 확신해요!

44 Lady: 네 말이 맞아!

45 Bob: 오, 안 돼! 이제 우리는 반지를 찾기 위해 이 도넛들을 모두 쪼개야 해요.

46 Homer: 걱정하지 마세요, 삼촌. 저에게 아이디어가 있어요.

47 Homer는 종이 한 장을 가져와 안내판을 만들었다.

48 그러고 나서 그것을 가게 창문에 걸었다.

49 신선한 도넛 2개에 5센트

50 도넛 안에 있는 반지를 찾으면 100달러의 상금을 드려요.

51 추신. 반지를 돌려주어야 합니다.

52 그러자, 많은 사람들이 도넛을 사기 시작했다.

53 갑자기, 한 남자가 흥분해서 소리쳤다.

54 Man: 찾았어요! 내가 반지를 찾았어요!

55 Homer: 보세요, 제 아이디어가 통했어요!

56 Lady: 여기 100달러예요!

57 결국 모두가 행복했다.

58 남자는 100달러를 갖고 집으로 갔다.

59 귀부인은 다이아몬드 반지를 다시 찾았고, Bob 삼촌은 도넛을 많이 팔았다.

60 그러면, Homer는 어떻게 됐을까?

61 그는 자신의 아이디어가 아주 잘 통해서 행복했다!

※ 다음 우리말을 영어로 쓰시오.

1 도넛
➡ _____

2 Homer의 삼촌인 Bob은 도넛 가게를 가지고 있었다.
➡ _____

3 Bob 삼촌은 기계를 좋아해서, 가게는 요리 기계들로 가득 차 있었다.
➡ _____

4 어느 날, Homer가 Bob 삼촌의 가게를 방문했다.
➡ _____

5 Homer: 안녕하세요, Bob 삼촌!
➡ _____

6 Bob: 안녕, Homer. 만나서 반갑구나. 이 새 도넛 기계 좀 봐. 멋지지 않니?
➡ _____

7 Bob: Homer, 내가 잠시 집에 가 봐야 해.
➡ _____

8 나 대신 가게를 봐 주고 도넛을 좀 만들어 줄 수 있겠니?
➡ _____

9 Homer: 네, 해 볼게요, 그런데….
➡ _____

10 Bob: 하기 쉬워. 먼저, 도넛 반죽을 만들고 그것을 기계에 넣으렴.
➡ _____

11 그런 다음에 기계를 작동하기만 하면 돼. 여기 요리법이 있어.
➡ _____

12 Homer: 그건 할 수 있어요. 걱정하지 마세요.
➡ _____

13 Bob 삼촌이 떠난 후, 큰 차 한 대가 가게 앞에 섰고, 한 귀부인이 내렸다.
➡ _____

14 Lady: 도넛과 커피 한 잔 주겠니?
➡ _____

15 Homer: 죄송하지만, 도넛이 준비가 안 됐어요.
➡ _____

16 Lady: 지금 도넛 반죽을 만들고 있는 거니?
➡ _____

17 Homer: 네, 하지만 처음 만드는 거예요.
➡ _____

18 그 귀부인은 외투를 벗고 커다란 다이아몬드 반지를 뺐다.
➡ _____

19 그녀는 반죽을 섞기 시작했다.
➡ _____

20 Lady: 내가 도와줄게. 나는 맛있는 도넛을 만들 수 있단다.
➡ _____

21 ▶ Homer: 아, 좋아요.

　➡ _____

22 ▶ Homer: 반죽이 많군요.

　➡ _____

23 ▶ Lady: 좀 기다려 보렴. 도넛이 아주 맛있을 거야.

　➡ _____

24 ▶ Homer는 도넛 기계를 작동했다.

　➡ _____

25 ▶ 링 모양의 반죽들이 뜨거운 기름 속으로 떨어지기 시작했다.

　➡ _____

26 ▶ Lady: 첫 번째 도넛을 맛보렴. 여기 있어.

　➡ _____

27 ▶ Homer: 와! 정말 맛있네요!

　➡ _____

28 ▶ Lady: 난 이제 가 봐야 해. 정말 재미있었어! 잘 있으렴!

　➡ _____

29 ▶ Homer: 도와주셔서 감사해요. 안녕히 가세요!

　➡ _____

30 ▶ Homer는 도넛이 충분하게 있어서 정지 버튼을 눌렀지만, 아무 일도 일어나지 않았다.

　➡ _____

31 ▶ 도넛이 계속해서 기계에서 나오고 있었다.

　➡ _____

32 ▶ Homer: 흐음 … 뭐가 잘못된 거지? Bob 삼촌에게 전화를 해야겠어.

　➡ _____

33 ▶ 가게는 이제 도넛으로 가득 찼다. Homer는 도넛들을 계산대 위로 쌓아 올렸다.

　➡ _____

34 ▶ Homer: Bob 삼촌! 지금 당장 돌아와 주세요.

　➡ _____

35 ▶ 도넛 기계에 이상이 있어요.

　➡ _____

36 ▶ Bob: 오, 이런! 이 도넛들을 모두 어떻게 팔지?

　➡ _____

37 ▶ 바로 그때 그 귀부인이 다시 가게로 돌아왔다.

　➡ _____

38 ▶ Lady: 내 다이아몬드 반지를 잃어버렸어. 내 생각엔 계산대 위에 그것을 놓은 것 같은데.

　➡ _____

39 ▶ Homer: 오, 기억나요. 반죽을 섞기 전에 그것을 뺐어요.

　➡ _____

40 ▶ 모두가 다이아몬드 반지를 찾았지만, 찾을 수 없었다.

　➡ _____

41 Homer: 저는 못 찾겠어요.
➡ _____

42 Lady: 그 반지를 찾는 사람에게 100달러의 보상금을 드릴게요!
➡ _____

43 Homer: 알겠어요! 그 반지는 반죽 속으로 떨어졌어요. 반지는 이 도넛들 중 하나 안에 있다고 확신해요!
➡ _____

44 Lady: 네 말이 맞아!
➡ _____

45 Bob: 오, 안 돼! 이제 우리는 반지를 찾기 위해 이 도넛들을 모두 쪼개야 해요.
➡ _____

46 Homer: 걱정하지 마세요, 삼촌. 저에게 아이디어가 있어요.
➡ _____

47 Homer는 종이 한 장을 가져와 안내판을 만들었다.
➡ _____

48 그리고 나서 그것을 가게 창문에 걸었다.
➡ _____

49 신선한 도넛   2개에 5센트
➡ _____

50 도넛 안에 있는 반지를 찾으면 100달러의 상금을 드려요.
➡ _____

51 추신. 반지를 돌려주어야 합니다.
➡ _____

52 그러자, 많은 사람들이 도넛을 사기 시작했다.
➡ _____

53 갑자기, 한 남자가 흥분해서 소리쳤다.
➡ _____

54 Man: 찾았어요! 내가 반지를 찾았어요!
➡ _____

55 Homer: 보세요, 제 아이디어가 통했어요!
➡ _____

56 Lady: 여기 100달러예요!
➡ _____

57 결국 모두가 행복했다.
➡ _____

58 남자는 100달러를 갖고 집으로 갔다.
➡ _____

59 귀부인은 다이아몬드 반지를 다시 찾았고, Bob 삼촌은 도넛을 많이 팔았다.
➡ _____

60 그러면, Homer는 어떻게 됐을까?
➡ _____

61 그는 자신의 아이디어가 아주 잘 통해서 행복했다!
➡ _____

MEMO

영어 기출 문제집

적중100

2학기

정답 및 해설

동아 | 윤정미

중 2

적중100

2학기

정답 및 해설

동아 | 윤정미

중 2

Life in Space

시험대비 실력평가
p.08

01 secret   02 ①   03 ④   04 ⑤
05 are covered with   06 ③   07 recently
08 ④

01 한 사람이나 몇 사람만 알고 다른 사람에게는 말하지 말아야 하는 정보: secret(비밀)

02 Jonny가 우유 용기를 열고는 흔들었다. 우유가 공기 중으로 떠서 공 모양이 되었다.

03 손을 이용하여 무언가를 아래로 옮기다: pull down(아래로 끌어내리다)

04 물이나 다른 액체로 덮여 있거나 가득 차 있는: wet(젖은)

05 be covered with: ~로 덮여 있다

06 동사로 '삼키다'라는 의미와 명사로 '제비'의 뜻을 가지고 있는 swallow가 적절하다. 두 번째 문장은 '제비 한 마리가 왔다고 해서 여름이 온 것은 아니다.'라는 뜻으로 작은 조짐 하나를 너무 확대 해석하지 말라는 의미이다.

07 유의어 관계이다. 놀라운 = 최근의

08 • 그들은 서로(each other)를 쳐다보고 웃었다. • Rada 와 Jonny는 부드러운 초록색의 잔디 위에 누워서(lay down) 언덕 아래로 굴러갔다.

서술형 시험대비
p.09

01 (1) pulls   (2) covered   (3) exciting   (4) curious
02 (1) shaking   (2) rolling down   (3) landing
03 (1) (f)orm   (2) (l)and
04 (1) were born   (2) surprise
   (3) don't have to, space suit, everywhere
05 (1) air: 공기   (2) secret: 비밀   (3) space suit: 우주복

01 (1) 또한 그곳에서는 지구가 끌어당기고 있기 때문에 뛰어오르는 것이 어렵지. (2) 언덕들은 초록색의 잔디로 덮여 있지. (3) 그들이 보고, 그리고 하게 될 새로운 모든 것들에 대해서 생각하는 것은 흥미로웠다. (4) 나는 우주 마라톤에 대해 정말 궁금하다.

02 be동사와 함께 현재진행형(be+동사-ing) 형태를 사용한다.

03 (1) form: 양식; 형성하다, 만들다 (2) land: 육지; 착륙하다

04 (1) be born: 태어나다 (2) in surprise: 놀라서 (3) space suit: 우주복

[교과서] Conversation

핵심 Check
p.10~11

1 ③   2 Have, heard about   3 ⑤   4 ①, ②, ⑤

교과서 대화문 익히기

Check(√) True or False
p.12

1 T   2 T   3 F   4 T

교과서 확인학습
p.14~15

Listen and Talk A-1
hear about, that / curious about / to buy

Listen and Talk A-2
Did, hear about / I'm really curious about / right here, about

Listen and Talk A-3
Did you hear about / I didn't / Look at / I'm really curious about

Listen and Talk A-4
about / a type / hear it is / curious about

Listen and Talk B
1 about / heard / curious about
2 Look at, hear about / it has great songs/ curious

Listen and Talk C
about / good / curious about, about / about, who, to live / interesting / is plaing / What time / begins / Let's, and then / hungry

Review 1
did you / heard / curious, about / about, who

Review 2
about / right, living / curious about

01 curious about   02 ④   03 ①, ③

04 hear about

01 궁금증을 표현하거나 보다 많은 정보를 알고 싶을 때 사용하는 표현으로 be curious about을 쓴다.

02 B의 No, I didn't.와 어울리는 질문은 ④번이 적절하다. ④번은 새로운 정보를 알고 있는지 물어 보는 말이다.

03 새로운 정보에 대하여 궁금증을 표현하는 것으로 'I want to know ~. I'd like to know ~, I'm curious about ~' 등을 사용할 수 있다.

04 '~에 대해서 들어 봤니?'라는 표현으로 'Did you hear about ~?'을 사용한다.

01 ④   02 ④, ⑤   03 ⑤   04 ②

05 here it is   06 ④

07 It's about a father who saves his son.   08 ①

09 ③   10 ⑤   11 ②

12 (c)urious

01 G가 No, I didn't.로 과거시제로 답하고 있기 때문에 과거 시제 의문문이 적절하다. 그리고 G의 마지막 말에 I want to buy it.이라고 관심을 가지고 있다는 것을 알 수 있으므로 ⑤는 적절하지 않다.

02 새로운 정보에 대해 궁금증을 나타내는 표현이 적절하다.

03 (D) 우주 마라톤에 대해 들어 봤니?'에 대한 답으로 (C) 부정의 답이 오고 → (B) 우주 마라톤에 대한 설명과 비디오를 보라는 말에 → (A) 동의의 답과 함께 궁금증을 나타내는 표현이 적절하다.

04 '~에 관해 듣다'는 hear about, '~이 궁금하다'는 be curious about을 사용한다.

06 ④ 새로운 뮤지컬에 대해 들어본 적이 없다고 답하고 나서 좋은 노래들이 나온다고 들었다고 말하는 것은 어색하다.

07 '~에 관한 것이다'는 be about이고, a father를 수식하는 관계대명사절을 이용한다. 선행사가 단수 명사 a father이므로 save는 단수 형태 saves로 쓴다.

08 Did you hear about ~?은 상대방이 어떤 정보를 알고 있는지 묻는 표현이다.

09 선행사가 단수 명사 a man이므로 주격 관계대명사 뒤의 동사도 단수인 is가 적절하다.

10 영화를 본 후에 그들이 무엇을 할 것인지는 대화에서 언급되어 있지 않다.

11 '그건 일종의 아이스크림이야'라고 말하고 있으므로 알고 있다는 것을 알 수 있다.

12 어떤 것을 알고 싶거나 세상에 대해 배우고 싶어 하는: 궁금한, 호기심 많은

01 Did you hear about the new book, Living in a Foreign Country?

02 I'm really curious about this book.

03 (A) Did you hear about the new running shoes, Speed?

    (B) What about them?

    (C) I'm curious about them.

04 about a father who[that] saves his son

05 That sounds interesting.

01 '~에 관해 들어 봤니?'라는 표현은 Did you hear about ~?으로 시작한다. 그리고 the new book과 Living in a Foreign Country는 동격 관계로 동격의 comma를 사용한다.

02 형용사 curious는 be curious about 형태로 '~에 관해 궁금해 하다'의 의미다.

04 '~에 관한 것이다'는 be about을 사용하고, 사람을 선행사로 하는 관계대명사 who나 that을 사용한다. 주격 관계대 명사의 동사는 단수 동사인 saves를 쓴다.

05 (B) 새로운 영화에 대해 알고 있는지 묻고 → (F) 알지 못한다는 대답을 하고 → (A) 정말 좋다고 들었다고 이야기 해주고 → (C) 정말로 궁금해진다는 말로 관심을 표현하고 무엇에 관한 내용인지 묻는다. → (D) 영화 내용을 말해준다 → (E) 마지막으로 그거 재미있겠다는 문장이 오는 것이 자연스럽다.

교과서

Grammar

1 (1) has studied   (2) heard   (3) Have, met

2 (1) is it important to   (2) It, to

    (3) for me to play

01 ①   02 ③

03 (1) return → returned

    (2) has eaten → ate

    (3) do you have been → have you been

    (4) for → since

    (5) That → It

    (6) reads → to read

01 it을 가주어로 하고 to부정사를 진주어로 쓸 수 있는 ①번이 적절하다.

02 ③ 'have gone to'는 '~에 가고 없다'는 결과를 나타내는 것으로 3인칭만 주어로 쓸 수 있다. I have been to Hong Kong. 으로 고쳐야 한다.

03 (1) 현재완료는 'have[has]+과거분사'의 형태이다. (2) 현재완료는 과거를 나타내는 어구와 함께 쓸 수 없다. (3) 현재완료의 의문문은 have 동사를 주어 앞으로 보낸다. (4) 현재완료에서 'since+시간 명사', 'for+기간 명사'를 쓴다. (5) 가주어로는 That이 아니라 It을 쓴다. (6) 진주어로 to부정사가 적절하다.

시험대비 실력평가   p.23~25

01 ④   02 ⑤   03 ③   04 ①
05 ③   06 (1) has   (2) haven't   (3) gone
(4) went   (5) to sleep   (6) for 07 ④   08 ②
09 ①   10 It is necessary to take a break
regularly.   11 ⑤   12 ②   13 ①
14 (1) It is difficult for me to guess the ending of story.
   (2) It is boring to read a science book.
   (3) It is important to read for an hour every day.
   (4) I worked in the hospital snack bar then.
   (5) Jim has had a cat for three years.
   (6) Garry has gone to New York on business and he stays there now.
15 (1) Josh has lost his smartphone.
   (2) Sophia has lived in Georgia for five years.
16 ⑤   17 ③   18 ②, ④

01 ④ 언제 영화를 봤는지 묻는 문장으로 특정한 과거의 한 시점을 묻는 것이므로 현재완료가 아니라 과거시제가 되어야 한다. when은 현재완료와 쓰이지 않는다.

02 '가주어(It) ~ 진주어(to부정사) …' 구문이 적절하다. ②번은 It is so kind of you to lend me the book.이 적절하다.

03 현재완료의 의문문은 'Have[Has]+주어+과거분사 ~?'이다. It이 나와 있으므로 It을 가주어로 하고 빈칸에는 진주어로 이용할 수 있는 to부정사가 나와야 한다. 그러므로 ③번이 적절하다.

04 가주어로 It이 적절하다.

05 부정문이므로 yet이 적절하다.

06 (1) 주어가 3인칭 단수이므로 has가 적절하다. (2) 현재완료의 부정문은 'have[has]+not[never]+과거분사'로 나타낸다. (3) have[has] gone to는 '~에 가고 없다'는 결과를 나타낸다. (4) 현재완료는 과거를 나타내는 어구와 함께 쓸 수 없다. (5) 진주어로 to부정사가 적절하다. (6) to부정사의 의미상 주어는 to부정사 바로 앞에 'for+명사의 목적격'의 형태로 쓴다.

07 ① Angie bought a new smartphone yesterday. ② Has she told you the good news yet? ③ I have been to England once. ⑤ I've been learning English for ten years.

08 ②번은 인칭대명사로 '그것'이라고 해석 가능하지만 나머지는 모두 가주어로 쓰인 it이다.

09 현재완료형의 질문에 대한 답은 have[has]를 이용하여 답한다.

10 '규칙적으로 휴식을 취하는 것(to take a break regularly)'을 진주어로 하고 가주어 It을 이용하여 'It ~ to …' 형식으로 쓴다.

11 현재완료의 결과적 용법(…해서 (그 결과) 지금 ~하다)을 이용하여 과거에 집으로 가서 지금 여기에 없다는 결과를 나타내도록 한다.

12 가주어로 it을 쓰고 진주어로 to부정사를 쓰는 것이 적절하다.

13 ①과 <보기>는 계속 용법이다. ②, ⑤ 결과 용법 ③ 경험 용법 ④ 완료 용법

14 (1) 진주어로 to guess를 쓴다. (2) 가주어로는 This가 아니라 It을 쓴다. (3) 진주어로 to부정사를 쓴다. (4) 현재완료는 과거를 나타내는 어구와 함께 쓸 수 없다. then은 '그때, 그 당시'라는 뜻으로 과거를 나타내는 말이다. (5) 현재완료에서 'since+시간 명사', 'for+기간 명사' (6) have[has] been to는 '~에 가 본 적이 있다'는 경험을 나타내고, have[has] gone to는 '~에 가고 없다'는 결과를 나타내므로 have gone to로 고쳐야 한다.

15 (1) 스마트폰을 잃어버려서 지금 가지고 있지 않으므로 현재완료의 '결과' 용법으로 나타낸다. (2) 5년 전에 살기 시작해서 아직도 살고 있으므로 현재완료의 '계속' 용법으로 나타낸다.

16 현재완료는 과거를 나타내는 어구와 함께 쓸 수 없으며, 현재완료에서는 'since+시간 명사', 'for+기간 명사'를 쓴다.

17 '가주어(It) ~ 진주어(to부정사: to hang out with my friends after finals) …' 구문으로 쓴 ③번이 적절하다.

18 문장에 쓰인 형용사가 사람의 성향, 성격을 나타내는 말일 때는 to부정사의 의미상의 주어로 'of+목적격'을 쓴다. 현재완료는 과거의 특정 시점을 나타내는 의문사 when과는 함께 쓰이지 않는다.

서술형 시험대비   p.26~27

01 (1) Kelly has lived in LA since she was 10 years old.
   (2) The government has become more interested in education.
   (3) He has heard about the rumor.
   (4) It is wonderful to travel to other countries.
   (5) Is it possible for him to get tickets for the game?
02 (1) To drive at night is dangerous.
   (2) It is dangerous to drive at night.

(1) To steal things is wrong.

(2) It's wrong to steal things.

03 (1) |모범답안| I have eaten nacho several times.

I have never eaten nacho.

(2) |모범답안| I have never been to Jeju-do before.

I have been to Jeju-do two times.

04 (1) Sonya has visited New York three times.

(2) I have eaten dinner.

05 (1) It was exciting to think about all the new things.

(2) It was great to swim in the cool blue sea.

(3) It's good to eat a lot of vegetables.

(4) It is true that the pen is mightier than the sword.

06 (1) I have never seen a sunrise.

(2) He has taught English for 20 years.

(3) Is it safe to drink this water?

(4) It's lucky for me to play soccer on the team.

(5) It is important to brush your teeth every day.

07 (1) When did you hear from Susan?

(2) Mr. Brown has lived in Jeju-do since 2010.

(3) Have you been to Canada before?

(4) To use a ticket machine in the theater is easy.
또는 It is easy to use a ticket machine in the theater.

(5) It's important for her to understand him.

08 They haven't finished their project yet. /
Have they finished their project yet?

09 (1) has rained since[has been raining since]

(2) has gone

01 (1)~(3) 현재완료를 이용하여 배열한다. (4)~(5) '가주어(it) ~ 진주어(to부정사) …' 구문을 이용한다. (5)번에서 to부정사의 의미상의 주어로 for him을 써야 하는 것에 주의한다.

02 to부정사가 문장의 주어로 쓰일 때 주어 자리에 가주어 It을 두고 to부정사 부분(진주어)을 문장 뒤로 보낸다.

03 현재완료의 '경험' 용법을 이용하여 쓴다.

04 (1) 현재완료의 '경험' 용법을 이용한다. (2) 현재완료의 '결과' 용법을 이용한다.

05 (1)~(3) 문장의 주어로 쓰인 to부정사를 뒤로 보내고 대신 주어 자리에 가주어 it을 쓴다. (4) 주어로 쓰인 that절의 경우에도 긴 that절을 뒤로 보내고 주어 자리에 가주어 it을 쓴다.

06 (1) 현재완료의 '경험' 용법을 이용한다. (2) 현재완료의 '계속' 용법을 이용한다. (3)~(5) '가주어(It) ~ 진주어(to부정사) …' 구문을 이용한다. (4) 내가 축구를 하는 것이므로 의미상의 주어 for me를 써 주어야 한다.

07 (1) 현재완료는 과거의 특정 시점을 나타내는 어구와 함께 쓸 수 없다. (2) 현재완료에서 'since+시간 명사', 'for+기간 명사' (3) have[has] been to는 '~에 가 본 적이 있다'는 경험을 나타

내고, have[has] gone to는 '~에 가고 없 다'는 결과를 나타내므로 3인칭만 주어가 될 수 있다. 주어 가 you이므로 been to 로 고쳐야 한다. (4) to부정사를 주 어로 하거나 전체 문장을 '가주어(It) ~ 진주어(to부정사) …' 구문으로 고쳐 쓴다. (5) for her가 to understand의 의 미상의 주어가 되도록 고쳐야 한다.

08 현재완료의 부정문은 'have[has]+not[never]+과거분사'로, 의문문은 'Have[Has]+주어+과거분사 ~?'로 나타낸다. already는 부정문이나 의문문에서 yet이 되어야 함에 주의한다.

09 (1) 현재완료의 '계속' 용법을 이용한다. (2) 현재완료의 '결과' 용법을 이용한다.

확인문제   p.28

1 T   2 T   3 F   4 T

확인문제   p.29

1 T   2 F   3 F   4 T

교과서 확인학습 A   p.30~31

01 Best   02 far out in space

03 lived there with   04 worked on

05 Only, were born   06 going back to

07 in surprise   08 What's it like   09 is different

10 For example   11 I've never seen

12 is always black

13 don't have to, there is air   14 pulls you down

15 What else   16 are covered with

17 roll down   18 have you ever rolled down

19 amazing   20 opened, shook

21 floated, formed   22 swallowed

23 get wet   24 Later that night

25 exciting, all the new things   26 one new thing

27 all night   28 their secret   29 got on

30 It's going to be   31 so excited

32 finally   33 to walk

34 pulling you down

35 couldn't float anymore

36 the first new thing   37 What's

38 is singing   39 I've never heard

40 I've never felt   41 These   42 the nearest

43 each other   44 lay down, rolled down

45 their secret   46 best new thing
47 up to the top

1 The Best New Thing

2 Rada lived on a little world, far out in space.

3 She lived there with her father, mother, and brother Jonny.

4 Rada's father and other people worked on spaceships

5 Only Rada and Jonny were children, and they were born in space.

6 One day, Dad told Rada and Jonny, "We're going back to Earth tomorrow."

7 Rada and Jonny looked at Dad in surprise and floated towards him.

8 Rada asked Dad, "What's it like on Earth?"

9 "Everything is different there.

10 For example, the sky is blue," answered Dad.

11 "I've never seen a blue sky," said Jonny.

12 "The sky is always black here," said Rada.

13 "You don't have to wear your big heavy space suits because there is air everywhere.

14 It's also hard to jump there because Earth pulls you down," said Dad.

15 "What else?" asked Rada.

16 "There are hills, and they are covered with soft green grass.

17 You can roll down the hills," answered Mom.

18 "Dad, have you ever rolled down a hill?" asked Rada.

19 "Yes, it's really amazing!" answered Dad.

20 Jonny was thirsty, so he opened a milk container and shook it.

21 The milk floated in the air and formed balls.

22 Jonny swallowed the balls.

23 "Jonny, if you drink milk that way on Earth, you'll get wet," said Mom.

24 Later that night, Rada and Jonny talked a long time about Earth.

25 It was exciting to think about all the new things they were going to see and do.

26 There was one new thing Rada and Jonny really wanted to do.

27 They thought about it all night and didn't tell Mom and Dad about it.

28 It was their secret.

29 The next day, Rada's family got on a spaceship.

30 "It's going to be a long trip," said Mom.

31 That's alright. I'm so excited!" said Rada.

32 The spaceship finally landed.

33 "Dad, it's difficult to walk on Earth," said Rada.

34 "I know. Earth is pulling you down," said Dad.

35 Rada and Jonny couldn't float anymore.

36 That was the first new thing.

37 "What's that sound?" asked Rada.

38 "A bird is singing," said Mom.

39 "I've never heard a bird sing," said Rada.

40 "And I've never felt the wind," said Jonny.

41 These were all new things.

42 Rada and Jonny ran up the nearest hill.

43 At the top, they looked at each other and laughed.

44 Then they lay down on the soft green grass and rolled down the hill.

45 That was their secret!

46 "This is the best new thing of all!" shouted Rada and Jonny.

47 And they ran up to the top of the hill again.

01 ③   02 ②, ⑤   03 ⑤   04 ③

05 shook   06 ②   07 if you drink milk that way on Earth, you'll get wet 08 ②

09 (A) to think about all the new things they were going to see and do

(B) one new thing Rada and Jonny really wanted to do

(C) one new thing Rada and Jonny really wanted to do

10 (A) exciting (B) night (C) on   11 ⑤

12 (A) landed (B) pulling (C) new

13 lie → lay 14 ④   15 ③   16 ②

17 (A) shake (B) balls (C) swallow   18 ④

19 Rada and Jonny couldn't float anymore

20 familiar → new   21 they lay down on the soft green grass and rolled down the hill.

22 ⓐ ridden ⓑ ride ⓒ rode

23 오전: 공원에서 자전거를 탔다.

오후: 해변으로 가서 수영을 했다.

밤: 지구에서 사는 것에 대해 Rada와 Jonny

24 Rada thought it was wonderful to live on Earth and Jonny thought it was great to be on Earth.

25 ②　　　　**26** do them → do　　　**27** one

new thing they really wanted to do　　**28** ②

29 to sing → sing 또는 singing　　　**30** ⑤

01 ⓐ in space: 우주에서, ⓑ on Earth: 지구(상)에서

02 (A)와 ②, ⑤번: 막연한 상황을 나타내는 비인칭 주어, As it happened: 공교롭게도, ① 가목적어, ③ It is[was] ... that 의 구문으로 문장의 어떤 부분을 강조할 때 씀, ④ 가주어

03 위 글은 '공상 과학 소설(SF)'이다. ① 독후감, ② (신문, 잡지의) 글, 기사, ③ 전기, ④ 수필

04 ③ 'space'를 'Earth'로 고치는 것이 적절하다.

05 opened와 병렬구문을 이루도록 shook이라고 쓰는 것이 적절하다.

06 ⓑ와 ②, ⑤: 경험 용법, ① 결과 용법 ③ 계속 용법 ④ 완료 용법

07 조건의 부사절에서는 현재시제가 미래를 대신하므로, 'if you drink'라고 하는 것이 적절하다.

08 지구에서는 점프하는 것이 '어렵다'고 했다.

09 ⓐ It은 가주어로서 진주어인 to think about all the new things they were going to see and do를 대신 한다. ⓑ와 ⓒ: Rada와 Jonny가 정말로 하고 싶었던 한 가지 새로운 것을 가리킨다.

10 (A) 모든 새로운 것들을 생각하는 것이 '흥미로웠던' 것이므로 exciting이 적절하다. (감정을 나타내는 동사는 감정을 유발할 때 현재분사를 쓰는 것이 적절하다.) (B) all+단수 명사는 그 기간 내내 어떤 일이 계속 됨을 나타내므로 night가 적절하다. (C) 우주선에 '오르는' 것이므로 on이 적절하다. get on: 타다, 오르다, get off: 내리다

11 ⑤ (특히 좋거나 신나는 일을) 기대하는, Rada와 Jonny는 지구 여행을 기대하고 있다. ① 속상한, ② 혼란스러워 하는, ③ 걱정[우려]하는, ④ 실망한

12 (A) 우주선이 마침내 '착륙했다'고 해야 하므로 landed가 적절하다. take off: 이륙하다, (B) 지구가 너를 '끌어당기고' 있다고 해야 하므로 pulling이 적절하다. push: 밀다, (C) 지구에서 겪 는 모든 새로운 것들에 대해 이야기하고 있으므로 new를 써서 최고의 '새로운 것'이라고 하는 것이 적절하다. familiar: 친숙한

13 과거시제로 써야 하므로 lay로 고치는 것이 적절하다. lie-lay-lain: 눕다

14 이 글은 지구에서 겪는 모든 새로운 것들에 대해 이야기하는 글이므로, 제목으로는 '그들이 지구에서 겪은 새로운 것들'이 적절하다.

15 Rada는 새가 노래하는 것을 들어 본 적이 '없다'.

16 주어진 문장의 else에 주목한다. ②번 앞 문장에서 우주 와 지구의 다른 점을 설명한 것 외에 "그 밖에 또 뭐가 있어요?"라고 묻는 것이므로 ②번이 적절하다.

17 우주에서는 지구에서 사람들이 하는 방식으로 우유를 마실 수

없다. 먼저, 당신은 우유 용기를 열어 그것을 '흔든다'. 그 다음, 우유가 공기 중으로 떠서 '방울'을 형성한다. 마지막으로 그 우유 방울을 '삼킨다.'

18 아빠가 언제 언덕을 굴러 내려갔는지는 대답할 수 없다. ① Because there is air everywhere. ② Because Earth pulls you down. ③ You can roll down the hills. ⑤ He swallowed the balls of milk.

19 'Rada와 Jonny가 더 이상 떠다닐 수 없었던 것'이 첫 번째 새로운 것이었다.

20 These가 앞에서 말한 새로운 것들을 받은 것이기 때문에, 이러한 것들이 모두 '새로운' 것이었다라고 고치는 것이 적절하다. familiar: 익숙한

21 'lie'의 과거 'lay'를 사용하여 영작하는 것이 적절하다.

22 ⓐ 현재완료 시제이므로 과거분사로 쓰는 것이 적절하다. ⓑ Let's 다음에 동사원형으로 쓰는 것이 적절하다. ⓒ 과거에 일어난 일이므로 과거시제로 쓰는 것이 적절하다.

23 오전에는 자전거를 탔고, 오후에는 수영을 했고, 밤에는 지구에서 사는 것에 대해 Rada와 Jonny가 이야기를 했다.

24 Rada와 Jonny는 지구에서 사는 것이 '멋있다'고 생각했다.

25 ⓐ와 ②, ④: 가주어, ① 비인칭주어, ③ 인칭대명사, 그것(앞에 이미 언급되었거나 현재 이야기되고 있는 사물·동물을 가리킴), ⑤ 가목적어

26 all the new things와 they 사이에 see and do의 목적어에 해당하는 목적격 관계대명사 which/that이 생략되어 있는데, 목적어 them을 또 쓰는 것은 옳지 않다.

27 Rada와 Jonny의 비밀은 '그들이 정말로 하고 싶었던 한 가지 새로운 것'이다.

28 이 글은 Rada와 Jonny가 지구에서 겪는 새로운 것들에 대해 이야기하는 글이다.

29 hear는 지각동사로서 'hear+목적어+동사원형/-ing'의 형태로 쓰인다.

30 Rada와 Jonny가 언덕 꼭대기로 몇 번 뛰어올라갔는지는 대답할 수 없다. ① Because Earth is pulling you down. ② No. ③ No. ④ They lay down on the soft green grass and rolled down the hill.

서술형 시험대비　　　　　　　　　　p.40~41

01 (A) children　(B) who[that]

02 Rada and Jonny looked at Dad in surprise and floated towards him.

03 color

04 (A) must(또는 have to)　(B) hard(또는 difficult)　(C) balls

05 I have

06 will drink → drink

07 never

08 no more

09 lay down, rolled down

10 (A) other (B) What (C) different

11 ran → floated

12 ⓑ on Earth ⓒ in space

---

21 ③, ⑤   22 What's it like on Earth?

23 (A) because (B) What (C) if   24 ⑤

25 ①, ③, ④   26 There was one new thing which(또는 that) Rada and Jonny really wanted to do.

27 It's going to be a long trip   28 ①

29 has ever heard → has never heard
has ever felt → has never felt

30 best new thing

---

01 우주에는 그곳에서 태어난 Rada와 Jonny를 제외하고는 '아이들'이 없었다. (B)에는 주격 관계대명사 who[that]를 쓰는 것이 적절하다.

02 'in'을 보충하면 된다.

03 지구의 하늘은 파란색이고, 우주의 하늘은 항상 검은색이라고 했으므로 하늘의 '색깔'이 서로 다르다.

04 (A) 우주에서는 크고 무거운 우주복을 입을 '필요가 있다.' have to = must (B) 지구에서는 점프하는 것이 '어렵다.' (C) 우주에서는 '우유 방울'을 삼킨다.

05 현재완료로 물었기 때문에 Yes, I 'do'가 아니라 Yes, I 'have'로 답하는 것이 적절하다.

06 조건의 부사절에서는 현재시제가 미래를 대신하므로, 'if you drink'라고 하는 것이 적절하다.

07 (A) 이번이 새가 노래하는 것을 처음 들어 본 때이다. = 나는 새가 노래하는 것을 들어 본 적이 없다. (B) 이번이 내가 바람을 처음 느껴 본 때이다. = 나는 바람을 느껴 본 적이 없다.

08 not ~ anymore = no more: 더 이상 … 아닌[하지 않는], no longer도 가능하다.

09 부드러운 초록 잔디에 '누워서' 언덕 '아래로 굴러 내려간' 것이 그들의 비밀이었다.

10 (A) 뒤에 복수명사가 나오므로 other가 적절하다. another+단수 명사, (B) is like의 목적어가 와야 하므로 What이 적절하다. (C) 바로 뒤에 하늘의 색이 다른 예가 나오고 있으므로, 그곳에선 모든 것이 '다르다'고 하는 것이 적절하다. similar: 비슷한, 유사한

11 우주에서 일어나고 있는 일이므로, 그에게 '달려서' 가는 것이 아니라 '둥둥 떠서 갔다'로 고치는 것이 적절하다.

12 ⓑ는 '지구(상)에서', ⓒ는 '우주에서'를 가리킨다.

영역별 핵심문제   p.43~47

01 land   02 ④   03 ③   04 ①

05 space   06 ⑤   07 ④   08 ②

09 It's about a man who is trying to live on the moon.

10 ①   11 (1) Did you hear about (2) I'm really curious about it. (3) What's it about?   12 ②

13 ②   14 ①   15 ⑤

16 (1) for Tony to hand in his report by tomorrow
(2) for you to be careful when you cross the street

17 ③   18 ④   19 ⑤   20 ④

---

01 반의어 관계이다. 신난 : 지루한 = 이륙하다 : 착륙하다

02 모든 곳에 공기가 있기 때문에 크고 무거운 우주복을 입을 필요가 없다(don't have[need] to). 또한 그곳에서는 지구가 너희를 끌어당기고 있기(pulls you down) 때문에 뛰어 오르는 것이 어렵다. pull down은 이어 동사(동사+부사)로 대명사 you는 동사와 부사 사이에 위치한다.

03 엄마의 몸에서 나오다: 태어나다(be born)

04 공중에서 아래로 이동한 후 땅이나 다른 표면에 도착하다

05 • 저 책상은 너무 많은 공간을 차지한다. • 이 주차장에는 90대의 주차 공간이 있다. • 6월 18일, 중국은 첫 여성우주 비행사를 우주로 보냈다.

06 lie down은 '눕다'라는 뜻이다

07 (C) 새로운 우주 음식에 대해 들어 봤는지 묻고 → (B) 긍정의 답과 함께 우주 음식이 일종의 아이스크림이라고 말한다. → (A) 그 말에 동의하고 그 음식을 가리키며 맛있어 보인다고 말한다. → (D) 마지막으로 맛이 궁금하다고 말한다.

08 영화 내용을 설명하는 말 앞인 ②가 적절하다.

09 영화 'Life on the Moon'은 무엇에 관한 것인가?

10 ① 새 영화가 정말로 좋다는 말을 들은 사람은 Subin이 아니라 B다.

12 ⓑ의 'right'은 부사로 '바로'의 의미이다.

13 ②에는 사람의 성격이나 성질을 나타내는 형용사(foolish)가 왔으므로 의미상의 주어 앞에 of가 들어가야 한다. 나머지는 모두 for가 들어간다.

14 since(~한 이래로)는 보통 현재완료와 함께 많이 쓰인다. 이때 since절에는 과거 시제가 많이 쓰인다.

15 ⑤번은 '계속' 용법이지만 나머지는 '경험' 용법이다.

16 '~해야 한다'는 의미를 가주어 it을 이용하여 '~할 필요가 있다'라고 쓰려면 진주어로 to부정사를 이용한다. 이때 의미상의 주어를 빠뜨리지 않도록 주의한다.

17 ⓐ Has Daniel found → Did Daniel find ⓒ gone → been ⓔ since → for ⓕ follows → to follow ⓖ That → It

18 ④번은 to부정사의 부사적 용법이지만 나머지는 모두 진주어로 쓰인 명사적 용법으로 쓰였다.

19 ⑤ 현재완료는 과거를 나타내는 어구와 함께 쓸 수 없다.

20 앞의 내용의 예가 나오고 있으므로 For example이 가장 적절하

다.① 그러나, ② 그러므로, ③ 게다가, ⑤ 즉

21 ⓐ와 ③, ⑤번: 미래를 나타내는 부사(구)와 함께 쓰여 현재진행되는 의미가 아니라 가까운 미래를 나타낸다. 나머지는 다 현재 진행되는 의미를 나타낸다.

22 be like: ~와 같다

23 (A) 크고 무거운 우주복을 입을 필요가 없는 이유를 말해야 하므로 because가 적절하다. though: 비록 ~이지만(양보), (B) 그 밖에 또 '뭐가' 있냐고 물어야 하므로 What이 적절하다. (C) '만약' 그런 식으로라고 해야 하므로 if가 적절하다. unless = if ~ not

24 Jonny는 우유 용기를 열어 흔들었을 때 우유가 공기 중으로 떠서 형성된 '우유 방울을 삼켰다.'

25 ⓐ와 ②, ⑤: 명사적 용법, ①, ④ 부사적 용법, ③ 형용사적 용법

26 'ne new thing과 Rada and Jonny 사이에 do의 목적어에 해당하는 목적격 관계대명사 which/that이 생략되어 있다.

27 "긴 여행이 될 거야."라는 엄마의 말을 가리킨다.

28 주어진 문장의 These에 주목한다. ①번 앞 문장의 내용들을 받고 있으므로 ①번이 적절하다.

29 Rada는 새가 노래하는 것을 들어 본 적이 '없고', Jonny는 바람을 느껴 본 적이 '없다.'

30 Rada와 Jonny에게 모든 것들 중에서 '최고의 새로운 것'은 부드러운 초록 잔디에 누워서 언덕 아래로 굴러 내려간 것이었다.

단원별 예상문제 p.48~51

01 smooth　　02 ③　　　03 I'm interested in it.
04 ③　　　　05 ⑤　　　06 hear about, that, into
07 ②　　　　08 who is trying to live on the moon
09 have you heard about the new movie
10 I'm really curious about the movie.　11 ③
12 (1) He has slept for thirty minutes.
　(2) The celebrity has just arrived at the airport.
　(3) Sue has never been to France before.
　(4) I have forgotten the new student's name.
　(5) It is important to share various opinions.
　(6) It is nice of you to remember my birthday.
13 ⑤　　14 ②　　15 ⑤　　16 ③
17 ②　　18 ③　　19 ②, ⑤
20 ⓒ the hills　ⓓ to roll[rolling] down the hills
　ⓔ the milk container
21 ④　　22 ①, ③　　23 ④　　24 ②
25 (1) Rada와 Jonny가 더 이상 떠다닐 수 없었던 것.
　(2) Rada가 새가 노래하는 것을 들어 본 것.
　(3) Jonny가 바람을 느껴 본 것.

01 반의어 관계이다. 똑똑한 : 어리석은 = 거친 : 부드러운
02 누군가나 어떤 것의 방향으로 또는 더 가까이: '~을 향해'
03 새로운 정보에 관심이 있다는 표현으로 be curious about, be

interested in, want to know 등을 사용할 수 있다.

04 전치사 about 뒤에 있는 부정사 to live를 동명사 living으로 바꾸는 적절하다.

05 get on은 '~을 타다, 탑승하다'라는 의미로 '우주선에 올랐다'가 맞다.

06 'hear about ~'은 '~에 관해 듣다'는 뜻이고, 선행사에 the first(서수)가 있을 때는 보통 관계대명사 that을 사용하는 것이 적절하다.

07 G의 첫 번째 말에 우주선에 대해 궁금하다고 했으므로 빈칸에는 긍정의 대답이 오는 것이 적절하다. ⑤번은 대화와 관련이 없는 말이다.

08 관계대명사 who 뒤에 동사 is를 사용하고 be동사 뒤에 현재분사 trying이 오는 것이 적절하다. 그 다음 'trying to+ 동사원형' 형태가 온다.

09 현재완료를 사용해 'Have you heard about ~?'이라고 들어 본 적이 있는지 물을 수 있다.

10 부사 really는 be동사 뒤에 오고 be curious about을 사용하여 문장을 완성한다.

11 현재완료에서 'since+시간 명사', 'for+기간 명사'

12 (1) 현재완료의 '계속' 용법을 이용한다. (2) 현재완료의 '완료' 용법을 이용한다. (3) 'have[has] been to'는 '~에 가본 적이 있다'는 경험을 나타낸다. (4) 현재완료의 '결과' 용법을 이용한다. (5) '가주어(it) ~ 진주어(to부정사) …' 구문을 이용한다. (6) 문장에 쓰인 형용사가 사람의 성향, 성격을 나타내는 말일 때는 to부정사의 의미상의 주어로 'of+목적격'을 쓴다.

13 ① It's great to be here. ② It's fun to play with friends. ③ It is boring to fish in the lake. ④ It's exciting for us to have you here

14 ② Have you been to London before?

15 가주어 it을 이용하여 바꿔 쓰는 것으로 원래 문장의 to부정사를 진주어로 쓴다.

16 ⓒ in

17 (A)와 ②번: (외관·내용 등이) …을 닮아, 유사하여; …일 것 같아, …과 다름없이(전치사), be like: ~와 같다, ①, ③, ⑤: ~을 좋아하다(동사), ④ [외관·형태·성질 등이] 같은 (same) (형용사)

18 '그곳에는 모든 곳에 공기가 있기 때문에' 크고 무거운 우주복을 입을 필요가 없다고 하는 것이 적절하다.

19 It은 가주어로서 진주어인 to jump there를 대신한 것이므로 to jump there나 jumping there를 가주어 It 자리에 쓸 수 있고, 의미상의 주어인 for you를 써도 된다.

20 ⓒ 언덕들, ⓓ 언덕을 굴러 내려가는 것, ⓔ 우유 용기를 가리킨다.

21 Rada는 지구 여행을 기대하고 있으므로 "괜찮아요. 정말 신나요!"라고 하는 것이 적절하다. ② 감정을 나타내는 동사는 사람을 수식할 때 보통 과거분사를 써야 하므로 interested가 적절하다. ③ pleasant는 '상냥한'이라는 뜻일 때를 제외하고는 사

람을 주어로 해서 쓸 수 없다. pleased로 쓰는 것이 적절하다.

22 all the new things와 they 사이에 see and do의 목적어에 해당하는 목적격 관계대명사 which/that이 생략되어 있다.

23 Rada와 Jonny는 정말로 하고 싶었던 한 가지 새로운 것에 대해서 엄마와 아빠에게 말하지 않았다.

24 consequently: 그 결과, 따라서, finally와 나머지는 다 '마침내'

25 앞의 세 문장들의 내용을 가리킨다.

서술형 실전문제
p.52~53

01 (A) Did you hear about the new snack?
   (B) I'm curious about it.
02 You can choose a player who you like and play.
03 (1) for   (2) before   (3) since
04 (1) They are talking about the new movie.
   (2) They will eat[have] lunch.
05 (1) It was easy to answer his questions.
   (2) It is easy to cook camping food.
   (3) It is safe and comfortable to live in Seoul.
   (4) It was very wise of her to say so.
06 (1) has live, since   (2) have read, three times
   (3) has taken
07 (A) don't have to   (B) hard   (C) amazing
08 pulls down you → pulls you down
09 (A) get wet   (B) shake

02 조동사 can 뒤에 동사원형 choose를 쓰고 관계대명사절 'who you like'가 선행사인 목적어 'a player'를 꾸며주고 and 뒤에 play가 choose와 병렬구조로 문장을 완성한다.

03 (1), (3) 현재완료에서 'since+시간 명사', 'for+ 기간 명사' (2) ago는 현재완료와 함께 사용할 수 없으나 before는 사용할 수 있다.

04 (1) Subin과 Andy는 새 영화에 관해 이야기하고 있다. (2) 영화를 보기 전에 점심을 먹을 것이다.

05 (1) It을 가주어로 하고 to부정사를 진주어로 쓴다. (2) It을 가주어로 하고 진주어 to cook의 목적어로 camping food를 쓴다. (3) 전치사 in의 목적어로 Seoul을 쓴다. (4) to say의 주어가 she이므로 of her로 의미상의 주어를 나타내야 한다.

06 (1) 현재완료의 '계속' 용법을 이용한다. (2) 현재완료의 '경험' 용법을 이용한다. (3) 현재완료의 '결과' 용법을 이용한다.

07 (A) 그곳에는 모든 곳에 공기가 있기 때문에 크고 무거운 우주복을 입을 '필요가 없다'고 해야 하므로 don't have to가 적절하다. (B) 지구가 너희들을 끌어당기기 때문에 거기에서는 점프하는 것도 '어렵다'고 해야 하므로 hard가 적절하다. (C) 언덕을 굴러 내려가는 것이 '놀라운' 것이므로 amazing이 적절하다. (감정을 나타내는 동사는 감정을 일으킬 때 현재분사를 쓰는 것이 적

절하다.)

08 목적어가 인칭대명사일 때는 타동사와 부사 사이에 목적어를 쓰는 것이 적절하다.

09 지구에서 우유 용기를 열어 그것을 '흔들면' 우유가 용기에서 쏟아져 나와서 당신을 '젖게' 만들 것이기 때문이다.

창의사고력 서술형 문제
p.54

|모범답안|
01 (1) It is exciting to learn a new language.
   (2) It's necessary for me to see a doctor.
   (3) It is important to exercise regularly.
   (4) It's difficult to learn Chinese.
   (5) It's fun to go to the beach.
02 (A) ridden a bike   (B) rode bikes
   (C) swum before   (D) to swim   (E) living on Earth

단원별 모의고사
p.55~58

01 ④   02 arrive / reach   03 ①
04 ④   05 ③   06 ⑤   07 ②
08 They are going to eat lunch.
09 about, who   10 (1) F   (2) T   11 ⑤
12 ④   13 ②   14 ③
15 (1) Have you found → Did you find
   (2) played the piano since → have played the piano for
   (3) gone → been
   (4) Search → To search[Searching]또는 Search information using the Internet is easy. → It is easy to search information using the Internet.
   (5) of → for
16 (1) He has known her since he was ten years old.
   (2) He hasn't finished his homework yet.
   (3) They have seen the movie four times.
   (4) She has gone to Paris.
   (5) It was helpful to visit this web site.
   (6) It is hard for a child to wash a big dog.
17 (A) different   (B) blue   18 ①, ②, ④   19 (e)lse
20 have you ever rolled down a hill?   21 ④

01 ④번은 'pull down'에 대한 설명이다. roll down은 'to move downward by turning over and over(반복해서 돌면서 아래로 내려오다)'가 적절하다.

02 반의어 관계이다. 다른 : 같은 = 도착하다 : 출발하다

03 '액체의 표면에 머무르고 가라앉지 않다'는 float '뜨다'가 적절하다.

04 '새 노래에 대해 들어 봤느냐'는 A의 물음에 '아니, 못 들어 봤다'

고 말하고는 새 노래에 대한 설명을 하는 건 자연스럽지 않다.

05 대화는 화성에 관한 책에 대한 이야기다.

06 G의 답으로 보아 영화의 내용을 묻는 말이 적절하다.

07 빈칸 다음의 말이 영화의 내용이 무엇인지 묻고 있으므로 그 영화에 관심이 있다는 것을 알 수 있다.

10 (1) 두 사람은 새로운 책에 대해 이야기 중이다. (2) 소년은 새 책에 대해 궁금해 하기 때문에 관심이 있다는 것을 알 수 있다.

11 B가 그 영화가 정말 궁금하다고 말하는 것으로 보아 G는 영화에 대해 좋은 평가를 내리고 있다고 추측할 수 있다.

12 (D)에서 새 책에 대한 정보를 알고 있는지 묻고, (A)에서 부정의 답이 오고 이어서 (C)에서 책에 관한 내용을 이야기해 주고 나서 (B)에서 이 책이 궁금하다고 말하는 것이 자연스럽다.

13 현재완료는 과거의 특정 시점을 나타내는 의문사 when과 함께 쓸 수 없다. When did you visit Italy?

14 주어진 문장과 ③번은 가주어로 쓰이고 있다. ①, ⑤ 비인칭 주어 ② It ~ that 강조구문 ④ 인칭대명사

15 (1) 현재완료는 과거를 나타내는 ~ ago와는 함께 쓰이지 않는다. (2) 오래전에 시작해서 아직도 즐기고 있다고 했으므로 현재완료의 '계속' 용법으로 나타내는 것이 적절하다. 'since+시간 명사', 'for+ 기간 명사'임에 유의한다. (3) have[has] been to는 '~에 가 본 적이 있다'는 경험을 나타내고, have[has] gone to 는 '~에 가고 없다'는 결과를 나타내므로 have been to로 고쳐야 한다. (4) to부정사나 동명사가 주어가 되도록 하거나 가주어 it을 사용하고 진주어로 to부정사를 쓴다. (5) to부정사의 의미상 주어는 to부정사 바로 앞에 'for+명사의 목적격'의 형태로 쓴다.

16 (1) 현재완료의 '계속' 용법을 이용한다. (2) 현재완료의 '완료' 용법 을 이용한다. 부정문이므로 yet을 쓰는 것에 주의한다. (3) 현재완료의 '경험' 용법을 이용한다. (4) 현재완료의 '결과' 용법을 이용한다. have[has] been to는 '~에 가 본 적이 있다'는 경험을 나타내고, have[has] gone to 는 '~에 가고 없다'는 결과를 나타낸다. (5) '가주어(it) ~ 진주어(to부정사) …' 구문을 이용한다. (6) '가주어(it) ~ 진주어(to부정사) …' 구문을 이용하고 to 부정사의 의미상의 주어로 'for+목적격'을 쓴다

17 지구에서 하늘의 색깔은 우주의 그것과는 다르다. 그것은 검은 색이 아니라 '파란색'이다.

18 ⓐ와 ③, ⑤번: 경험 용법, ①, ④: 계속 용법, ② 완료 용법

19 else: 그 밖에

20 'down'을 보충하면 된다. roll down: 굴러 내려가다

21 지구가 끌어당기기 때문에 지구에서 점프하는 것이 어려운 것이므로, 우주복을 입는 것과 점프하는 것은 상관이 없다.

Pride of Korea

01 • 상자가 금과 은과 같은 보물로 가득 차 있었다. • 이 그림의 가치는 약 백만 달러이다.

02 '멈추지 않고서 어떤 일을 계속하다'

03 '누군가가 무엇을 할 수 있다고 말하다'는 allow(허락하다)가 적절하다.

04 '당신이 한 일에 대한 만족감과 즐거움'은 pride(긍지, 자부심)가 적절하다.

05 as soon as는 접속사로 '~하자마자'라는 뜻이다.

06 글의 흐름상 도서관 상사들이 심지어 필자를 한국의 스파이라고 생각했기 때문에 '해고했다'가 적절하다.

07 반의어 관계이다. 멈추다: 계속하다 - 실패하다 : 성공하다

08 해외에 있는 우리의 문화재에 더 많은 관심을 갖고 그것의 반환을 위해 애써 주기를 바란다는 내용이 적절하다.

01 (1) 조사를 끝내기 위해 매일 도서관에 갔다는 뜻으로 research 가 적절하다. (2) 해금에 관한 내용이다. 전통적인 한국 악기라는 뜻으로 주어진 단어 'tradition'을 형용사 형태로 바꾸어 준다. (3) but 뒤에 그가 곧 그의 나라로 돌아 갈 것이라고 했기 때문에 그가 지금 'abroad(해외에)' 있다는 것을 알 수 있다. (4) 잔디에 앉는 것이 금지되어 있다는 수동의 의미로 주어진 단어 allow를 과거분사 allowed로 바꾸어 주어야 한다.

02 (1) '~ 덕분에'란 뜻으로 thanks to를 사용하고, 발견되었다는 수동의 의미로 were found가 적절하다. (2) 이 문장에서 'return'은 명사로 사용이 되었다.

03 (1) • 대부분의 동물들은 불을 두려워한다. • 우리는 그가 정직

11

하지 못해서 해고해야 했다. (2) • 여가 시간은 어떻게 보내세요? • 나의 부모님은 매달 책을 사는 데 많은 돈을 쓰신다. (3) • 그는 재생 가능한 에너지원에 대한 연구 조사를 수행해 왔다. • 많은 연구원들이 그 문제를 철저히 조사한다. (4) • 우리는 인생에서 성공하기 위해 열심히 일해야 한다. • 많은 실패 후에, 과학자들은 마침내 그들의 이론을 증명하는데 성공했다.

04 (1) 어떤 것이 사실이라는 것을 보여주다 (2) 다른 누군가에게 속해 있는 물건을 가져가다 (3) 왕이나 여왕과 관련되거나 속해 있는 (4) 전기와 열을 잘 전달하는 철, 금 또는 철강과 같은 단단한 물질 conduct: (열, 전기를) 전달[전도]하다

Conumation [교과서] Conversation

핵심 Check
p.64~65

1 ⑤ **2** ⑤

교과서 대화문 익히기

Check(√) True or False
p.66

1 T **2** T **3** T **4** T

교과서 확인학습
p.68~69

Listen and Talk A-1
I've never seen, like / dessert / Is it OK to / ahead, delicious

Listen and Talk A-2
to sit / mean / sitting, is not allowed

Listen and Talk A-3
looks interesting / traditional, instrument / Is it OK to play / I'm sorry, for display, allowed

Listen and Talk A-4
Excuse, Is it OK to take / How about using / afraid, Using, not allowed

Listen and Talk B
Is it OK to sit here / afraid not, Sitting, not allowed

Talk and Play
Which, to go / Why don't you / Is it OK to eat / Eating, allowed / Is it OK to take / is not allowed / got it

---

Listen and Talk C
Is it OK / fitting room / over there / traditional, for, worn, wedding / Is it OK to try it on / for display, on, allowed / try on

Review 1
looks interesting / traditional, musical instrument / Is it OK to / for display, allowed

Review 2
is it OK / ahead / Can I / but, one more / not allowed

시험대비 기본평가
p.70

01 Using, is, allowed **02** ② **03** ⑤
04 ② **05** ①

01 동명사 주어 using을 사용하고, 'be not allowed'가 '허용되지 않다'라는 뜻이다.

02 'Is it OK if I ~?'는 '~해도 될까요?'라는 뜻으로 'Is it OK to+동사원형 ~?'과 같은 표현이다.

03 '여기에 앉는 것이 허용되지 않는다'고 했으므로 허락을 하지 않는 부정의 답이 적절하다.

04 금지를 나타내는 표현이 아닌 것은 don't have to(~할 필요가 없다)이다.

시험대비 실력평가
p.71~72

01 ④ **02** I've never seen any food like this.
03 ④ **04** Sitting is not allowed **05** ③
06 ⑤ **07** Playing the haegeum is not allowed. **08** is it OK to take pictures here? → is it OK if I take pictures here? **09** ②
10 ④ **11** ③ **12** ⑤

01 허가 여부를 묻는 표현으로 ④는 어색하다.

02 현재완료 부정문 형태는 'have never+과거분사'이다. like는 전치사로 '~와 같은'의 의미다.

03 (C) 저기에 앉아도 되는지 허가 여부를 묻고 (B) 저기가 잔디 위를 말하는 건지 확인하는 말이 오고 (D)의 긍정의 답이 온다. 마지막으로 (A)의 앉으면 안 된다는 금지의 말이 오는 것이 적절하다.

04 동사 sit을 동명사 sitting으로 바꾸어 주어로 쓴다. '~이 허용되지 않는다.'는 수동태 be not allowed로 쓴다.

05 'Should I use it ~?'은 상대방에게 허가를 묻는 표현으로는 자연스럽지 않다.

06 ⓔ be동사 뒤에 일반동사 allow를 또 사용할 수 없다. be동사

뒤에 과거분사 형태로 수동태(is not allowed)가 적 절하다.

07 해금을 연주하는 것이 허락되지 않는다.

08 '~해도 될까요?'라는 의미로 허가 여부를 묻는 표현으로 'Is it OK to+동사원형 ~?', 'Is it OK if+주어+동사 ~?'의 형태가 가능하다.

09 'Can I eat food here?'에 대한 답으로 'I'm sorry'라고 말하고 있으므로 먹을 수 없다는 부정의 답이 온다는 것을 알 수 있다.

10 제시문은 '그것은 보통 결혼식 날 착용된다.'는 의미로 It은 'jokduri'를 나타내므로 ④에 들어가는 것이 적절하다.

11 ⓒ의 try on은 '동사+부사' 형태의 이어동사로 대명사 it은 반드시 '동사와 부사' 사이에 위치해야 한다.

12 족두리만 전시용이다.

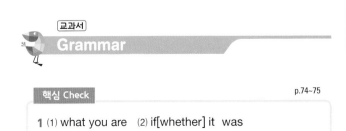

01 (A) Eating food is allowed.
   (B) Taking pictures is not allowed.
02 Using a flash is not allowed here.
03 Is it OK to play it?
04 (A) is it OK to take pictures here?
   (B) Can I use a flash, too?
   (C) I have one more question.
   (D) that's not allowed.

01 (A) 음식을 먹어도 되는지에 대한 허락의 표현으로 동명사 Eating food로 문장을 시작하고, 음식을 먹는 것이 허락된다. 수동의 의미로 is allowed를 쓴다. (B) 사진을 찍는 것에 대한 금지의 표현으로 동명사 Taking pictures로 문장을 시작하고 부정문 수동태로 is not allowed를 쓰면 된다.

02 허가 여부를 묻는 'Can I ~?'의 질문에 'I'm afraid not.'이라는 부정의 답을 하고 있기 때문에, 금지의 표현인 'is not allowed'를 이용하는 것이 적절하다. 주어는 동명사 'Using a flash'를 쓴다.

03 허가 여부를 묻는 표현으로 'Is it OK ~?' 구문을 이용한다. 조건에 맞게 장구(a janggu)는 대명사 it을 사용한다.

교과서
Grammar

핵심 Check   p.74~75

1 (1) what you are (2) if[whether] it was
2 (1) because[as, since] (2) because of

01 ②   02 ⑤   03 ②
04 He quit the job because of his health.

01 의문사가 있는 간접의문문은 '의문사+주어+동사'의 형태로 다른 문장 안에서 주어, 목적어, 보어 역할을 한다.

02 간접의문문은 '의문사+주어+동사'의 어순이다.

03 because는 접속사이므로 뒤에는 주어와 동사가 있는 절이 나오고, because of는 부사구이므로 뒤에는 명사 또는 명사구가 나온다.

04 동사가 하나뿐이므로 접속사가 아닌 부사구 because of를 써야 하므로 of를 추가하여 문장을 배열한다.

01 ④   02 ②   03 ⑤
04 (1) because of (2) because of (3) because
   (4) his name was (5) you are (6) if
05 ③   06 Do you know when the movie starts?
07 ①   08 ⑤   09 ③   10 ④
11 (1) Because it was getting dark, we had to hurry.
   (2) Jim couldn't take a nap because his little sister cried a lot.
   (3) We didn't go camping because of the bad weather.
12 ③
13 (1) Can I ask you why you decided to become a teacher?
   (2) I want to know where you were born.
   (3) Who do you think the girl is?
   (4) He asked me if[whether] I am Simon's sister.
   (5) I took some medicine because of a bad cold.
   (6) You can't watch the movie because you're not old enough.
14 ⑤   15 ③   16 ①   17 ⑤
18 ⑤   19 Please tell me what the thief stole.

01 간접의문문의 어순은 '의문사+주어+동사'의 형태임에 유의한다.

02 because는 접속사이므로 뒤에는 주어와 동사가 있는 절이 나오고, because of는 부사구이므로 뒤에는 명사 또는 명사구가 나온다.

03 ① Can you tell me where you were born? ② Minho doesn't know where Kevin lives. ③ I stayed home because I had a high fever. ④ The picnic was canceled because of the bad weather.

04 (1), (2) because of는 부사구이므로 뒤에는 명사 또는 명사구

13

가 나온다. (3) because는 접속사이므로 뒤에는 주어와 동사가 있는 절이 나온다. (4), (5) 간접의문문의 어순은 '의문사+주어+동사'이다. (6) 간접의문문에서 의문사가 없는 경우에는 의문사 대신에 if나 whether를 쓴다.

05 ③번은 간접의문문에 쓰인 것이지만 나머지는 모두 조건의 부사절을 이끌고 있다.

06 간접의문문의 어순은 '의문사+주어+동사'이다.

07 because 다음에는 '이유'가 나오고, so 다음에는 '결과'가 나온다.

08 간접의문문의 어순은 '의문사+주어+동사'의 형태임에 유의한다.

09 ③은 뒤에 '결과'가 이어지고 있으므로 so가 들어가야 하고, 나머지는 모두 이유를 이끌고 있는 because가 들어가야 한다.

10 의문사가 없는 간접의문문의 어순은 'if[whether]+주어+동사'이며 if는 or not과 붙여 쓰지 않는다.

11 because+절(주어+동사 ~), because of+명사 또는 명사구

12 ⓐ I want to know where she is. ⓒ I wonder if he is at home. ⓕ Peter couldn't play soccer because of the rain.

13 (1), (2) 간접의문문의 어순은 '의문사+주어+동사'이다. (3) do you think가 있을 때에는 의문사가 문장 앞에 위치한다. (4) 의문사가 없는 간접의문문의 어순은 'if[whether]+ 주어+동사'로 쓴다. (5) 뒤에 명사구가 나오므로 because of가 적절하다. (6) 뒤에 절이 나오므로 because가 적절하 다.

14 간접의문문의 어순은 '의문사+주어+동사'이다. 의문문에 쓰인 조동사 did를 안 쓰는 대신, did의 시제를 간접의문문의 동사에 반영한다.

15 뒤에 명사구가 나오므로 because of가 적절하다.

16 간접의문문의 어순은 '의문사+주어+동사'이며 의문사가 없는 경우는 'if[whether]+주어+동사'로 쓴다.

17 뒤에 '이유'가 이어지고 있으므로 because가 들어가야 한다.

18 의문사가 없는 간접의문문은 'if[whether]+주어+동사'로 쓴다.

19 간접의문문의 어순은 '의문사+주어+동사'이다. 의문문에 쓰인 조동사 did의 시제를 간접의문문의 동사에 반영한다.

01 (1) I'd like to know what you wanted to be when you were young.

(2) Can you tell me when and where you were born?

(3) I don't know who borrowed your book.

(4) I wonder if[whether] my child expresses himself well in English.

(5) Do you know if[whether] it will rain today?

(6) What do you believe you were in a previous life?

02 (1) There is no school today because it's snowing a lot. 또는 Because it's snowing a lot, there is no school today.

(2) We couldn't start the meeting because Jaemin didn't arrive. 또는 Because Jaemin didn't arrive, we couldn't start the meeting.

03 (1) when you found (2) where you found them

04 because riding a bike is not allowed

05 (1) I'd like to know. Who is your best friend?

(2) She didn't tell me. Whom did she meet yesterday?

(3) He wondered. Was something wrong with him?

(4) Do you think? What will you wear on Monday?

06 (1) Can you tell me what happened to Jessie?

(2) He asked me if[whether] I had any money.

(3) I want to know who wrote this book.

(4) What do you think the secret of your health is?

(5) I didn't go to his birthday party because of a cold.

(6) I sat down because I was feeling dizzy.

(7) Everyone left early because Michael and Jane had an argument.

07 (1) I don't remember what the thief was wearing.

(2) I don't know who stole my camera.

(3) Can you tell me how you became interested in Uigwe?

(4) I asked her if[whether] she was ready to go.

(5) What do you suppose most American teenagers seek help for?

(6) Jane woke up in the middle of the night because of a bad dream.

(7) Yesterday Mary went shopping because she wanted to buy a gift for her dad.

08 because[as, since]

01 간접의문문의 어순은 '의문사+주어+동사'이며 의문사가 없는 경우는 'if[whether]+주어+동사'로 쓰며 의문사가 주어인 경우에는 의문사가 주어 역할을 동시에 하므로 직접의문문처럼 '의문사+동사'의 어순임에 유의한다. believe 동사가 주절에 있을 경우 간접의문문의 의문사를 문장 맨 앞으로 배치한다. 또한 의문문에 쓰인 조동사 do를 안 쓰는 대신, do의 시제를 간접의문문의 동사에 반영한다.

02 'so+결과'를 'because+이유'로 바꿔 쓸 수 있다.

03 간접의문문의 어순은 '의문사+주어+동사'이며 (1)에는 언제 발견했는지를 묻는 표현이, (2)에는 어디서 발견했는지를 묻는 표현이 들어가는 것이 적절하다.

04 why로 묻고 있으므로 'because+주어+동사'로 '이유'를 답하면 된다.

05 간접의문문의 어순은 '의문사+주어+동사'이며 의문사가 없는 경우는 'if[whether]+주어+동사'로 쓴다. think 동사가 주절에 있을 경우 간접의문문의 의문사를 문장 맨 앞으로 배치한다.

또한 의문문에 쓰인 조동사 do를 안 쓰는 대신, do의 시제를 간접의문문의 동사에 반영한다.

06 간접의문문과 because를 이용하여 영작한다.

07 (1)~(5) 간접의문문의 어순은 '의문사+주어+동사'이며 의문사가 없는 경우는 'if[whether]+주어+동사'로 쓴다. 의문사가 주어인 경우에는 의문사가 주어 역할을 동시에 하므로 '의문사+동사'의 어순으로 쓴다. suppose 동사가 주절에 있을 경우 간접의문문의 의문사를 문장 맨 앞으로 배치한다. 또한 의문문에 쓰인 조동사 do를 안 쓰는 대신, do의 시제를 간접의문문의 동사에 반영한다. (6) 뒤에 명사구가 나오므로 because of가 적절하다. (7) 뒤에 절이 나오므로 because가 적절하다.

08 'so+결과'를 'because[as, since]+이유'로 바꿔 쓸 수 있다.

Reading

확인문제
p.82

1 T 2 F 3 F 4 T

확인문제
p.83

1 T 2 F 3 T 4 T 5 F

교과서 확인학습 A
p.84~85

01 Interview with

02 On, a collection of, came back to

03 behind this return, searching for, abroad

04 how, became interested in   05 studied history

06 to continue   07 As you know   08 while

09 one of them   10 297 books of *Uigwe*

11 how   12 As soon as, look for

13 finally   14 looked at, 30 million

15 I'm sure   16 more difficulties

17 should be returned to, that idea

18 even thought, fired

19 as a visitor, do research on   20 However

21 For more than 22 the value of *Uigwe*

23 were published as   24 because of

25 asked, for, are here now

26 I'd like to ask, printing

27 in my first year   28 right away

29 to prove its value

30 was displayed as, movable metal type

31 thanks to, thank, for

32 our national treasures abroad, return

교과서 확인학습 B
p.86~87

1 An Interview with Dr. Park Byeong-seon

2 On May 27, 2011, 297 books of Uigwe , a collection of royal books the French army took in 1866, came back to Korea.

3 the person behind this return is Dr. Park Byeong-seon, a historian who spent her whole life searching for Korean national treasures abroad.

4 Q: Can you tell me how you became interested in *Uigwe* ?

5 Dr. Park: I studied history in college.

6 I went to France to continue my studies in 1955.

7 As you know, the French army took many of our national treasures in 1866.

8 I wanted to find them while I was studying there.

9 *Uigwe* was one of them.

10 Q: You found 297 books of *Uigwe* in the National Library of France, in Paris.

11 Please tell me how you found them.

12 Dr. Park: As soon as I became a researcher at the National Library in 1967, I began to look for *Uigwe*.

13 After 10 years, in 1977, I finally found the books.

14 I think I looked at more than 30 million books.

15 Q: I'm sure you were very excited when you found the books.

16 Dr. Park: Yes, I was, but more difficulties were waiting for me.

17 I thought that the books should be returned to Korea, but my bosses at the library didn't like that idea.

18 They even thought that I was a Korean spy and fired me.

19 After that, I had to go to the library as a visitor, so it was not easy to do research on *Uigwe* .

20 However, I didn't give up.

21 For more than ten years, I went to the library every day to finish my research.

22 I wanted to show people the value of *Uigwe* .

23 Q: The results of your research were published as a book in Korea in 1990.

24 Many Koreans became interested in *Uigwe* because of your book.

25 Dr. Park: Yes. In 1992, the Korean government asked the French government for its return and, finally, the 297 books are here now.

26 Q: Before I finish this interview, I'd like to ask you about *Jikji*, a book that changed the history of

printing.

27 Dr. Park: I found it in my first year at the library.

28 I knew right away that it was very special.

29 I worked hard to prove its value and finally succeeded.

30 At a book exhibition in Paris in 1972, *Jikji* was displayed as the oldest book in the world that was printed with movable metal type.

31 Q: Dr. Park, thanks to your hard work, *Jikji* and Uigwe were found, and all Koreans thank you for that.

32 Dr. Park: I hope people will become more interested in our national treasures abroad and work for their return.

시험대비 실력평가
p.88~93

01 ①번 In → On   02 As you know 03 ⑤
04 Please tell me how you found them.   05 ①, ③
06 her idea, a Korean spy   07 ②   08 ①, ⑤
09 metal type 10 in spite of → thanks to   11 ③
12 ①, ④   13 ②   14 ③   15 ④
16 ③   17 ②, ⑤   18 ⑤   19 ③
20 ④   21 ①   22 ③
23 (1) in order to finish   (2) so as to finish
   (3) in order that, could[might] finish
   (4) so that, could[might] finish
24 (A) special   (B) exhibition   (C) was displayed
25 ⓐ 박 박사님의 노고 덕분에 "직지"와 "의궤"가 발견된 것
   ⓑ 해외에 있는 우리의 문화재
26 ④
27 ⓐ when and where you were born
   ⓑ what you like about your job
28 ⓐ to know
   ⓑ to make와 making
   ⓒ to help와 helping

01 ① 특정한 날 앞에는 전치사 on을 쓴다. ② 297 books of Uigwe: "의궤" 297권, [동격 관계] …의, …라고 하는, …인, e.g.: the five of us(우리 다섯 사람), ③ 연도 앞에는 in을 쓴다. ④ search for: ~을 찾다, ⑤ become interested in: ~에 관심을 갖게 되다

02 as: -하다시피[~이듯이](접속사)

03 Dr. Park은 프랑스에서 공부하는 동안, 프랑스군이 1866년에 가져간 우리 문화재를 '찾고' 싶었고 "의궤"는 그것들 중의 하나였다.

04 의문문이 다른 문장의 일부로 쓰이면 '의문사＋주어＋동사' 어

순의 간접의문문이 된다. Please tell me에 맞춰 부호는 마침표를 찍는 것이 적절하다.

05 ① 적어도, ③ 마지막으로, 끝으로(무엇을 열거하면서 마지막 요소 앞에 붙이는 말), ⓐ와 나머지는 다 '마침내'

06 도서관의 그녀의 상사들이 '그녀의 생각'을 좋아하지 않았고. 그들은 심지어 그녀가 '한국의 스파이'라고 생각했기 때문이다.

07 ② 의지가 강한[확고한], ① 다정한, ③ 공손한, ④ 창의적인, ⑤ 호기심 많은

08 ⓐ와 ①, ⑤번: 관계대명사, ② 지시부사(그렇게), ③ 접속사, ④ 지시대명사

09 metal type: 금속 활자, movable: 이동시킬 수 있는, 움직이는

10 당신의 노고 '덕분에'라고 해야 하므로, 'thanks to'로 고치는 것이 적절하다. in spite of: ~에도 불구하고

11 이 글은 "직지"의 가치를 증명하기 위해 열심히 연구한 Dr. Park에 대한 인터뷰 내용이므로, 제목으로는 'Dr. Park이 직지의 가치를 증명했다'가 적절하다.

12 the French army took in 1866는 앞에 있는 선행사 a collection of royal books를 수식하는 관계대명사절이며 목적격 관계대명사 which 또는 that이 생략되었다.

13 ⓑ와 ②번: ~다시피[~이듯이](접속사), As you see: 보다 시피, ① 때, ③ 이유, ④ ~처럼(전치사), ⑤ ~함에 따라, ~할수록

14 누가 그것을 만들었는지 그리고 무엇이 그 안에 기록되어 있는지는 알 수 없다. ① It's a collection of royal books. ② It has 297 books. in all: 총, ④ The French army did. ⑤ It came back on May 27, 2011.

15 앞에 나오는 내용과 상반되는 내용이 뒤에 이어지므로 However가 가장 적절하다. ① 그러므로, ② 예를 들어, ③ 게다가, ⑤ 즉, 다시 말해

16 ③은 Dr. Park이 "의궤"를 찾기 시작한 뒤부터 그 책들을 발견할 때까지 본 책들을 가리키고, 나머지는 다 "의궤"를 가리킨다.

17 ② 뜻이 있는 곳에 길이 있다. ⑤ 낙숫물이 바위를 뚫는다. (성실하게 꾸준

18 위 글만으로는 "의궤"의 가치가 무엇인지를 대답할 수 없다. ① As soon as she became a researcher at the National Library in 1967. ② It took 10 years. ③ More than 30 million books. ④ She thought that the books should be returned to Korea.

19 ③ as the oldest book: 가장 오래된 책으로, 나머지 빈칸들은 모두 that을 쓰는 것이 적절하다. ①과 ④ 주격관계 대명사, ② 접속사, ⑤ 지시대명사

20 1972년에 구텐베르크 성경(Gutenberg Bible)이 세계에서 가장 오래된 책으로 증명된 것이 아니라, "직지"가 금속 활자로 인쇄된 세계에서 가장 오래된 책으로 전시되었다.

21 ①번 다음 문장의 They에 주목한다. 주어진 문장의 my bosses at the library를 받고 있으므로 ①번이 적절하다.

22 ⓐ와 ③번: 해고하다, ① (화살을) 쏘다, ② (질문·비난 등을)

퍼붓다, ④ (감정·정열 따위를) 타오르게 하다, (사람을) 흥분[감격]하게 하다(up), ⑤ 사격[발사/발포]하다

23 in order to 동사원형 = so as to 동사원형 = in order that 주어 can[may] = so that 주어 can[may]: ~하기 위하여(목적)

24 (A) 그것이 아주 '특별하다'는 것을 바로 알았다고 해야 하므로 special이 적절하다. common: 흔한, 보통의, 평범한, (B) 도서 '박람회'라고 해야 하므로 exhibition이 적절하다. explanation: 설명, (C) 가장 오래된 책으로 '전시되었다'고 해야 하므로 was displayed가 적절하다.

25 ⓐ 'thanks to Dr. Park's hard work, Jikji and Uigwe were found' ⓑ 'our national treasures abroad'를 가리킨다.

26 두 사람은 '인터뷰 진행자'와 '인터뷰 받는 사람, 인터뷰 대상자'의 관계이다. ① employer: 고용주, employee: 종업원, ② applicant: 지원자, ③ trainer: 교육시키는 사람, 트레이너, trainee: 교육을 받는 사람, 수습 (직원), ⑤ manager: 경영자, candidate: (선거의) 입후보자[출마자], (일자리의) 후보자

27 의문문이 다른 문장의 일부로 쓰이면 '의문사＋주어＋동사' 어순의 간접의문문이 된다.

28 (A) would like는 목적어로 to부정사만 쓸 수 있다. (B) 보어 자리에는 to부정사와 동명사를 둘 다 쓸 수 있다. (C) like는 목적어로 to부정사와 동명사를 둘 다 쓸 수 있다.

서술형 시험대비
p.94~95

01 (A) collection (B) behind (C) abroad
02 (A) France (B) Korea
03 how you became interested in *Uigwe*
04 looking
05 I thought that the books should be returned to Korea
06 hired → fired
07 (A) As soon as (B) difficulties (C) value
08 in proving its value
09 (A) printing (B) oldest (C) movable metal type
10 behind
11 many of our national treasures (that/which) the French army took in 1866
12 (A) royal books (B) Dr. Park Byeong seon

01 (A) 왕실 서적인 "의궤" 297권이라고 해야 하므로, '소장품'이라는 의미의 collection이 적절하다. correction: 정정[수정], (B) 이 반환 '뒤에 있는' 인물이라고 해야 하므로 behind가 적절하다. in front of: ~의 앞쪽에[앞에], (C) '해외에 있는' 한국의 문화재라고 해야 하므로 abroad가 적절하다. abroad: 해외에서, aboard: (배·기차·비행기 등에) 탄, 탑승[승선]한

02 '프랑스'로부터 '한국'으로의 "의궤"의 반환을 가리킨다.

03 의문문이 다른 문장의 일부로 쓰이면 '의문사＋주어＋동사' 어순의 간접의문문이 된다.

04 begin은 목적어로 to부정사와 동명사를 모두 취할 수 있다.

05 return(돌려주다, 반납하다)을 수동태로 쓰면 된다.

06 그들이 저를 '해고했다'고 해야 하므로 'fired'로 고치는 것이 적절하다. hire: 고용하다

07 Dr. Park은 1967년에 국립도서관의 연구원이 '되자마자', "의궤"를 찾기 시작했다. 그녀는 사람들에게 "의궤"의 '가치'를 보여 주고 싶었기 때문에 많은 '어려움'에도 불구하고 포기하지 않았고, 10년 후, 마침내 그 책들을 발견했다.

08 succeed in ~ing: ~하는 데 성공하다

09 "직지"는 '금속 활자'로 인쇄된 세계에서 '가장 오래된' 책으로 드러났기 때문에, '인쇄'의 역사를 바꾼 책이다. turn out: ~인 것으로 드러나다[밝혀지다]

10 이 반환 '뒤에 있는' 인물 = 이 반환을 가능하게 만든 인물, behind: ~ 뒤에 (숨은), ~의 배후에

11 '1866년에 프랑스군이 가져간 우리 문화재'를 가리킨다.

12 그것은 프랑스군이 1866년에 가져갔던 한국 '왕실 서적'이다. 하지만, '박병선 박사'의 노력 덕분에 2011년 5월 27일에 그것은 프랑스로부터 한국으로 돌아왔다.

영역별 핵심문제
p.97~101

01 ②   02 ④   03 ③   04 ①
05 give up   06 ③   07 ③   08 ②
09 wants to try on the hanbok and the jokduri
10 it's only for display.   11 ④   12 ⑤
13 (A) Is it OK to sit over there?
   (B) sitting on the grass is not allowed
14 No, it isn't / for display   15 because
16 ⑤
17 (1) I'm not sure. Will my grandfather like my present?
   (2) Can you tell me? Where is the bathroom?
   (3) I'd like to know. Who did you meet at the party?
   (4) Did you know? Who was in the classroom?
   (5) Do you think? What is Jane's secret?
   (6) I'm curious. Can you lend me the book?
18 ③   19 ④   20 took them → took
21 during   22 ④   23 ⑤   24 bosses, fired   25 to   26 ③   27 ④
28 immediately   29 ②

01 나머지는 모두 동사와 명사의 뜻을 가지는 단어이지만, allow는 동사로만 사용된다.

02 ⓐ 프랑스 정부가 우리의 문화재(national treasures)를 가져갔다는 뜻이다. ⓑ 책 박람회에서 '직지'가 전시되었다 (displayed)는 의미가 적절하다.

03 '누군가나 무언가가 일어난 좋은 일에 책임이 있다고 말하는 데 사용되는'의 의미로 'thanks to(~ 덕분에)'가 적절하다.

04 어떤 것에 관한 사실들을 알아내는 일

05 • 그에게는 쉽지 않은 일이었지만, 그는 포기하지 않았습니다.
• 그들은 여러 번 실패할지라도 쉽게 포기하지 않습니다.

06 publish는 '출판하다'라는 의미이고, prove가 '입증하다'라는 의미이다.

08 제시문의 That은 그 다음에 나오는 the little hat을 가리키므로 ②가 적절하다.

09 소녀가 입고 싶어 하는 두 가지는 무엇인가?

10 'for display'는 '전시를 위한'의 의미이다.

11 Using smartphones는 동명사 주어로 단수 취급을 하므로 are를 is로 바꾸어야 한다.

12 헬스장은 fitness room이다. fitting room은 탈의실이다.

14 족두리를 써 보는 것은 허락되지 않는다. 족두리는 단지 전시만 하는 것이다.

15 뒤에 '이유'가 이어지고 있으므로 because가 들어가야 한다.

16 의문사가 없는 간접의문문의 어순은 'if[whether]+주어+동사'이다. However, she is not sure if[whether] she will return in the future.

17 간접의문문의 어순은 '의문사+주어+동사'이며 의문사가 없는 경우는 'if[whether]+주어+동사'로 쓴다. think 동사가 주절에 있을 경우 간접의문문의 의문사를 문장 맨 앞으로 배치한다.

18 ③번은 조건의 부사절에 쓰인 것이지만 나머지는 모두 간접 의문문을 이끌고 있다.

19 간접의문문의 어순은 '의문사+주어+동사'이다. how long 은 의문사 how가 long을 수식하는 부사로 쓰여 how long을 함께 의문사 취급을 한다.

20 the French army took in 1866는 앞에 있는 선행사 a collection of royal books를 수식하는 관계대명사절이며 took 의 목적어인 them은 목적격 관계대명사 which 또는 that으로 바 꾼 다음에 생략되었는데 또 them을 쓰는 것은 적절하지 않다.

21 while+주어+동사, during+기간을 나타내는 명사, for study: 공부를 위하여

22 Dr. Park이 "의궤"를 찾는 데 얼마나 오래 걸렸는지는 대답할 수 없다. ① On May 27, 2011. ② History. ③ In 1866. ⑤ While she was studying in France.

23 ⓐ와 ⑤번: (역할·자격 따위를 나타내어) ~으로서, ① ~ 때문에, ② ~함에 따라서, ③ ~와 같을 만큼(지시부사, 보통 as ~ as …로 형용사·부사 앞에서), ④ ~할 때

24 도서관의 '상사들'이 그녀를 한국의 스파이라고 생각해서 그녀를 '해고했기' 때문이다.

25 show는 간접목적어를 직접목적어 뒤로 보낼 때 'to'를 붙인다.

26 그 책들이 한국에 반환되어야 한다고 생각한 것은 '도서관의 상 사들'이 아니라 'Dr. Park'이었다.

27 ④는 일반적인 '도서'를 가리키고, 나머지는 다 '직지'를 가리 킨다.

28 right away = immediately: 즉시

29 위 글은 직지의 가치를 증명하기 위해 열심히 연구한 Dr. Park에 관 한 인터뷰 내용이므로, 주제로는 'Dr. Park 덕분에 직지의 가치가 발견되었다'가 적절하다.

01 royal   02 ③   03 ⑤   04 ②
05 ③   06 ②   07 Taking, is, allowed
08 ③   09 the little hat
10 ⓐ is allowed   ⓑ is allowed   11 ②

12 (1) What do you think the best way to encourage kids to study more is?
(2) Can you tell me who your favorite actor is?
(3) The car accident happened because[as, since] the road was slippery.
(4) Tina ran into the house because[as, since] it started to rain.

13 what you like doing in your free time / because[as, since] it is really fun

14 (1) I went to the school health room because I had a headache. I went to the school health room because of a headache.
(2) He got food poisoning because he ate undercooked chicken. He got food poisoning because of undercooked chicken.

15 (A) royal   (B) interested   (C) while

16 a historian who spent her whole life searching for Korean national treasures abroad

17 ①, ④   18 ③   19 ③   20 ②
21 millions → million   22 tried to find → found

01 '왕실의 책'이란 의미로 royal이 적절하다. loyal은 '충실한 의 미이다.

02 사진을 찍을 때 충분한 빛을 제공하기 위해 번쩍이는 카메라의 밝은 빛

03 (A) 그 책이 한국으로 반환되어야 한다고 생각했다. (B) 도서관 의 상사 들이 필자를 해고시켰기 때문에 그 후에는 방문객으로 방 문했다가 적절하다 (C) 의궤의 가치를 사람들에게 보여주기를 원했다가 적절하다.

04 about은 전치사이므로 뒤에 동명사(-ing)가 와야 한다.

05 (C)의 prove는 '입증하다, 증명하다'라는 의미이다. 발견하다 는 find이다.

06 빈칸 다음의 말이 'Eating food is allowed.'이므로 음식을 먹어도 되는지 여부를 묻는 말이 적절하다. ⑤번의 'Do you mind if I ~?' 표현도 허가 여부를 묻는 말이지만, B의 답이 'Yes'이기 때문에 허락하지 않는다는 뜻이 되어 어색하다.

08 ⓐ에는 '~을 입어 보다'라는 의미로 try on이 적절하다. ⓑ에는 족두리에 대해 설명을 하는 말로, 전통적인(traditional) 한국 모자가 적절하다. ⓒ에는 써 봐도 되는지 묻는 말에 미안하다고 했기 때문에 써 볼 수 없다는 것을 알 수 있다.

09 저쪽에 있는 작은 모자를 가리킨다는 것을 알 수 있다.

10 ⓐ, ⓑ 모두 허락 여부를 묻는 말에 대해 Yes와 OK로 답하고 있기 때문에 모두 허락을 해주는 표현이 오는 것이 적절하다.

11 ① I want to know how you spent your vacation. ③ I wonder if she got angry at me. ④ We didn't win the game because of my mistake. ⑤ You can't watch the movie because you're not old enough.

12 (접의문문의 어순은 '의문사+주어+동사'이며 think 동사가 주절에 있을 경우 간접의문문의 의문사를 문장 맨 앞에 써야 함에 유의한다. 두 개의 문장을 연결하는 것이므로 because를 이용하여 because 뒤에 이유에 해당하는 것을 쓴다. So를 이용하여 두 문장의 순서를 바꾸어 써도 좋다.

13 첫 번째 빈칸에는 간접의문문을 이용하여 '의문사+주어+동사'의 어순으로 쓰고 두 번째 빈칸에는 'really fun'이라는 이유에 해당하는 말이 있으므로 because[as, since]를 이용하여 답한다.'

14 because+절(주어+동사 ~), because of+명사 또는 명사구

15 (A) '왕실' 서적이라고 해야 하므로 royal이 적절하다. loyal: 충실한, 충성스러운, (B) 감정을 나타내는 동사는 수식받는 명사가 감정을 느끼게 되는 경우에 과거분사를 써야 하므로 interested가 적절하다. (C) while+주어+동사, during+기간을 나타내는 명사

16 spend+시간+~ing: ~하는 데 시간을 보내다, search for: ~을 찾다

17 ⓑ와 ②, ③, ⑤는 부사적 용법, strong will: 강한 의지, ①, ④ 명사적 용법

18 프랑스에 갔을 때 그녀가 몇 살이었는지는 알 수 없다. ① She searched for Korean national treasures abroad throughout her lifetime.(She spent her whole life searching for Korean national treasures abroad.) ② History. ④ To continue her studies. ⑤ Many of our national treasures the French army took in 1866.

19 (A) look for: ~을 찾다, (B) look at: ~을 보다, ① look after: ~을 돌보다

20 as soon as = the moment = the instant= immediately = directly: ~하자마자, ② exactly: 정확히, 꼭, 틀림없이

21 more than 30 million books: 3천만 권 이상의 책, million은 구체적인 숫자와 함께 쓰일 때 단수로 쓴다.

22 1977년에 그 책들을 '찾으려고 노력한 것'이 아니라, 마침내 그 책들을 '발견했다.'

서술형 실전문제
p.106~107

01 (A) Is it OK if I play it?
   (B) You must not play it.
02 (A) Using smartphones is allowed
   (B) Taking pictures is not allowedt.
03 (1) What do you like to do?
   (2) Will my boss accept my idea?
   (3) I worked all day yesterday.
04 (1) I stayed home because of a heavy rain.
   (2) Because of a high fever, I couldn't sleep last night.
05 (1) She couldn't run because of her uncomfortable shoes.
   (2) Mark didn't join us because he had to work.
   (3) Do you know where she went?
   (4) She could not remember if[whether] she watched the movie.
06 (A) in 1955   (B) national treasures   (C) in 1866
07 were returned
08 to search → searching
09 (A) found   (B) was   (C) visitor
10 (1) 그 책들이 한국에 반환되어야 한다는 Dr. Park의 생각을 도서관의 상사들이 좋아하지 않았다.
   (2) 도서관의 상사들이 Dr. Park을 한국의 스파이라고 생각했고 그녀를 해고했다.
   (3) 해고당한 뒤 방문객으로 도서관에 가야만 해서 "의궤"를 연구하는 것이 쉽지 않았다.
11 they should return the books to Korea

---

03 (1), (2) 간접의문문의 어순은 '의문사+주어+동사'이며 의문사가 없는 경우는 'if[whether]+주어+동사'로 쓴다. (3) because를 이용하여 '이유'를 밝히고 있다. 이것을 따로 써주면 된다.

04 'because of' 다음에는 명사 또는 명사구가 나온다. 'because of'는 문장의 앞이나 뒤 모두 올 수 있다.

05 (1), (2) because+절(주어+동사 ~), because of+명사 또는 명사구 (3), (4) 간접의문문의 어순은 '의문사+주어+동사'이다. 의문사가 없는 경우에는 의문사 대신 if나 whether를 쓴다.

06 그녀는 '1955년에' 역사를 계속 공부하기 위해 프랑스에 갔다. 그녀는 그곳에서 공부하는 동안 프랑스군이 '1866년에' 가져갔던 많은 우리 '문화재'를 찾고 싶었고 "의궤"는 그것들 중의 하나였다.

07 return(돌려주다, 반납하다)을 수동태로 쓰면 된다.

08 spend+시간+-ing: ~하는 데 시간을 보내다

09 (A) 그 책들을 '발견했을' 때 무척 흥분한 것이므로 found가 적절하다. find-found-found: ~을 찾다, found-founded-founded: ~을 설립하다, (B) 그 책들을 발견했을 때 무척 '흥분

했다'고 하는 것이므로 was가 적절하다. (C) 도서관에서 해고당한 뒤 '방문객'으로 도서관에 가야 만 했다고 해야 하므로 visitor가 적절하다. librarian: 사서

10 뒤에 이어지는 내용을 쓰는 것이 적절하다.

11 조동사가 있는 문장의 능동태는 '조동사+동사원형'의 형태로 쓰인다.

창의사고력 서술형 문제   p.108

|모범답안|

01 Is it OK to set up a tent / How about / afraid not / is no allowed

02 (1) I got up late this morning because I stayed up late last night.

   (2) I couldn't go out today because of a bad cold.

   (3) I don't know what my friend wants me to do.

03 (A) to continue   (B) a researcher   (C) *Uigwe*

   (D) *Jikji*   (E) more than 30 million books

   (F) were published

단원별 모의고사   p.109~112

01 ⑤   02 (r)esult   03 ①   04 ④

05 ②   06 ③   07 ④

08 going to try on a hanbok

09 traditional, women, display, allowed, wedding day

10 ④   11 ③   12 ②   13 ④

14 ②, ⑤

15 (1) I don't know who broke the window.

   (2) Tell me how you found the key.

   (3) I have no idea if[whether] he loves me or not?

   (4) Who do you think will be selected as the best player of the game?

16 (1) I don't see my grandparents often because they live far away.

   (2) They moved to Japan because of her job.

   (3) The accident happened because of his carelessness.

   (4) Minho knows what Kevin wants to be in the future.

   (5) Daniel is not sure where he put his phone.

   (6) I will check if the president can meet you now.

17 who 또는 that

18 (A) a historian   (B) abroad

19 the books should be returned to Korea

20 ②   21 ④

01 ⑤번의 'aboard'는 '(비행기에, 배에) 탄, 탑승하여'의 의미로 'on or onto a ship, aircraft, bus, or train'이 적절한 설명이다. 'in or to a foreign country'는 abroad(해외로, 해외에서)에 대한 설명이다.

02 • 최고의 결과를 얻기 위해, 당신은 최선을 다해야 한다. • 질병은 가난으로부터 발생할 수 있다.

03 '주의 깊게 봄으로써 누군가나 무언가를 찾으려고 하다'라는 뜻으로 '찾아보다'는 search가 적절하다.

04 해금은 전시를 위한 것이라고 했으므로, 연주하는 것이 허락되지 않는다는 대답이 적절하다.

05 B가 'Yes'라는 긍정의 답을 하고 있기 때문에 ④번의 'Do you mind if I ~?'는 적절하지 않다.

06 ③번은 저기에 앉아도 되는지 물어보는 말에 B가 미안하지만 앉는 것이 허락되지 않는다고 말하는 것이 자연스럽다. is allowed를 is not allowed로 바꾸어야 한다.

07 남자가 탈의실은 저기에 있다고 말하는 것으로 보아 옷을 입어봐도 되는지 물어보는 것이 적절하다.

08 Kate는 한복을 입어 볼 것이다.

09 Kate는 여자들을 위한 한국 전통 모자인 족두리를 써보려고 했지만 전시용이었기 때문에 써 볼 수가 없었다. 족두리는 주로 결혼식 날 쓴다.

10 빈칸 다음에 G가 '플래시도 사용할 수 있나요?'라고 묻고 있기 때문에 사진을 찍는 것이 가능하다는 것을 알 수 있다. 그래서 긍정의 답이 적절하다.

11 사진을 찍어도 되는지 묻는 말에 No라고 답하고 있으므로 사진을 찍는 것은 허락되지 않는다는 것을 알 수 있다.

12 ②번은 의미상 결과를 나타내는 so가 적절하다. 나머지는 다 because가 적절하다.

13 ④번은 조건절에 쓰인 if이지만 나머지는 모두 간접의문문을 이끌고 있다.

14 빈칸 뒤에 '이유'에 해당하는 내용이 나오며 절이 왔으므로 접속사 because나 since가 알맞다.

15 간접의문문의 어순은 '의문사+주어+동사'이며 의문사가 없는 경우 에는 'if[whether]+주어+동사'로 쓴다. think 동사가 주절에 있을 경우 간접의문문의 의문사를 문장 맨 앞으로 배치한다.

16 (1)~(3) 뒤에 '이유'를 이끄는 because나 because of를 이용하여 쓴다. (4)~(6) 간접의문문을 이용하여 쓴다. 어순이 '의문사+주어+동사'이 며 의문사가 없는 경우는 'if[whether]+주어+동사'로 쓰는 것에 유의한다.

17 주격 관계대명사 who 또는 that이 적절하다.

18 박병선 박사는 '해외에 있는' 한국의 문화재를 찾기 위해 전생애를 바친 '역사학자'였다.

19 '그 책들이 한국에 반환되어야 한다'는 것을 가리킨다.

20 ⓑ와 ③, ⑤: 명사적 용법, ①, ④ 부사적 용법, ② 형용사적 용법

21 because of+명사(구), because+절, because of = thanks to = owing to = due to = on account of: ~ 때문에

Lesson

S

Creative Ideas in Stories

교과서
Reading

확인문제   p.116

| 1 T   2 F   3 F |

확인문제   p.117

| 1 T   2 T   3 F |

확인문제   p.118

| 1 F   2 T |

교과서 확인학습 A   p.119~121

01 Doughnuts   02 had   03 so, was full of
04 visited   05 Uncle   06 Isn't it great
07 for a while   08 for me
10 doughnut batter   11 recipe
12 Don't worry 13 front, stepped out
14 Can I have   15 aren't ready
16 Are you making   17 my first time
18 took off   19 to mix   20 I can help you
22 a lot of   23 wait and see, great
24 turned on   25 dropping into 26 first
27 delicious   28 so much fun ! 29 for helping
30 enough, nothing happened   31 kept coming
32 should call   33 was, full of, piled
34 right away   35 Something's wrong
36 all these   37 came back   38 left
39 took it off   40 looked for   41 can't find
42 give a reward 43 I'm sure   44 right
45 break up, to find   46 Don't worry
47 made a sign 48 put it   49 2 for 5 cents
50 for finding   51 give, back   52 to buy
53 All of a sudden   54 found it
55 worked   56 Here's   57 In the end
58 with   59 got, back, lots of

교과서 확인학습 B   p.122~124

1 The Doughnuts

2 Homer's uncle, Bob, had a doughnut shop.

3 Uncle Bob liked machines, so the shop was full of cooking machines.

4 One day, Homer visited Uncle Bob's shop.

5 Homer: Hello, Uncle Bob!

6 Bob: Hi, Homer. Nice to see you. Look at this new doughnut machine. Isn't it great?

7 Bob: Homer, I need to go back home for a while.

8 Can you watch the shop for me and make some doughnuts?

9 Homer: OK, I'll try but ....

10 Bob: It's easy to do. First, make the doughnut batter and put it in the machine.

11 Then just start the machine. Here's the recipe.

12 Homer: I can do that. Don't worry.

13 After Uncle Bob left, a big car stopped in front of the shop, and a lady stepped out.

14 Lady: Can I have some doughnuts and a coffee?

15 Homer: I'm sorry, but the doughnuts aren't ready.

16 Lady: Are you making the doughnut batter now?

17 Homer: Yes, but this is my first time.

18 The lady took off her coat and her big diamond ring.

19 She started to mix the batter.

20 Lady: I can help you. I can make delicious doughnuts.

21 Homer: Uh, OK.

22 Homer: This is a lot of batter.

23 Lady: Just wait and see. The doughnuts will taste great.

24 Homer turned on the doughnut machine.

25 Rings of batter started dropping into the hot oil.

26 Lady: You try the first doughnut. Here.

27 Homer: Wow! It's really delicious!

28 Lady: I have to go now. This was so much fun! Good-bye!

29 Homer: Thank you for helping me. Good-bye!

30 Homer had enough doughnuts, so he pushed the stop button, but nothing happened.

31 The doughnuts kept coming out of the machine.

32 Homer: Hmm... What's wrong? I think I should call Uncle Bob.

33 The shop was now full of doughnuts. Homer

21

piled the doughnuts on the counter.

34 Homer: Uncle Bob! Please come back right away.

35 Something's wrong with the doughnut machine.

36 Bob: Oh, no! How can we sell all these doughnuts?

37 Just then the lady came back to the shop.

38 Lady: I lost my diamond ring. I think I left it on the counter.

39 Homer: Oh, I remember. You took it off before you started to mix the batter.

40 Everyone looked for the diamond ring, but they couldn't find it.

41 Homer: I can't find it.

42 Lady: I'll give a reward of one hundred dollars to the person who finds that ring!

43 Homer: I know! The ring fell into the batter. I'm sure it's inside one of these doughnuts!

44 Lady: You're right!

45 Bob: Oh, no! Now we have to break up all of these doughnuts to find the ring.

46 Homer: Don't worry, Uncle. I have an idea.

47 Homer took a piece of paper and made a sign.

48 He then put it in the shop's window.

49 Fresh Doughnuts 2 for 5 cents

50 $100 prize for finding a ring inside a doughnut

51 P.S. You have to give the ring back.

52 Then many people began to buy the doughnuts.

53 All of a sudden, a man shouted with excitement.

54 Man: I found it! I found the ring!

55 Homer: See, my idea worked!

56 Lady: Here's one hundred dollars!

57 In the end, everybody was happy.

58 The man went home with one hundred dollars.

59 The lady got her diamond ring back, and Uncle Bob sold lots of doughnuts.

60 And, what about Homer?

61 He was happy that his idea worked so well!

서술형 실전문제
p.125~127

01 have

02 (1) reward (2) dropping[to drop] into
   (3) stepped out

03 (1) remember: 기억하다 (2) compare: 비교하다
   (3) excitement: 흥분 (4) work: 효과가 있다

04 (1) (o)wned (2) (f)or a while (3) (t)ook off

05 (1) Bob liked books, so his room was full of books.
   (2) It is easy to make doughnuts.

(3) Homer thinks that the doughnuts smell great.

(4) After Bob made doughnuts with the doughnut machine, he turned it off.

(5) We ordered three pieces of pizza and two cans of cola at the restaurant.

06 (1) Have you met the girl who[that] is talking to Judy?

(2) Yuna is good at figure skating which[that] is hard to learn.

(3) The hotel (which/that) I stayed at was clean and beautiful. 또는 The hotel at which I stayed was clean and beautiful.

07 Because he liked machines.

08 batter

09 (1) 먼저, 도넛 반죽을 만든다.
   (2) 그 반죽을 기계에 넣는다.
   (3) 그런 다음에 기계를 작동시킨다.

10 You took it off before you started to mix the batter.

11 I'll give the person who finds that ring a reward of one hundred dollars!

12 (1) in order to find (2) so as to find
   (3) in order that (4) so that, can[may]

13 25 cents 14 work

15 100달러를 갖고 집으로 갔다. / 다이아몬드 반지를 다시 찾았다. / 도넛을 많이 팔았다. / 자신의 아이디어가 아주 잘 통해서 행복했다.

16 ③

01 (1) 해석: 도넛과 커피 한 잔 주겠니?, 이 문장에서 have는 '먹다'와 '마시다'의 의미로 사용된다. (2) 해석: 난 이제 가 봐야 해. 정말 재미있었어. 잘 있으렴. 'have to+동사원형'은 '~해야 한다'는 의미다.

02 (1) 그 반지를 찾는 사람에게 100달러의 보상을 드릴게요. (2) 링 모양의 반죽들이 뜨거운 기름 속으로 떨어지기 시작했다. start는 뒤에 동명사나 to부정사를 취한다. (3) Bob 삼촌이 떠난 후, 큰 차 한 대가 가게 앞에 섰고, 한 귀부인이 내렸다. 시제가 과거이므로 step의 과거형 stepped를 써야 한다.

03 (1) 과거에 일어났거나 말하여진 어떤 것의 이미지를 마음속에 갖다 (2) 둘 또는 그 이상의 것이 어떻게 다르거나 같은지에 관해 생각하다 (3) 당신이 신날 때 갖는 느낌 (4) 효과적이거나 성공하다

05 (1) so는 결과를 이끌고 because는 이유를 이끈다. (2) 가주어로 It이 적절하다. (3) 감각동사+형용사 (4) turn off는 '동사+부사'의 형태로, 목적어가 인칭대명사일 때 목적어를 동사와 부사 사이에 써야 한다. (5) 물질명사를 셀 때는 세는 단위를 복수로 표시한다.

06 (1) 선행사가 사람이고 is의 주어 역할을 해야 하므로 관계대명사 who나 that을 써야 한다. (2) 선행사가 사물이고 is의 주어 역할을 해야 하므로 관계대명사 which나 that을 써야 한다. (3) 선행사가 사물이고 at의 목적어 역할을 해야 하므로 관계대명사 which나 that을 써야 한다. 목적격이므로 생략할 수도 있다. 또한 that은 전치사 다음에는 쓸 수 없음에 유의한다.

07 Bob은 '기계를 좋아해서', 그의 도넛 가게는 요리 기계들로 가득 차 있었다.

08 batter: 반죽(요리에서 사용되는 밀가루, 달걀, 우유의 혼합 물)

09 먼저, 도넛 반죽을 만들고 그것을 기계에 넣은 다음에 기계 를 작동하기만 하면 된다고 했다.

10 'off'를 보충하면 된다. take ~ off(~을 벗다, ~을 빼다)는 '동사＋부사'의 형태로 목적어가 인칭대명사일 때는 동사와 부사 사이에 쓰는 것이 적절하다

11 전치사 'to'를 빼고 '간접목적어＋직접목적어'의 어순으로 바꾼다.

12 in order to 동사원형 = so as to 동사원형 = in order that ~ can[may] = so that ~ can[may]: ~하기 위하여(목적)

13 2개에 5센트이므로 10개를 사면 가격은 '25센트'이다.

14 이 글의 요지는 문제를 해결할 때 창의적인 아이디어가 어떻게 '잘 되어 갈 수 있는가'이다. text: 본문, 지문, work: (계 획 등이) 잘 되어 가다

15 남자는 100달러를 갖고 집으로 갔다. 귀부인은 다이아몬드 반지를 다시 찾았다. Bob 삼촌은 도넛을 많이 팔았다. Homer는 자신의 아이디어가 아주 잘 통해서 행복했다.

16 ⓒ와 ③번: (계획 등이) 잘 되어 가다, ①, ⑤ 일하다, ② (광산· 농장· 사업 등을) 경영하다, ④ (기계 등을) 작동시키다(타동사)

123서술형

단원별 예상문제
p.128~132

01 ⑤   **02** drop   **03** ①   **04** batter
05 All of a sudden   **06** ②   **07** ④
08 back
09 (1) Homer is the person who[that] is very creative.
  (2) Bob had to fix the machine to make doughnuts.
  (3) Homer found the lost ring with ease.
  (4) Sean was happy that his idea was finally accepted.
10 ④, ⑤   **11** ④
12 (1) Grace bought a skirt and put it on.
  (2) Charlie Brown is a boy who has bad luck.
  (3) The metal felt smooth and cold.
  (4) She started playing the piano to make her fingers strong.
13 ②   **14** ③   **15** the doughnut batter
16 (A) watch the shop   (B) make some doughnuts
17 (A) took off   (B) great   (C) turned on   **18** ④

19 ④   **20** ①   **21** filled with
22 He pushed the stop button, but nothing happened. The doughnuts kept coming out of the machine.
23 ④   **24** ①   **25** ①   **26** ③, ④
27 ⑤   **28** ②, ④   **29** Here're → Here's

01 ⑤번은 'drop'에 대한 설명이다. 'step out'은 'to go out for a short time(잠시 밖으로 나가다)'이 적절하다.

02 유의어 관계이다. 섞다 : 떨어지다

03 '음식을 준비하거나 요리하는 방법을 말해주는 일련의 설명서'

04 그림은 소년이 밀가루 반죽을 만들고 있는 모습이다.

05 • 갑자기 어두워졌다. • 나는 집에 물건을 두고 온 것이 갑자기 생각났다.

06 • drop into: ~속으로 떨어지다. drop by: 잠시 들리다 • be full of: ~으로 가득 차다(= be filled with) • break up: 쪼개다, break down: 고장나다, 분해하다

07 모두 반의어 관계이고, ④번은 '외치다'라는 유의어 관계이다.

08 • go back: 돌아가다 • come back: 돌아오다 • give 목적어 back: ~을 돌려주다 • get 목적어 back: ~을 돌 려받다

09 (1) 선행사가 사람이므로 주격 관계대명사 who나 that이 적절하다. (2) 부사적 용법으로 '목적'을 나타내는 to부정사가 적절하다. (3) 'with+추상명사'로 부사의 의미를 나타낸다. with ease = easily (4) 감정의 원인을 나타내는 부사절을 이끄는 that이 적절하다. (because로 써도 좋다.)

10 뒤에 형용사 delicious가 보어로 나오고 있으므로 감각동사가 적절하다. buy나 bring, ask 등은 형용사를 보어로 쓰지 않는다.

11 <보기>와 ④ 부사적 용법의 '목적' ① 명사적 용법(진주어) ② 명사적 용법(목적어) ③ 형용사적 용법 ⑤ 명사적 용법(보어)

12 (1) put on은 '동사+부사'의 형태로, 목적어가 인칭대명사 일 때 목적어를 동사와 부사 사이에 써야 한다. (2) 선행사가 사람이므로 주격 관계대명사 who나 that을 이용하여 쓴다. (3) 감각 동사의 보어로 형용사가 적절하다. (4) to부정사의 부사적 용법의 '목적'을 이용하여 쓴다.

13 a person을 선행사로 하고 있고 teaches의 주어 역할을 해야 하므로 who나 that이 적절하다. whom을 대신해서 who를 쓸 수는 있지만 who를 대신해서 whom을 쓸 수는 없다.

14 이유를 나타내는 접속사 As를 쓰는 것이 적절하다.

15 '도넛 반죽'을 가리킨다.

16 Bob 삼촌은 Homer가 자기 대신 '가게를 봐 주고', '도넛을 좀 만들어 주기'를 원했다.

17 (A) 외투를 '벗고' 커다란 다이아몬드 반지를 '뺐다'고 해야 하므로 took off가 적절하다. put on: ~을 입다, (B) 감각동사의 보어로 형용사를 써야 하므로 great이 적절하다. (C) 도넛 기계를 '작동시키자' 링 모양의 반죽들이 뜨 거운 기름 속으로 떨어지기 시작한 것이므로 turned on이 적절하다. turn off: (전기·가스·수도 등을) 끄다

23

18 귀부인은 자발적으로 Homer가 도넛 반죽을 만들고 있는 것을 도와주었으므로, '친절한[다정한]' 성격이라고 하는 것이 적절하다. ① 호기심 많은, ② 공손한, ③ 끈기 있는, ⑤ 창의적인

19 Homer가 반죽을 만든 것이 아니라 '귀부인'이 반죽을 만들 었다.

20 주어진 문장은 ①번 앞 문장의 내용을 부연 설명하는 것이므 로 ①번이 적절하다.

21 be full of = be filled with: ~로 가득 차 있다

22 정지 버튼을 눌렀지만, 아무 일도 일어나지 않고, 도넛이 계속해서 기계에서 나오고 있었던 것을 가리킨다.

23 leave: ~에 두다, 놓다, ① lie-lay-lain: 눕다, 놓여 있다, lay-laid-laid: 놓다[두다], 과거시제를 써야 하므로 laid로 쓰는 것이 적절하다.

24 ⓑ와 ①: 부사적 용법(목적), ②, ④ 명사적 용법. ③, ⑤: 형용사적 용법

25 반지를 찾기 위해 도넛을 모두 쪼개야 했기 때문에 '당황스러운' 심경이라고 하는 것이 적절하다. ① 당황스러운, ② 흥분한, ③ 부끄러운, ④ 지루한, ⑤ 안도하는

27 이 글은 Homer의 창의적인 아이디어 덕분에 문제를 해결 하는 내용의 글이므로, 제목으로는 '창의적인 아이디어가 잘 통했다!' 가 적절하다.

28 all of a sudden = suddenly = all at once: 갑자기, ① 한꺼번에, 동시에, ③ 실제로, 정말로, ⑤ 즉시, 즉각

29 금액은 단수 취급한다.

교과서 파헤치기

단어 TEST Step 1 p.02

01 도착하다	02 모험	03 맛
04 놀라운	05 어려운	06 뜨다, 떠가다
07 외치다	08 풍선	09 그릇, 용기
10 다른	11 궁금한, 호기심이 많은	
12 목마른	13 모든 곳에	14 우주 정거장
15 탐험, 탐사	16 마침내	17 ~한 이래로
18 외국의	19 신남, 흥분한	20 눕다
21 삼키다	22 흔들다	
23 ~쪽으로, ~을 향하여		24 우주선
25 고치다	26 젖은	27 웃다
28 구하다	29 최근에	30 우주복
31 형성하다, 만들어 내다		32 비밀, 기밀
33 부드러운	34 아주 신나는	35 ~할 필요 없다
36 (둘 사이의) 서로	37 ~으로 뒤덮이다	38 아래로 끌어내리다
39 눕다	40 예를 들어	
41 ~에 관해 궁금해 하다		42 ~으로 달려가다
43 더 이상 ~ 않다		

단어 TEST Step 2 p.03

01 dventure	02 balloon	03 difficult
04 float	05 excited	06 different
07 exploration	08 soft	09 amazing
10 finally	11 since	12 fix
13 foreign	14 spaceship	15 secret
16 everywhere	17 wind	18 shout
19 shake	20 curious	21 towards
22 space suit	23 thirsty	24 container
25 swallow	26 hill	27 lie
28 thrilling	29 laugh	30 wet
31 grass	32 recently	33 save
34 taste	35 be curious about ~	
36 try to+동사원형	37 in surprise	38 not ~ anymore
39 be covered with		40 get on
41 for example	42 each other	43 roll down

단어 TEST Step 3 p.04

1 amazing, 놀라운 2 float, 뜨다 3 spaceship, 우주선
4 form, 형성하다, 만들다 5 arrive , 도착하다
6 save, 구하다 7 curious, 호기심 많은 8 wet, 젖은
9 exploration, 탐험, 탐사 10 foreign, 외국의

---

11 towards, ~을 향해   12 space station, 우주 정거장
13 adventure, 모험   14 swallow, 삼키다
15 land, 착륙하다   16 secret, 비밀

대화문 TEST Step 1 p.05~06

Listen and Talk A-1

hear about, that went into space / curious about /
spaceship / want to buy

Listen and Talk A-2

Did, hear about / I'm really curious about / right here,
about / buy

Listen and Talk A-3

Did you hear about / I didn't / space station, Look at /
I'm really curious about

Listen and Talk A-4

about, space food / a type of / hear it is, looks good /
curious about the taste

Listen and Talk B

1 about / heard / curious about
2 Look at, hear about / No, didn't / it has great
   songs/ realy curious about

Listen and Talk C

hear about / didn't / heard good / curious about,
about / about, who, trying to live / sounds interesting
/ is playing / What time / begins at / Let's eat lunch,
and then / hungry, Let's go

Review 1

did you hear about / No, didn't / heard / curious
about, about / about, who saves his son

Review 2

Did, hear about / right, about living / really curious
about / Me, too

대화문 TEST Step 2 p.07~08

Listen and Talk A-1

B: Did you hear about the first spaceship that went
   into space?
G: No, I didn't. I'm curious about it.
B: This is a poster of the spaceship.
G: Really? I want to buy it.

Listen and Talk A-2

G: Did you hear about the new book about Mars?
B: No, I didn't. I'm really curious about Mars.
G: Look. It's right here. It's about Mars and its moons.
B: Great. I think I'll buy the book.

25

Listen and Talk A-3

G: Did you hear about the space marathon?

B: No, I didn't.

G: It's a marathon on a space station. Look at this video.

B: OK. I'm really curious about it.

Listen and Talk A-4

G: Did you hear about the new space food?

B: Yes, I did. It's a type of ice cream.

G: Yes, and here it is. It looks good.

B: I'm really curious about the taste.

Listen and Talk B

1 A: Look at this. Did you hear about the new musical?

B: Yes, I did. I heard it has great songs.

A: Oh, I'm really curious about it.

2 A: Look at this. Did you hear about the new musical?

B: No, I didn't.

A: I heard it has great songs.

B: Oh, I'm really curious about it.

Listen and Talk C

B: Subin, did you hear about the new movie, Life on the Moon?

G: No, I didn't.

B: I heard it's really good.

G: I'm really curious about the movie. What's it about?

B: It's about a man who is trying to live on the moon.

G: That sounds interesting.

B: Look. The movie is playing at the Space Theater here.

G: What time is the movie?

B: It begins at 2:30.

G: Let's eat lunch first and then see the movie.

B: OK. I'm hungry. Let's go!

Review 1

G: Tony, did you hear about the movie, My Hero?

B: No, I didn't.

G: Well, I heard it's really good.

B: I'm really curious about the movie. What's it about?

G: It's about a father who saves his son.

Review 2

G: Did you hear about the new book, Living in a Foreign Country?

B: No, I didn't.

G: Look. It's right here. It's about living in New York. B: Great. I'm really curious about this book.

G: Me, too.

01 Best, Thing   02 like, far out   03 lived there with

04 other, worked on   05 Only, were born

06 One, going back

07 in surprise, floated towards   08 What's it like

09 Everything, different

10 For example, answered

11 never seen, said

12 is always black

13 don't have, suits, there

14 hard, because, pulls, down

15 What else   16 covered with, grass

17 roll down, answered

18 have, ever rolled down

19 amazing, answered

20 thirsty, opened, shook

21 floated, air, formed

22 swallowed, balls

23 if, way, get wet

24 Later, talked, long

25 exciting, all, things, going   26 one new thing

27 thought, all night, about   28 their secret

29 next, got on   30 going, be, trip

31 alright, so excited   32 finally landed

33 difficult to walk

34 pulling you down

35 couldn't float anymore   36 first new thing

37 What's, sound   38 bird singing

39 never heard, sing

40 never felt, wind   41 These, all new

42 ran up the nearest

43 top, each other, laughed

44 lay down, soft, rolled   45 their secret

46 best new, shouted   47 ran up to, top

01 Best, Thing   02 far out in space

03 lived there with, brother

04 other, worked on

05 Only, were born in space

06 One day, going back to

07 in surprise, floated towards   08 What's it like

09 Everything is different   10 For example

11 I've never seen   12 is always black

13 don't have to, because there is air

14 jump, pulls you down   15 What else

16 are covered with

17 roll down　　18 have you ever rolled down

19 really amazing 20 thirsty, so, opened, shook

21 floated, formed　　　　22 swallowed

23 if, that way, get wet

24 Later that night, a long time

25 exciting, think, all the new things, going to

26 one new thing, wanted to do

27 all night　　28 their secret　　29 got on

30 It's going to be

31 alright, so excited

32 finally landed　33 to walk

34 pulling you down

35 couldn't float anymore

36 the first new thing　　　37 What's, sound

38 is singing　　39 I've never heard, sing

40 I've never felt　41 These, all new things

42 ran up the nearest

43 each other, laughed

44 lay down, rolled down

45 their secret　　46 best new thing

47 up to the top

1 최고의 새로운 것

2 Rada는 먼 우주의 작은 세계에 살고 있었다.

3 그녀는 아빠, 엄마 그리고 남동생 Jonny와 함께 그곳에서 살고 있었다.

4 Rada의 아빠와 다른 사람들은 우주선에서 일했다.

5 Rada와 Jonny만이 아이들이었고, 그들은 우주에서 태어났다.

6 어느 날, 아빠가 Rada와 Jonny에게, "우리는 내일 지구로 돌아갈 거야."라고 말했다.

7 Rada와 Jonny는 깜짝 놀라 아빠를 바라보았고, 그에게 둥둥 떠서 갔다.

8 Rada가 아빠에게, "지구는 어떤 곳인가요?"라고 물었다.

9 "그곳에선 모든 것이 다르단다.

10 예를 들어, 하늘은 파란색이지."라고 아빠가 대답했다.

11 "전 한 번도 파란 하늘을 본 적이 없어요."라고 Jonny가 말했다.

12 "여기는 하늘이 항상 검은색이잖아요."라고 Rada가 말했다.

13 "그곳에는 모든 곳에 공기가 있기 때문에 크고 무거운 우주복을 입을 필요가 없단다.

14 또한 지구가 너희들을 끌어당기기 때문에 거기에서는 점프하는 것도 어렵단다." 아빠가 말했다.

15 "그 밖에 또 뭐가 있어요?" Rada가 물었다.

16 "언덕들이 있는데 그것들은 부드러운 초록색의 잔디로 뒤덮여 있단다.

17 언덕을 굴러 내려갈 수도 있어." 엄마가 대답했다.

18 "아빠, 언덕을 굴러 내려가 본 적 있어요?" Rada가 물었다.

19 "그럼, 정말 놀라워!" 아빠가 대답했다.

20 Jonny는 목이 말라서 우유 용기를 열어 그것을 흔들었다.

21 우유가 공기 중으로 떠서 방울을 형성했다.

22 Jonny는 그 우유 방울을 삼켰다.

23 "Jonny, 만약 네가 지구에서 그런 식으로 우유를 마신다면, 다 젖을 거야." 엄마가 말했다.

24 그날 밤 늦게, Rada와 Jonny는 지구에 대해서 오랜 시간 이야기했다.

25 그들이 보고, 하게 될 모든 새로운 것들을 생각하는 것은 흥미로웠다.

26 Rada와 Jonny가 정말로 하고 싶었던 한 가지 새로운 것이 있었다.

27 그들은 밤새 그것에 대해서 생각했고 엄마와 아빠에게는 그것을 말하지 않았다.

28 그것은 그들의 비밀이었다.

29 다음날, Rada의 가족은 우주선에 올랐다.

30 "긴 여행이 될 거야." 엄마가 말했다.

31 "괜찮아요. 정말 신나요!" Rada가 말했다.

32 우주선이 마침내 착륙했다.

33 "아빠, 지구에서는 걷는 것이 어려워요." Rada가 말했다.

34 "그래. 지구가 너를 끌어당기고 있거든." 아빠가 말했다.

35 Rada와 Jonny는 더 이상 떠다닐 수 없었다.

36 그것이 첫 번째 새로운 것이었다.

37 "저건 무슨 소리죠?"라고 Rada가 물었다.

38 "새가 노래하는 거야." 엄마가 말했다.

39 "새가 노래하는 것을 들어 본 적이 없어요."라고 Rada가 말했다.

40 "그리고 저는 바람을 느껴 본 적도 없어요."라고 Jonny가 말했다.

41 이러한 것들이 모두 새로운 것들이었다.

42 Rada와 Jonny는 가장 가까운 언덕으로 뛰어 올라갔다.

43 꼭대기에서, 그들은 서로를 쳐다보고 웃었다.

44 그러고 나서 그들은 부드러운 초록 잔디에 누워서 언덕 아래로 굴러 내려갔다.

45 그것이 그들의 비밀이었다!

46 "이것이 모든 것들 중에서 최고의 새로운 것이에요!" Rada와 Jonny는 외쳤다.

47 그리고 그들은 언덕 꼭대기로 다시 뛰어 올라갔다.

1 The Best New Thing

2 Rada lived on a little world, far out in space.

3 She lived there with her father, mother, and brother Jonny.

4 Rada's father and other people worked on spaceships

5 Only Rada and Jonny were children, and they were born in space.

6 One day, Dad told Rada and Jonny, "We're going back to Earth tomorrow."

7 Rada and Jonny looked at Dad in surprise and floated towards him.

8 Rada asked Dad, "What's it like on Earth?"

9 "Everything is different there.

10 For example, the sky is blue," answered Dad.

11 "I've never seen a blue sky," said Jonny.

12 "The sky is always black here," said Rada.

13 "You don't have to wear your big heavy space suits because there is air everywhere.

14 It's also hard to jump there because Earth pulls you down," said Dad.

15 "What else?" asked Rada.

16 "There are hills, and they are covered with soft green grass.

17 You can roll down the hills," answered Mom.

18 "Dad, have you ever rolled down a hill?" asked Rada.

19 "Yes, it's really amazing!" answered Dad.

20 Jonny was thirsty, so he opened a milk container and shook it.

21 The milk floated in the air and formed balls.

22 Jonny swallowed the balls.

23 "Jonny, if you drink milk that way on Earth, you'll get wet," said Mom.

24 Later that night, Rada and Jonny talked a long time about Earth.

25 It was exciting to think about all the new things they were going to see and do.

26 There was one new thing Rada and Jonny really wanted to do.

27 They thought about it all night and didn't tell Mom and Dad about it.

28 It was their secret.

29 The next day, Rada's family got on a spaceship.

30 "It's going to be a long trip," said Mom.

31 That's alright. I'm so excited!" said Rada.

32 The spaceship finally landed.

33 "Dad, it's difficult to walk on Earth," said Rada.

34 "I know. Earth is pulling you down," said Dad.

35 Rada and Jonny couldn't float anymore.

36 That was the first new thing.

37 "What's that sound?" asked Rada.

38 "A bird is singing," said Mom.

39 "I've never heard a bird sing," said Rada.

40 "And I've never felt the wind," said Jonny.

41 These were all new things.

42 Rada and Jonny ran up the nearest hill.

43 At the top, they looked at each other and laughed.

44 Then they lay down on the soft green grass and rolled down the hill.

45 That was their secret!

46 "This is the best new thing of all!" shouted Rada and Jonny.

47 And they ran up to the top of the hill again.

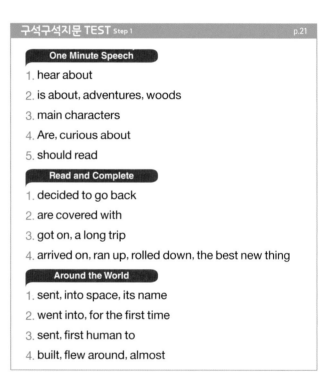

구석구석지문 TEST Step 1　　p.21

One Minute Speech

1. hear about
2. is about, adventures, woods
3. main characters
4. Are, curious about
5. should read

Read and Complete

1. decided to go back
2. are covered with
3. got on, a long trip
4. arrived on, ran up, rolled down, the best new thing

Around the World

1. sent, into space, its name
2. went into, for the first time
3. sent, first human to
4. built, flew around, almost

구석구석지문 TEST Step 2　　p.22

One Minute Speech

1. Did you hear about the new book, Dave's Adventures?
2. This book is about Dave and his adventures in the woods .
3. The main characters are Dave and a big bear. The story is fun.
4. Are you curious about the book? 5. Then you should read it!

Read and Complete

1. Rada's family lived in space. One day, they decided to go back to Earth.
2. Rada's family talked about life on Earth. They talked about the blue sky and hills which are covered with green grass.
3. The next day, Rada's family got on a spaceship. It was a long trip to Earth.
4. When they arrived on Earth, Rada and Jonny ran up the nearest hill and rolled down it. That was the best new thing to them.

Around the World

1. Russia sent the first dog into space . It was small, and its name was Laika.
2. Yuri Gagarin went into space for the first time .
3. The USA sent the first human to the moon. His name was Neil Armstrong.
4. Russia built the first space station. It flew around the Earth almost 3,000 times.

Lesson 8

단어 TEST Step 1   p.23

01 대학	02 잔디, 풀	03 전시
04 박람회, 전시회	05 부채춤	06 계속하다
07 해외에서, 해외로	08 보물	09 군대, 육군
10 ~ 뒤에, ~ 배후에	11 연구, 조사	12 결혼식
13 폭풍	14 연구가	15 허락하다, 허용하다
16 전통적인	17 박물관	18 탈의실
19 정부	20 결과, 결실	21 역사학자
22 인쇄	23 악기	24 성공하다
25 가치	26 왕실의	27 마침내, 결국
28 자부심, 긍지	29 입증하다, 증명하다	
30 맛있는	31 도둑질하다, 훔치다	
32 출판하다, 발행하다		33 어려움
34 전부의, 전체의	35 ~ 때문에	36 포기하다
37 ~로 가득 차 있다	38 ~하고 싶다	39 ~하자마자
40 ~을 입어 보다	41 바로, 즉시	42 ~ 덕분에
43 ~하면서 시간을 보내다		

단어 TEST Step 2   p.24

01 abroad	02 pride	03 government
04 college	05 delicious	06 succeed
07 allow	08 return	09 prove
10 royal	11 exhibition	12 difficulty
13 display	14 historian	15 treasure
16 continue	17 instrument	18 storm
19 finally	20 researcher	21 fitting room
22 result	23 fire	24 metal
25 traditional	26 steal	27 army
28 noise	29 million	30 wedding
31 publish	32 research	33 thief
34 value	35 thanks to	
36 as soon as+주어+동사		37 right away
38 try on	39 give up	40 spend+시간+ -ing
40 because+주어+동사, because of+명사		
41 be full of	42 look for	

단어 TEST Step 3   p.25

1 spend, (시간을) 보내다   2 abroad, 해외로, 해외에서
3 prove, 입증하다   4 pride, 자부심, 긍지
5 allow , 허락하다   6 research, 조사   7 result, 결과
8 succeed, 성공하다   9 royal, 왕실의   10 steal, 훔치다

11 search, 찾아보다   12 treasure, 보물

13 publish, 출판하다   14 government, 정부

15 flash, 플래시   16 fitting room, 탈의실

대화문 TEST Step 1   p.26~27

Listen and Talk A-1

Excuse, I've never seen, like / dessert / Is it OK to try / Go ahead, delicious

Listen and Talk A-2

to sit over there / mean / all right / sitting, is not allowed / understand

Listen and Talk A-3

looks interesting / traditional, musical instrument / Is it OK to play / I'm sorry, for display, Playing, allowed

Listen and Talk A-4

Excuse, Is it OK to take / all right / How about using, too / afraid not, Using, not allowed

Listen and Talk B

Is it OK to sit here / afraid not, Sitting, not allowed

Talk and Play

Which, to go / Why don't you / Is it OK to eat / Eating food, allowed / Is it OK to take / is not allowed / got it, thinking of going

Listen and Talk C

Is it OK / fitting room, over there / minute / over there / traditional, for women, worn, wedding / Is it OK to try it on / for display, on, not allowed / try on

Review 1

Excuse me, looks interesting / traditional, musical instrument / Is it OK to / for display, allowed

Review 2

is it OK / ahead / Can I use, too / also / but, one more / not allowed

대화문 TEST Step 2   p.28~29

Listen and Talk A-1

B: Excuse me. What's this? I've never seen any food like this.

W: Oh, it's Tteok, a Korean dessert.

B: Is it OK to try some?

W: Sure. Go ahead. It's really delicious.

Listen and Talk A-2

G: Excuse me. Is it OK to sit over there?

M: You mean, on the grass?

G: Yes. Is it all right?

M: I'm sorry, but sitting on the grass is not allowed.

G: OK, I understand.

Listen and Talk A-3

B: Excuse me. What's this? It looks interesting.

W: Oh, that's a haegeum, a traditional Korean musical instrument.

B: Is it OK to play it?

W: I'm sorry, but it's only for display. Playing it is not allowed.

B: I see.

Listen and Talk A-4

G: Excuse me. Is it OK to take pictures here?

M: Yes, it's all right.

G: How about using a flash? Can I use it, too?

M: I'm afraid not. Using a flash is not allowed here.

G: Oh, I see. Thank you.

Listen and Talk B

A: Is it OK to sit here?

B: I'm afraid not. Sitting is not allowed here.

A: Oh, I see.

Talk and Play

A: Which place do you want to go first in the museum?

B: Why don't you guess?

A: OK. Is it OK to eat food there?

B: Yes. Eating food is allowed.

A: Is it OK to take pictures?

B: No. Taking pictures is not allowed.

A: I got it. You're thinking of going to the Video Room.

B: You're right.

Listen and Talk C

G: Excuse me, but is it OK to try on this hanbok?

M: Sure. The fitting room is over there.

G: Thanks. Wait a minute. That's also very pretty.

M: Oh, the little hat over there?

G: Yes. What is it?

M: It's a jokduri, a traditional Korean hat for women. It's usually worn on a wedding day.

G: Really? Is it OK to try it on, too?

M: I'm sorry, but it's only for display. Trying it on is not allowed.

G: Oh. Then, I'll just try on this hanbok.

Review 1

G: Excuse me. What's this? It looks interesting.

B: Oh, that's a janggu, a traditional Korean musical instrument.

G: Is it OK to play it?

B: I'm sorry, but it's only for display. Playing it is not allowed.

G: I see.

Review 2

G: Excuse me, but is it OK to take pictures here?

M: Yes. Go ahead.

G: Can I use a flash, too?

M: Yes. That's also OK.

G: I'm sorry, but I have one more question. Can I eat food here?

M: I'm sorry, but that's not allowed.

본문 TEST Step 1   p.30~31

01 Interview with

02 On, collection, took, back

03 behind, return, searching, abroad

04 how, became interested

05 studied history, college

06 to continue, studies

07 As, army, treasures

08 find, while, studying   09 one of them

10 found, books, in

11 tell, how, found

12 As soon, look for

13 After, finally found

14 looked at, than, million

15 sure, excited, found

16 more difficulties, waiting for

17 thought, should, returned, but

18 even thought, fired

19 as, so, do, on   20 However, give up

21 more, every, to, research

22 wanted, show, value

23 results, research, published as

24 interested in, because of

25 asked, for, return, finally

26 finish, like, changed, printing

27 found, in, year

28 right away, special

29 hard, prove, value, succeeded

30 exhibition, displayed as, metal

31 thanks to, thank, for

32 interested, treasures abroad, return

본문 TEST Step 2   p.32~33

01 Interview with

02 On, a collection of royal books, came back to

03 behind this return, spent, whole life searching for, abroad

04 how, became interested in

05 studied history in colleage

06 to continue   07 As you know, national treasures

08 while, was studying   09 one of them

10 297 books of *Uigwe*, National Library

11 tell me how, found

12 As soon as, researcher, look for

13 After, finally found

14 looked at, 30 million

15 I'm sure, excited

16 more difficulties, waiting for

17 should be returned to, that idea

18 even thought, fired

19 as a visitor so, do research on   20 However

21 For more than, to finish my research

22 the value of *Uigwe*

23 were published as

24 became interested in, because of

25 asked, for its return, are here now

26 I'd like to ask, changed, printing

27 in my first year

28 right away, very special

29 to prove its value, succeeded

30 was displayed as, oldest book, movable metal type

31 thanks to, thank, for

32 our national treasures abroad, return

본문 TEST Step 3   p.34~35

1 박영선 박사와의 인터뷰

2 2011년 5월 27일에 프랑스군이 1866년에 가져갔던 왕실 서적인 "의궤" 297권이 한국으로 돌아왔다.

3 이 반환 뒤에 있는 인물이 해외에 있는 한국의 문화재를 찾기 위해 전 생애를 바친 역사학자 박병선 박사이다..

4 Q: "의궤"에 어떻게 관심을 갖게 되셨는지 말씀해 주시겠어요?

5 Dr. Park: 저는 대학에서 역사를 공부했어요.

6 저는 1955년에 학업을 계속하기 위해 프랑스에 갔습니다.

7 아시다시피, 프랑스군은 1866년에 우리 문화재를 많이 가져갔어요.

8 저는 그곳에서 공부하는 동안 그것들을 찾고 싶었어요.

9 "의궤"는 그것들 중의 하나였어요.

10 Q: 당신은 파리에 있는 프랑스 국립도서관에서 297권의 "의궤"를 발견하셨어요.

11 그것들을 어떻게 발견하셨는지 말씀해 주세요.

12 Dr. Park: 1967년에 국립도서관의 연구원이 되자마자, 저는 "

의궤"를 찾기 시작했어요.

13 10년 후인 1977년에 마침내 그 책들을 발견했죠.

14 제 생각에 3천만 권 이상의 책을 본 것 같아요.

15 Q: 그 책들을 발견했을 때 무척 흥분하셨겠어요.

16 Dr. Park: 네, 하지만 더 큰 어려움이 저를 기다리고 있었어요.

17 저는 그 책들이 한국에 반환되어야 한다고 생각했지만, 도서관의 제 상사들은 그 생각을 좋아하지 않았어요.

18 그들은 심지어 제가 한국의 스파이라고 생각했고 저를 해고했죠.

19 그 후에, 저는 방문객으로 도서관에 가야만 했고, 그래서 "의궤"를 연구하는 것이 쉽지 않았어요.

20 하지만 저는 포기하지 않았죠.

21 10년 넘게, 연구를 끝마치기 위해 매일 도서관에 갔어요.

22 저는 사람들에게 "의궤"의 가치를 보여 주고 싶었어요.

23 Q: 당신의 연구 결과가 1990년 한국에서 책으로 출판되었죠.

24 많은 한국인들이 당신의 책 때문에 "의궤"에 관심을 갖게 되었어요.

25 Dr. Park: 네. 1992년에 한국 정부는 프랑스 정부에 그것의 반환을 요청했고, 마침내 297권의 책이 지금 여기 있게 된 거죠.

26 Q: 인터뷰를 마치기 전에, 인쇄의 역사를 바꾼 책인 "직지"에 대해 여쭙고 싶어요.

27 Dr. Park: 저는 도서관에서 근무한 첫해에 그것을 발견했어요.

28 그것이 아주 특별하다는 것을 바로 알았어요.

29 저는 그것의 가치를 증명하기 위해 열심히 연구했고 마침내 성공했죠.

30 1972년에 파리 도서 박람회에서 "직지"는 금속 활자로 인쇄된 세계에서 가장 오래된 책으로 전시되었죠.

31 Q: 박 박사님, 당신의 노고 덕분에 "직지"와 "의궤"가 발견되었고, 모든 한국인들이 그 점을 당신에게 감사하고 있어요.

32 Dr. Park: 저는 사람들이 해외에 있는 우리의 문화재에 더 많은 관심을 갖고 그것의 반환을 위해 애써 주시기를 바랍니다.

본문 TEST Step 4~Step 5   p.36~39

1 An Interview with Dr. Park Byeong-seon

2 On May 27, 2011, 297 books of Uigwe , a collection of royal books the French army took in 1866, came back to Korea.

3 The person behind this return is Dr. Park Byeong-seon, a historian who spent her whole life searching for Korean national treasures abroad.

4 Q: Can you tell me how you became interested in Uigwe ?

5 Dr. Park: I studied history in college.

6 I went to France to continue my studies in 1955.

7 As you know, the French army took many of our national treasures in 1866.

8 I wanted to find them while I was studying there.

9 Uigwe was one of them.

10 Q: You found 297 books of Uigwe in the National Library of France, in Paris.

11 Please tell me how you found them.

12 Dr. Park: As soon as I became a researcher at the National Library in 1967, I began to look for Uigwe.

13 After 10 years, in 1977, I finally found the books.

14 I think I looked at more than 30 million books.

15 Q: I'm sure you were very excited when you found the books.

16 Dr. Park: Yes, I was, but more difficulties were waiting for me.

17 I thought that the books should be returned to Korea, but my bosses at the library didn't like that idea.

18 They even thought that I was a Korean spy and fired me.

19 After that, I had to go to the library as a visitor, so it was not easy to do research on Uigwe .

20 However, I didn't give up.

21 For more than ten years, I went to the library every day to finish my research.

22 I wanted to show people the value of Uigwe .

23 Q: The results of your research were published as a book in Korea in 1990.

24 Many Koreans became interested in Uigwe because of your book.

25 Dr. Park: Yes. In 1992, the Korean government asked the French government for its return and, finally, the 297 books are here now.

26 Q: Before I finish this interview, I'd like to ask you about Jikji, a book that changed the history of printing.

27 Dr. Park: I found it in my first year at the library.

28 I knew right away that it was very special.

29 I worked hard to prove its value and finally succeeded.

30 At a book exhibition in Paris in 1972, Jikji was displayed as the oldest book in the world that was printed with movable metal type.

31 Q: Dr. Park, thanks to your hard work, Jikji and Uigwe were found, and all Koreans thank you for that.

32 Dr. Park: I hope people will become more interested in our national treasures abroad and work for their return.

After You Read C Think and Talk

1. What, think about
2. think, will, difficulties, give up
3. great passion
4. As, passionate, finding, abroad

Think and Write Step 2

1. Interview with
2. following, local police officer
3. when and where you were born
4. was born, on
5. like to, what your goal in life is
6. My goal, to make
7. what you like
8. like helping
9. that, police officer

Team Project Create

1. South Korea's National Treasure
2. was printed
3. National Library
4. world's oldest book, metal type

After You Read C Think and Talk

1. A: What do you think about Dr. Park?
2. B: I think she had a strong will. She had many difficulties, but she didn't give up.
3. C: I think she had a great passion for her work.
4. As a historian, she was very passionate about finding Korean national treasures abroad.

Think and Write Step 2

1. An Interview with Kim Yubin
2. The following is the interview I had with Kim Yubin, a local police officer .
3. Q: Can you tell me when and where you were born ?
4. A: I was born in Seoul on March 11, 1980.
5. Q: I'd like to know what your goal in life is .
6. A: My goal in life is to make a better world.
7. Q: Can you tell me what you like about your job?
8. A: I like helping people.
9. I think that Kim Yubin is a great police officer .

Team Project Create

1. Jikji, South Korea's National Treasure No. 1132
2. Jikji was printed at Heungdeoksa in 1377.
3. It is now in the National Library of France, in Paris.
4. It is the world's oldest book that was printed with movable metal type .

Lesson
S

01 버튼, 단추	02 재미있는, 즐거운	03 창의적인
04 맛있는	05 충분한	06 ~한 맛이 나다
07 효과가 있다, 작동하다		08 쌓아 올리다, 쌓다
09 반죽	10 소유하다	11 계산대
12 요리법	13 섞다	14 떨어지다
15 신선한	16 팔다	17 ~ 안에
18 누르다	19 발생하다, 일어나다	
20 상금	21 표지판	22 기계
23 외치다, 소리치다	24 추신	25 준비된
26 시도하다, 먹어보다		27 잃어버리다
28 잘못된, 이상이 있는		29 떠나다, ~에 두다
30 기억하다	31 ~을 부수다, 쪼개다	
32 갑자기	33 흥분하여	34 잠시
35 결국, 마침내	36 ~ 으로 가득 차다	37 ~ 속으로 떨어지다
38 A를 B에 쌓아 올리다		39 ~을 돌려주다
40 즉시, 지금 당장	41 ~에서 나오다, 내리다	
42 포상금을 지급하다		43 계속해서 ~하다

01 doughnut	02 batter	03 pile
04 creative	05 sign	06 prize
07 taste	08 drop	09 lose
10 shout	11 counter	12 happen
13 before	14 try	15 ring
16 wrong	17 leave	18 mix
19 sell	20 recipe	21 machine
22 push	23 work	24 ready
25 inside	26 own	27 delicious
28 enough	29 fresh	30 remember
31 in front of	32 for a while	33 in the end
34 be full of	35 step out	36 take off
37 break up	38 all of a sudden	
39 one day	40 a piece of paper	
41 fall into	42 get ~ back	43 right away

1 step out, ~에서 나오다　　2 work, 효과가 있다
3 ring, 반지　　4 excitement, 흥분　　5 recipe, 요리법
6 shout, 외치다, 소리치다　　7 sell, 팔다
8 compare, 비교하다　　9 doughnut, 도넛

10 machine, 기계   11 counter, 계산대
12 give a reward, 포상금을 주다   13 batter, 반죽
14 prize, 상금   15 sign, 표지판   16 remember, 기억하다

01 The Doughnuts
02 uncle, had, shop
03 so, full of cooking
04 One, visited, shop   05 Uncle Bob
06 Nice, at, Isn't
07 back, for, while
08 watch, for, make   09 try but
10 easy, make, batter, put
11 just, machine, recipe
12 do, Don't worry
13 stopped, front, stepped out
14 Can, have some
15 but, aren't ready   16 making, batter
17 my first time   18 took off, her, ring
19 started to mix 20 can help, delicious
21 Uh, OK   22 a lot of
23 wait, taste great
24 turned on, machine
25 Rigs, dropping into   26 try, first
27 really delicious
28 have to, so much
29 Thank, for helping
30 enough, pushed, nothing happened
31 kept coming out
32 wrong, should call   33 full of, piled
34 back right away
35 Something's wrong with   36 How, all these
37 Just, came back
38 lost, ring, left, counter   39 took, off, mix
40 looked for, couldn't   41 can't find
42 give, reward, who finds   43 fell into, inside
44 You're right   45 break up, to find
46 Don't worry, have
47 took, piece, made, sign   48 put, it, shop's
49 for, cents   50 for finding, inside
51 have, give, back   52 many, to buy
53 All, sudden, with excitement   54 found, ring
55 idea worked   56 Here's, hundred
57 In, end, was   58 went, with, hundred
59 got, back, sold lots
60 what about   61 that, worked, well

01 Doughnuts   02 uncle, had
03 so, was full of cooking machines
04 One day, visited   05 Uncle
06 Look at, Isn't it great
07 for a while   08 for me   09 try
10 easy to do, doughnut batter, put, in
11 machine, recipe
12 can do, Don't worry
13 in front of, stepped out   14 Can I have
15 aren't ready
16 Are you making, batter   17 my first time
18 took off, ring   19 started to mix
20 I can help you, make delicious   21 OK
22 a lot of   23 wait and see, will taste great
24 turned on   25 dropping into, hot oil
26 try, first   27 delicious
28 have to go, so much fun   29 for helping
30 enough, nothing happened
31 kept coming out of
32 wrong, should call
33 was, full of, piled, on the counter
34 back right away
35 Something's wrong with
36 all these   37 came back to 38 lost, left
39 took it off, mix the batter
40 looked for, couldn't find   41 can't find
42 give a reward, who finds
43 fell into, I'm sure, inside   44 right
45 have to break up, to find   46 Don't worry
47 piece, made a sign   48 put it
49 2 for 5 cents   50 for finding
51 have to give, back   52 to buy
53 All of a sudden   54 found it
55 worked   56 Here's, hundred
57 In the end, was   58 with
59 got, back, lots of
60 what about   61 his idea worked

1 도넛
2 Homer의 삼촌인 Bob은 도넛 가게를 가지고 있었다.
3 Bob 삼촌은 기계를 좋아해서, 가게는 요리 기계들로 가득 차 있었다.
4 어느 날, Homer가 Bob 삼촌의 가게를 방문했다.
5 Homer: 안녕하세요, Bob 삼촌!

6 Bob: 안녕, Homer. 만나서 반갑구나. 이 새 도넛 기계 좀 봐. 멋지지 않니?

7 Bob: Homer, 내가 잠시 집에 가 봐야 해.

8 나 대신 가게를 봐 주고 도넛을 좀 만들어 줄 수 있겠니?

9 Homer: 네, 해 볼게요, 그런데….

10 Bob: 하기 쉬워. 먼저, 도넛 반죽을 만들고 그것을 기계에 넣으렴.

11 그런 다음에 기계를 작동하기만 하면 돼. 여기 요리법이 있어.

12 Homer: 그건 할 수 있어요. 걱정하지 마세요.

13 Bob 삼촌이 떠난 후, 큰 차 한 대가 가게 앞에 섰고, 한 귀부인이 내렸다.

14 Lady: 도넛과 커피 한 잔 주겠니?

15 Homer: 죄송하지만, 도넛이 준비가 안 됐어요.

16 Lady: 지금 도넛 반죽을 만들고 있는 거니?

17 Homer: 네, 하지만 처음 만드는 거예요.

18 그 귀부인은 외투를 벗고 커다란 다이아몬드 반지를 뺐다.

19 그녀는 반죽을 섞기 시작했다.

20 Lady: 내가 도와줄게. 나는 맛있는 도넛을 만들 수 있단다.

21 Homer: 아, 좋아요.

22 Homer: 반죽이 많군요.

23 Lady: 좀 기다려 보렴. 도넛이 아주 맛있을 거야.

24 Homer는 도넛 기계를 작동했다.

25 링 모양의 반죽들이 뜨거운 기름 속으로 떨어지기 시작했다.

26 Lady: 첫 번째 도넛을 맛보렴. 여기 있어.

27 Homer: 와! 정말 맛있네요!

28 Lady: 난 이제 가 봐야 해. 정말 재미있었어! 잘 있으렴!

29 Homer: 도와주셔서 감사해요. 안녕히 가세요!

30 Homer는 도넛이 충분하게 있어서 정지 버튼을 눌렀지만, 아무 일도 일어나지 않았다.

31 도넛이 계속해서 기계에서 나오고 있었다.

32 Homer: 흠음 … 뭐가 잘못된 거지? Bob 삼촌에게 전화를 해야겠어.

33 가게는 이제 도넛으로 가득 찼다. Homer는 도넛들을 계산대 위로 쌓아 올렸다.

34 Homer: Bob 삼촌! 지금 당장 돌아와 주세요.

35 도넛 기계에 이상이 있어요.

36 Bob: 오, 이런! 이 도넛들을 모두 어떻게 팔지?

37 바로 그때 그 귀부인이 다시 가게로 돌아왔다.

38 Lady: 내 다이아몬드 반지를 잃어버렸어. 내 생각엔 계산대 위에 그것을 놓은 것 같은데.

39 Homer: 오, 기억나요. 반죽을 섞기 전에 그것을 뺐어요.

40 모두가 다이아몬드 반지를 찾았지만, 찾을 수 없었다.

41 Homer: 저는 못 찾겠어요.

42 Lady: 그 반지를 찾는 사람에게 100달러의 보상금을 드릴게요!

43 Homer: 알겠어요! 그 반지는 반죽 속으로 떨어졌어요. 반지는 이 도넛들 중 하나 안에 있다고 확신해요!

44 Lady: 네 말이 맞아!

45 Bob: 오, 안 돼! 이제 우리는 반지를 찾기 위해 이 도넛들을 모두 쪼개야 해요.

46 Homer: 걱정하지 마세요, 삼촌. 저에게 아이디어가 있어요.

47 Homer는 종이 한 장을 가져와 안내판을 만들었다.

48 그리고 나서 그것을 가게 창문에 걸었다.

49 신선한 도넛   2개에 5센트

50 도넛 안에 있는 반지를 찾으면 100달러의 상금을 드려요.

51 추신. 반지를 돌려주어야 합니다.

52 그러자, 많은 사람들이 도넛을 사기 시작했다.

53 갑자기, 한 남자가 흥분해서 소리쳤다.

54 Man: 찾았어요! 내가 반지를 찾았어요!

55 Homer: 보세요, 제 아이디어가 통했어요!

56 Lady: 여기 100달러예요!

57 결국 모두가 행복했다.

58 남자는 100달러를 갖고 집으로 갔다.

59 귀부인은 다이아몬드 반지를 다시 찾았고, Bob 삼촌은 도넛을 많이 팔았다.

60 그러면, Homer는 어떻게 됐을까?

61 그는 자신의 아이디어가 아주 잘 통해서 행복했다!

1 The Doughnuts

2 Homer's uncle, Bob, had a doughnut shop.

3 Uncle Bob liked machines, so the shop was full of cooking machines.

4 One day, Homer visited Uncle Bob's shop.

5 Homer: Hello, Uncle Bob!

6 Bob: Hi, Homer. Nice to see you. Look at this new doughnut machine. Isn't it great?

7 Bob: Homer, I need to go back home for a while.

8 Can you watch the shop for me and make some doughnuts?

9 Homer: OK, I'll try but ....

10 Bob: It's easy to do. First, make the doughnut batter and put it in the machine.

11 Then just start the machine. Here's the recipe.

12 Homer: I can do that. Don't worry.

13 After Uncle Bob left, a big car stopped in front of the shop, and a lady stepped out.

14 Lady: Can I have some doughnuts and a coffee?

15 Homer: I'm sorry, but the doughnuts aren't ready.

16 Lady: Are you making the doughnut batter now?

17 Homer: Yes, but this is my first time.

18 The lady took off her coat and her big diamond ring.

19 She started to mix the batter.

20 Lady: I can help you. I can make delicious doughnuts.

21 Homer: Uh, OK.

22 Homer: This is a lot of batter.

23 Lady: Just wait and see. The doughnuts will taste great.

24 Homer turned on the doughnut machine.

25 Rings of batter started dropping into the hot oil.

26 Lady: You try the first doughnut. Here.

27 Homer: Wow! It's really delicious!

28 Lady: I have to go now. This was so much fun! Good-bye!

29 Homer: Thank you for helping me. Good-bye!

30 Homer had enough doughnuts, so he pushed the stop button, but nothing happened.

31 The doughnuts kept coming out of the machine.

32 Homer: Hmm... What's wrong? I think I should call Uncle Bob.

33 The shop was now full of doughnuts. Homer piled the doughnuts on the counter.

34 Homer: Uncle Bob! Please come back right away.

35 Something's wrong with the doughnut machine.

36 Bob: Oh, no! How can we sell all these doughnuts?

37 Just then the lady came back to the shop.

38 Lady: I lost my diamond ring. I think I left it on the counter.

39 Homer: Oh, I remember. You took it off before you started to mix the batter.

40 Everyone looked for the diamond ring, but they couldn't find it.

41 Homer: I can't find it.

42 Lady: I'll give a reward of one hundred dollars to the person who finds that ring!

43 Homer: I know! The ring fell into the batter. I'm sure it's inside one of these doughnuts!

44 Lady: You're right!

45 Bob: Oh, no! Now we have to break up all of these doughnuts to find the ring.

46 Homer: Don't worry, Uncle. I have an idea.

47 Homer took a piece of paper and made a sign.

48 He then put it in the shop's window.

49 Fresh Doughnuts   2 for 5 cents

50 $100 prize for finding a ring inside a doughnut

51 P.S. You have to give the ring back.

52 Then many people began to buy the doughnuts.

53 All of a sudden, a man shouted with excitement.

54 Man: I found it! I found the ring!

55 Homer: See, my idea worked!

56 Lady: Here's one hundred dollars!

57 In the end, everybody was happy.

58 The man went home with one hundred dollars.

59 The lady got her diamond ring back, and Uncle Bob sold lots of doughnuts.

60 And, what about Homer?

61 He was happy that his idea worked so well!

적중100

영어 기출 문제집

정답 및 해설

동아 | 윤정미